Eben Greenough Scott

Reconstruction During the Civil War in the United States of America

Eben Greenough Scott

Reconstruction During the Civil War in the United States of America

ISBN/EAN: 9783337009120

Printed in Europe, USA, Canada, Australia, Japan

Cover: Foto ©ninafisch / pixelio.de

More available books at **www.hansebooks.com**

RECONSTRUCTION
DURING THE CIVIL WAR IN THE UNITED STATES OF AMERICA

BY

EBEN GREENOUGH SCOTT

BOSTON AND NEW YORK
HOUGHTON, MIFFLIN AND COMPANY
The Riverside Press, Cambridge
1895

The Riverside Press, Cambridge, Mass., U. S. A.
Electrotyped and Printed by H. O. Houghton and Company.

PREFACE.

THE term "reconstruction," in American politics, applies more aptly to the revolted states than it does to the federal Union; for the mutilated form of the Union was restored by the mere ascendancy of the northern arms, but it was not until after this had occurred that the eleven states were reconstructed. The period during which the process of renewal was taking place is called, in popular speech, the Reconstruction Period, and it refers, somewhat indefinitely, to the time occupied by the single term of President Johnson and the succeeding two terms of President Grant, — the presidential terms during which the ancient governments of the subdued states were finally subverted, and new ones were erected in their places.

I intend to write the political history of the period of reconstruction, but, preliminary to doing so, I have set forth in this book certain things necessary to be known before taking up the subject and pursuing it in the sequence of time. It is a notable thing that, from the very beginning of the Civil War, the federal government never evinced a doubt of ultimate success, and it is significant that, even in moments of disaster which seemed irretrievable, it was occupied with the question, "What is to be done with the revolted states when the fortune of war shall have put their fate in our hands?"

At first, the notion prevailed that the seceded states would retake their places in the Union merely, and that, this done, "the Union as it was" would be restored. It was not long, however, before the slavery question made itself felt by transmuting restoration into reconstruction, and the distractions of the times were augmented by the conflicting opinions on this subject which divided the people and gained head in Congress. Nothing could be implied from the Constitution but restoration; yet restoration involved the continuance of slavery, and this was out of the question with the people, who were now demanding that no settlement should be made without the elimination of that which was certain to produce a recurrence of the intolerable evil under which they were laboring. President and Congress, accordingly, changed front, and the proclamations of one and the debates and legislation of the other showed how determinedly the North was bent upon a new order of things.

Though the object sought was manifest, and the demand for change was peremptory, the means by which this change was to be effected and this object was to be attained were not clear. The Constitution gave no help to a procedure which was foreign to the system of which it was the expression. The contrariety among the people betrayed itself on the floor of Congress in the dissension of factions. The President took one view of the relations of a state to the Union, a faction of the Republicans took another, while the Democrats, reduced to a party of mere protest, still clung unavailingly to the doctrine of restoration. There was much groping, much fault-finding, and much contention, but uppermost, out of the confusion, rose at length that which became known as the Presidential Plan of Reconstruction. This plan was actually in progress in several of the regained states when, by the assassination of President Lincoln, its furtherance devolved upon President Johnson. This plan had been prescribed by proclamation of the President.

It is to bring the genesis of "reconstruction" before the reader that this volume has been written. It is not a history of the contentions of parties and factions, but it is a presentation of the conception illustrated by the proclamations of the President, and by the debates (particularly those of the Senate) upon these proclamations, and upon matters which touched vitally the constitutional relations of the states to the federal Union: it shows, consequently, the great change of opinion and of sentiment which the people of the United States were then undergoing, and which at length found expression in three amendments of the Constitution.

In a written constitution, the people of the United States have a standard whereby to determine their constitutional character; for no matter how contrary the modes of construing this instrument, the written words remain. The Constitution, therefore, preserves the character of a landmark by which the fidelity or infidelity of the people to their ancient character can be judged. When the storm has cleared away, it reveals indubitably how far they have been swept from their moorings. It is absolutely essential to a people, the security of whose liberties is coincident with the preservation of their constitutional character, to ascertain if they have suffered this character to become impaired. Such an opportunity as that presented by the subsidence of the agitation which accompanied the most stormy days through which the United States have ever passed has not occurred before to the Americans, and the reader cannot close this painful chapter of our history without the question rising to his lips, Have we preserved the ancient character handed down to us along with the Constitution, or have we wandered from the faith of our fathers?

WASHINGTON, D. C., *March*, 1895.

CONTENTS.

CHAPTER I.

INTRODUCTORY.

CHAPTER II.

FEDERAL UNION; REPRESENTATIVE DEMOCRACY.

CHAPTER III.

POLITICAL SEPARATENESS OF THE BRITISH COLONIES.

CHAPTER IV.

SEPARATENESS OF THE BRITISH COLONIES — CONTINUED.

CHAPTER X.

CONSTITUTIONAL LEGISLATION.

CHAPTER XI.

COERCION, OR NON-COERCION?

CHAPTER XII.

DEVELOPMENT OF PRINCIPLES OF CONGRESSIONAL ACTION TOWARDS THE SOUTH.

CHAPTER XIII.

PLANS OF RECONSTRUCTION.

CHAPTER XIV.

THE CONGRESSIONAL PLAN OF RECONSTRUCTION.

CHAPTER XV.

THE CONGRESSIONAL PLAN OF RECONSTRUCTION — CONTINUED.

CHAPTER XVI.

ENFORCEMENT OF THE PRESIDENTIAL PLAN OF RECONSTRUCTION.

CHAPTER XVII.

ENFORCEMENT OF THE PRESIDENTIAL PLAN OF RECONSTRUCTION — CONTINUED.

CHAPTER XVIII.

ENFORCEMENT OF THE PRESIDENTIAL PLAN OF RECONSTRUCTION — CONTINUED.

CHAPTER XIX.

WHAT CONSTITUTES A STATE OF THE AMERICAN UNION?

CHAPTER XX.

RECONSTRUCTION

DURING THE CIVIL WAR IN THE UNITED STATES OF AMERICA.

CHAPTER I.

INTRODUCTORY

Withdrawal of southern senators from the Senate of the United States — Personality of the states; the Senate — Representation of the people; the House of Representatives — Contrast between the northern and the southern peoples — The compromise element in the Constitution — Equality of the states.

On the twenty-first of January, 1861,[1] the most impressive and painful scene in the annals of the United States of America was witnessed in the Senate Chamber. The rumor had gone abroad that the senators of several of the states which had seceded were about to withdraw from the Senate. The chamber was filled with members and with those who had the privilege of the floor, and the galleries were crowded with spectators. Every state was present except South Carolina; her senators had not come to the capitol, but had sent in their resignations in writing before the session began, and when the time came the chairs of these senators were empty. The first state to turn its back upon the Union was Florida, one which had been among the latest to be wel-

[1] Cong. Globe, 484 *et seq.*

comed with open arms by the sisterhood of states; it was also one of the weakest. Rising in his place, Yulee set forth briefly the reasons which had led his state to secede, and then he bade adieu to the Senate. He was followed by the other senator from this state, Mallory, who alluded to the fidelity with which the South had clung to the Union throughout her patient endurance of insult and wrong, and in the same breath announced that Florida had come into the Union only fifteen years before, and that, from the Union as their fathers had made it, there breathed not a secessionist upon the soil of this state. In spite of the solemnity of the moment, the inquiry forced itself upon the mind of the onlooker: Why did Florida enter the Union, if merely to share the insult and wrong of the other southern states? And, having accepted such a fate with her eyes open, with what consistency did she now turn her back upon a Constitution which she had been glad to accept, and which was the same at this moment as it had been when she had sought its protection? Censoriousness and argument were overwhelmed beneath the anguish which convulsed the breast of every listener, and which was augmented by the recital of each sister, who, through her representatives, uttered her sense of injury. Alabama followed Florida, and Mississippi, Alabama. The story of their griefs was told by these states in subdued and measured tones; the time for threat and defiance had gone by, the very parting itself had come, and the pain which wrung northerner and southerner alike was betrayed by twitching lips and by deep silence.

Every eye and every ear was intent upon Jefferson

Davis when he rose. He was not in good health, but to this alone could be attributed any faltering or agitation. There was none: this was the crowning hour of his existence, and he approached the culmination of his life-work with calmness and dignity. All his life long, he had maintained the right of a state to withdraw from the Union, and this as an attribute of sovereignty coequal with the right under which the state had entered into the Union. He was no nullifier; nullification implied union, and he was no unionist. To nullify was to parry, to palliate; it was to confess a right, yet to avoid its obligations. Nullification and secession were incompatible principles. Davis neither parried, nor compromised, nor sulked; he believed that the states were sovereign and unaccountable, and where there had been aggression he would not acknowledge superior power, but he was for meeting aggression on the threshold by denying the superiority; therefore, to Union he opposed dis-Union; to aggression, resistance. There was no middle course; so long as a state was a member of the Union, it was bound to obey the law that was common to all; if it would not obey, it must leave the Union, and of the necessity of such a course, there was no judge but the sovereign state. No one had the right to question, or to sit in judgment upon a sovereign, and unqualified obedience was the sole duty of the children of a state. This doctrine he had taught his people in season and out of season, and the hour had now come when he was reaping what he had sown. His eyes were beholding the success long striven for; the states were going out; he was seeing them take their departure; he was hearing them saying good-by; and, above all, he was beholding the deep emotion of those who were left behind. His tone was not exultant, neither did his voice falter; his manner was gentle, firm, determined.

Heretofore Davis had been the teacher, the seer, the leader of his people; but when he was made king he ceased to be prophet and priest. As President of the Confederate States, he became merely the official head, a figure-head of a government; he played a part which other men could have filled with equal benefit to his cause; he was no longer the soul of the South. In passing from the legislature to the field, the work of maintaining secession fell into other hands: and true it is, that, when Jefferson Davis bade farewell to the United States, he bade farewell to the real work of his life. He found but a barren sceptre in his gripe, and when he left the Senate Chamber he took the course, which he pursued with heroic resolution and with Promethean defiance of his enemies, until, a fugitive, his flight was ended in the woods of Georgia by the hand of a common soldier.

But prominent as this man was, and impressive as might be the personality of one upon whom men looked as being the embodiment of a cause, the spectacle owed its significance and solemnity to something deeper than that with which it was invested by one man. The departures from the House of Representatives were mostly signified by written missives, but there departure did not convey the intense and deeply moving force that it did in the Senate. For in the House it was representatives merely who were turning their backs upon their fellows, but in the Senate it was sovereign states that were deserting the common hearth. The *states* were going out. All that ever had been feared, or derided as improbable, or defied as impossible, or talked against, written against, prayed against, all this had actually come to pass, and in the visible physical forms of the departing senators, the states were leaving, never to return. Impenetrable gloom, foreboding, and thick darkness settled upon the Senate Chamber, and the soul was troubled: each man searched his heart to find if it were he who had dishonored his fathers, and had shortened the days of the land which the Lord his God had given him. The onlookers thought of Webster and his prayer, that his dying eyes, as they sought the sun, might not behold it shining upon a torn and rent land, and they cursed the hour in which they themselves were witnessing the dissolution of the Union. Woe worth the day!

When the scene was over and the open air had been reached, those who had been looking on this spectacle heaved a long breath and betook themselves to their homes. As the crowds streamed along the Avenue, it was apparent that something great, something direful, had happened. The southerners walked with their heads in the air, and talked in excited and defiant tones; the northerners had their heads down, and spoke in fitful and bated breath; then they tried to shake off their forebodings, and to throw the burden of the day upon the seceders. They recalled the ungracious conduct of Florida, who, with scarcely time enough to warm herself by the council fire, had been the first to reproach her fellows with inhospitality: how wrong it had been in her to come into the Union, knowing the unhappy condition of feeling which existed, when her presence increased the number of the discontented; for Florida had not added anything to the flag but her star; she had brought no increase of wealth or power; the sole dower it was possible for her to bring was fidelity, and this she had withheld; and soon the reproach of Florida had grown into a sense of injury against the whole South, which unquestionably, as far as material advantages were concerned, had gained from the Union more than she had contributed.

By the time that the people began to separate, and branch off into the different directions that led to their homes, the northerners had regained their voices, which, indeed, for some time had been pitched high in argument and in sharp retort, and when the doors closed upon them, the sense of the South's wrong towards the North was uppermost, the sense of the North's right controlled their minds, and the determination not to let the South go out, or, as it was expressed, the resolution to "maintain the Union," had become fixed and unalterable. The crowds at the hotels were divided: the southerners exulting in high voice over the event of the day, and asserting the resolution of the South to achieve its independence, and its capacity to maintain it against any attempt at prevention by the North. They were greatly elated, and their predictions of the course of secession assumed that every state south of Mason and Dixon's line, and of the Ohio and the Missouri rivers, would speedily follow, and that the year would not close without the South receiving applications from northern states for membership in the new confederation. The excited imagination of the southerner pictured the portions of Ohio, Indiana, and Illinois which bordered on the beautiful river, breaking off from their old allegiance and turning their faces southward, instead of towards Washington; even the greatest city and port of the country, New York, refusing to have its communication cut off from the most productive soil of the land and the greatest extent of territory, would join her fortunes to those of the South. Then her state would follow, and New England, the detested New England, would be completely isolated, and the day might come when the whole Union would be reorganized, with New England and her western progeny left out. Thus, in the strife for supremacy between New England on one side and South Carolina on the other, South Carolina was to be uppermost, with the northern firebrand quenched and cast aside. In the babel of voices the accentuated tone of the northerner was little heard; the southerner ruled the hour and his peculiar accent filled the air.

The southerners unquestionably relied upon the sympathy of the democratic party at the North for staying the hand of coercion. Nevertheless, wherever the news of this day's work reached in the North, it met but one reception. The northerner, Democrat though he might be, did not give way to his feelings: he brooded, and when he spoke, it was to tell his son that, come what may, the Union had to be preserved; that for the southerner to say he was going "out" was one thing, but for him to do it was another; the North would have something to say about that, too; never again should there be another such scene in the United States Senate. There was no mistaking the resolution of the northern people, and the South felt it.

That which took place in the Senate was something which never before had occurred in the recorded history of people, for the conditions under which it had taken place had never before existed. There had been confederations in plenty, and confederations which had broken up in dissension; but never before had there been a government delegated by sovereign states, which had been dissolved by the action of its individual constituents. Secession, as the American understood the term, was peculiar to the form of government known as the United States; for this was not a mere federation, it was a union, that is, a group of states consisting of a purely artificial central power, endued with attributes of sovereignty by the sovereign states, who delegated certain powers for the purpose of creating a qualified and limited sovereign. This artificial sovereign was *stella nova* in political history; but, artificial as it was, it was, within the purposes of its being and the limitations which had been set upon it, sovereign.[1] It presented the anomaly of a being with certain attributes of sovereignty (among which was perpetuity), created by agreement, and with its sovereignty delegated, limited, and defined by a written instrument.

To effect such a strange creation, it is evident that the parties to it must have been equal and willing; and as it contemplated multiplication of parties, and growth, or, rather, accretion of states from territory already possessed, but not contained within state lines, it is evident, too, that the new members of the family were also to be equal and willing. The result was a family of states, and the relations of members of a

[1] See Iredell's opinion in Chisholm *v.* Georgia, 2 Dallas, 435.

family, as well as the obligations of parties to a contract, implied equality and consent. There could not be, then, under the written instrument or Constitution, anything like inequality, and as the rule of the majority was inherent in the federal system, the consent of all was presumed when any act of the confederation had been ordained by a majority of voices. In order to effect this union, the two elements of people and states were represented in a House of two Chambers, in one of which sat the representatives of the states, and in the other those of the people. This frame of government constituted the Union. It is clear that it was neither a federation nor a confederation, merely, for then there would be no need of a representation of the people; a representation of states would be all that was required. Why was there a representation of the people? Because this government, created by the states, was intended to act, within its delegated powers, directly upon the citizens of a state, as well as upon a state. A chamber, then, in which would sit the representatives of the people, was as necessary as one in which would sit the representatives of the states. If the states alone met by their representatives, the body which these state-representatives composed would be a council, a collection of embassadors, for the states as sovereigns could be represented by plenipotentiaries only, and the form of government would be merely a federation. But, for the purposes of their being, the states which formed the new creature, considered it essential that, in their collective capacity, they should exercise power over the individuals who composed the citizens of the different states; they, therefore, ordained the representation of these individual citizens, but restricted its action to legislation strictly, and this legislation was to be shared by the states. This qualified the pure and simple executive character of the Senate, and made it legislative, as well as executive: for the primary character of the Senate, being an assembly of plenipotentiaries, was executive. No embassador can legislate for his government, he can execute only. A collection of plenipotentiaries may counsel and advise, but this is not legislation; and, even when it assents to an executive act, this is not pure legislation, but is confirmatory of executive action in the past, or, by anticipation, confirmatory of that in the future. This council of embassadors, therefore, would have remained a mere council, had not the Constitution gone farther, and ordained that the states, through their representatives, should take part in the legislation of the country, — a provision which modified the character of the council and invested it with a legislative character, and the Senate, consequently, was henceforth to be a legislature, as well as a council. Its character as an adviser was cut down to being adviser of the head of the executive branch of the government, who was to be styled President, and whose power was limited to executing the laws enacted by the legislature, except where special conditions and duties were laid down in the Constitution; its character as an executive branch of the government was restricted to foreign relations and to giving its assent to certain functions of the President, and its character as a legislature was fixed by requiring its passage of the laws.

Power, as we see, is greatly restricted in the House of Representatives, which can legislate merely. The power of the Senate to legislate is shared by the House and by the President, whose signature to an act cannot be supplied except under the limitations strictly prescribed by the Constitution; and its power to execute is shared also with the President. As for the President, he was to execute, and this in part under the control of the Senate; his power to legislate was restricted to allowance or disallowance, and this could be overridden by a two thirds vote of the legislature.

Here we see fusion of powers in different branches, but so restricted, divided, and balanced among these branches, or departments, of government, that neither could act at the expense of the other — if the Constitution, to support which the most solemn oaths were taken, was regarded, and if the people, whose watchfulness was taken for granted by the founders, were worthy of their liberties, and were equal to the task of preserving them.

Nothing could exceed the reverence with which the Americans regarded their Senate, so long as their reverence for the states retained its original vigor. The House of Representatives was an assemblage of themselves; but when they approached the Senate Chamber, their feelings were far different from those they entertained when approaching the House. In the latter case, they came as citizens, as individuals of the people; but, in the other, they came as sovereigns, and their hearts beat high with the pride of sovereignty. In that chamber sat their embassador in equality with other embassadors. In the House of Representatives they had little to call forth feelings other than those which accompanied them daily where-ever they might be, in their down-sitting and their uprising; but, in the Senate Chamber, — it was there that, above all plaçes in the world, they felt their state-hood. Could they not see their state, the state itself, before their very eyes, and hear it in the voices of the two men who sat in plain view?

Thus it was, that the American who looked upon the departure of the southern senators from the Senate Chamber was grieved and shocked beyond expression. To him the dissolution of the Union itself was going on before his eyes; than which there could be no more distressing spectacle, unless it were the rupture of his own family and its dispersion from the ancient hearth.

The great civil war, which, in the seventh decade of the XIXth century, for four years rent the United States of America in twain, was the result of the incongruous junction, under one government, of two conflicting forms of society. From the time in which the British colonies on the Atlantic seaboard revolted, asserted their existence as states, and united under the Articles of Confederation, there had been two peoples in this land calling themselves one people, and two forms of society passing themselves off as a single form. To all appearance, there was but one people, for they had had the same origin; they had, too, the same tongue and the same religion, but their localities were different, and so were their material interests and their habits. More significant than any other difference were the ways in which they viewed society, its foundation, its form, its spirit, and its end. Climate, topography, products of water and soil, tended to make the divergence between these elements wider, with a rapidity which the lack of every kind of the restrictions to which they had been subjected in the land of their origin, rendered marvellous. For, when the rebellious colonies came together at Philadelphia, the difference between the North and the South was greater than it is now that the South has undergone thirty years of assimilation with the North. In 1775 this difference was apparently fixed and unchangeable. The northerners presented the characteristics which the people of cold climates always display: they were prolific, insensible to change of temperature, saving, hard-working, of religious fervor, but tending to incredulity, skeptical in matters of politics, as well as in those of religion, and as venturesome in experiments of government as they were in scouring unknown seas; and the most striking and pregnant characteristic of all, and the one which exerted the greatest effect upon the settlement of the country, was that they were disposed to be migratory. The southerner's notion of home was a fixed habitation, around which was to cluster the traditions and associations of twenty generations: the longer it lasted, the more it was a home, and "home" was limited to "family." The northerner's notion was much more abstract; his neighborhood was more to him than the soil was; home was where his neighborhood was, and it might be said to include the neighborhood. The house might be a log-cabin, or, like the Virginian's, be built of bricks brought from England; but his pride in it depended upon the effect of the display his wealth had upon his importance in the community; his home lay where his family *and* the neighborhood were. The form of society characteristic of the northerner, therefore, was founded upon the neighborhood; it was centralized, consolidated; but, as the world knows, the form of society characteristic of the southerner was founded upon the plantation: it was dispersed, the members of it were isolated, and it was patriarchal in nature. The form each American lived under exerted a great influence upon his character, his affections, his ambition, his fears and hates, his mode of life, and, especially, upon the view he took of the end and aim of his life-work. The southern family was thrown upon its own resources: intercourse with the nearest, yet distant, neighbor, was a state affair; but the northerner lived in the midst of numbers; intercourse was the daily round of his life, and intercourse not formal and with his equals only, but informal, common, and with every class of society. To the seclusion of the southerner he opposed sociality; to his exclusion, freedom of intercourse; his sociability showed itself in every form and place; his servants were not restricted to "quarters;" they sat at the same board and broke the same bread, but they sat below the salt. It must be owned that when he went to church, that is, when he said his prayers in public instead of in private, the social line of demarcation was made more striking; then the servants who had knelt on the same floor with him in the morning, at high noon were gazing at him from "the loft." But the distinction between the northern and the southern social forms are unmistakable; one was where society lacked sociability, the other was where it was almost entirely sociable; in one region it was founded upon land, in the other, upon personal property; here labor was dishonorable and was owned, there it was honorable and compensated. The fact that all the northern colonies were slave colonies in the XVIIIth century signifies nothing, in view of the greater fact that northern society was getting rid of slavery as fast as it could do so. This fact has significance, for it shows that sentiment and interest in the North were already against slavery, while society in the South was actually founded upon it; for, in an agricultural slave country, land and slave cannot be separated; one implies the other. The South was restricted to agriculture; the North took to the sea, it navigated, it traded, it shaped materials into new forms, and already the signs were abounding that, but for the persistent opposition of Parliament to colonial manufacture, New England would be a manufacturing country.

The northern proclivities and habits of thought, too, differed greatly from those of the South. Religion entered into everything, down to the close of the XVIIth century, so much so as to impress the XVIIIth century very markedly. Ancient New England religious life was built upon the Old Testament, and was gloomy, severe, absorbing, and exacting. There was little mercy in the early New Englander's justice. Ancient southern religious life was built upon the New Testament; it did not affect manners austerely, and the justice of the southerner was humane. The middle class cut a small figure in the South; in the North it was all-important. Education in the South was exceedingly restricted, yet purer English was spoken nowhere than here; an exception to this defective education was to be found in the professional learning of the bar, which, crude as it may seem to us now, nevertheless produced not a few lawyers of erudition. In New England, education began in the cradle; as might be expected of the descendants of the most learned body of immigrants ever known. The atmosphere of the plantation was conducive to reflection and to self-analysis; that of the northern village and township favored the study of others, and was more conducive to observation than to meditation. The New Englander was a quick-witted being; he was acute — so much so as to be a standing target for the witticism of the South. There was no mechanical skill where society rested upon slavery; there were no artisans, for there were no towns, and the simple needs of the plantation were supplied by slaves. There was no demand for white mechanics, and this brought mechanical skill into disrepute. Even Jefferson[1] regarded mechanical labor unbecoming in a white person. The antipathy to white labor was inveterate; for, just preceding the secession of the eleven states, the northern laborers were stigmatized by a southern orator as "greasy mechanics," and as "the mudsills of society." No one ever heard of invention in the South, but in the Northeast every farmhouse had a brain busy in transferring the power of labor to wood and iron, and in multiplying its forces by machinery. From the beginning of the XVIIIth century, the New Englanders had displayed great aptitude for invention. In the South the planter made his journeys in his barge with half-a-dozen rowers, or in a coach and six; a carryall marked the possession of wealth in New England, and the great man generally went on horseback. As there was little or no home trade south of

[1] State of Virginia, 275.

the Potomac, there was no need of money; money, therefore, existed in little quantity, and for a long time did not circulate there at all. Tobacco provided the standard of values and was the circulating medium; trade was conducted by barter. In the North, on the contrary, except upon the frontiers, money was in active circulation. Then, as now, there were shops in every village and at the cross-roads, as well as taverns in plenty.

In several of the southern colonies there were but two classes of whites, the planters and "the poor whites;" an impassable gulf separated these social constituents. This low class is easily accounted for. In the XVIIth century Virginia and North Carolina were flooded with the scum of England, and especially of London. This was not altogether from free and voluntary immigration, but from immigration which was organized to supply the colonies with labor. The immigrants were in pawn until their labor had redeemed and enfranchised them. They were called "redemptioners," and they came over and were sent over by thousands. Criminals and the incorrigibly vicious were shipped along with them; sometimes as the result of municipal action, but often of their own motion, for undoubtedly these colonies became the retreat of many fugitives from justice, and of those who, if not criminals, had reason to shun the places where they were known. Much good, doubtless, would have been derived from the redemptioners had their force been sagaciously directed, but they were drowned out by the rapidly inflowing tide of slave labor, and thus that which might have proved beneficial to society became an evil. In the end, when slavery had possessed the land, there was no room for the low whites; the demand for their labor ceased, and they in turn ceased to labor. They sunk at once to a very low level, and they never rose again. Nothing at the South was held in such abhorrence as the "poor white." Slavery wronged him, indeed, for it permitted him to act no other part in life than that of a vicious drone, and to those above him he was a standing exemplification of the calamity in store for the white who relied on his own labor. He was really lower than the slave, if that were possible. This social pariah revenged himself upon the society into which unkind fortune had flung him, for he aggravated the contempt for labor entertained by his wealthy neighbor, and brought upon a succeeding and distant generation the punishment which the northern laboring classes inflicted. For the great mass of the northern army represented the laboring classes, of which it is safe to say, that they took the field against the South, not so much for the love of the slave as of hatred of the aristocrat who owned him.

Thus, alongside of each other lay two peoples: one, patriarchal, which, in the course of generations, became aristocratic, with labor owned and dishonorable; the other, tending more and more to democracy, with labor compensated and honorable. After the country had become subdued to settlement and tillage, commercial wealth flowed in greater stream into the hands of the democratic portion: this induced constant immigration into the North, which thus increased in numbers and wealth with astonishing rapidity, while the aristocratic portion lagged behind. Power gravitated to the North, and, therefore, when the States came together to form a confederation, the South eyed nervously every feature of the Constitution which might throw an overweight of political power into the hands of its neighbor. In order to preserve the balance of power between the two peoples, representation from the South in the general council was augmented by including the slave population distinctively in the basis of federal representation, or, rather, of the states represented in Congress. Equality of the states was secured by ordaining that all the states, irrespective of population, should be represented in the assembly of states styled the Senate, by the same number of representatives, to wit, two. Thus the South and the small states were protected against the menacing growth of the North and the great states, by equality in the chamber of states, and by a compensating increase of representatives in the chamber of the people. This compensation in representation was a precaution, and had the weakness of all precautions; it was liable to be rendered nugatory by change of conditions, and this change at last took place. As time wore on, it became clear that the enormous rapidity of growth on the part of the North had not been adequately forecast by the makers of the Constitution, and, as concurrent expansion was impossible, owing to the non-expansive capacity of slavery, the South apparently lagged behind: in reality, it had been distanced in the race. The black cannot keep up with the white race in any respect; and, as this contention for supremacy in the wealth of the country was a contention between the systems of labor which produced this wealth, white labor soon left black labor (and with it the society founded upon it) in the rear.

Moreover, the nature of slavery itself, by withholding the reward of exertion from the laborer, and by diverting the fruits of toil to the owner, rendered competition between free and slave labor a hopeless task. Except in the products to grow which white labor was unadaptable, slave labor could not hold even its own.

The career of the slaveholders as tillers of the soil, therefore, was easily forecast, and this forecast afforded slight comfort or even hope to the southerner. The supremacy of the North in wealth and population was speedily assured; its supremacy in political power was equally a matter of course, and became a question of time only. The most important legislation of this country, consequently, is that which relates to the preservation of the balance of power between the North and the South. From the nature of the Union, a family relation, this legislation necessarily took the form of compromise. The Constitution of the United States was so essentially a compromise in what related to slavery, that it has been acknowledged by contemporary writers, that, without such compromise, this Constitution could not have received adoption by the southern states. Later still, the very word "compromise" appears as the title, and, indeed, motive, of legislation in the famous "Missouri Compromise," and in "the Compromise of 1850," and the last efforts of the venerable Crittenden, when the pillars of the Union were actually falling around him, were aimed at compromise. "This is a government of 'compromise,'" said Henry Clay, "and I have passed my life in maintaining compromise."

There was a reason for vigilance other than that required by the contention for preponderance of sectional power, and this was the carefully guarded equality of the states; this, alone, would forbid any member of the family to admit the superiority of a fellow. Equality of the states was a great fundamental notion of Union. There could in nature be no union of unequals, and thus this principle of equality becomes of the utmost importance, the primal necessity, indeed, to the preservation of the Union. For union is not the mere physical, visible, and tangible collection of bodies politic; this would be union without spirit and soul. The greatest force of union is its moral force — the union of the different characters of the various sections, their ideas and their principles, and, to this end, the constituents of union must have absolute freedom of speech and of action under the limitations imposed by themselves upon themselves. Nothing can be clearer than that, to exert this freedom of action, equality of the members is of the first necessity, for how can there be absolute freedom where one is subject to another, directly or indirectly, immediately or remotely? For the maintenance of the Union, then, nothing was more strongly insisted upon by the founders of the government than the equality of the states, and no principle ever attained such sanctity in the eyes of the Americans as this one. It was supposed to be inviolable, for each and all recognized the fact that, if it ever failed to be the paramount principle, "this Union," as the Constitution styles it, would no longer exist; a "Union might exist (indeed, another union would have to be substituted for the ruined one), "a union whereof one section is pinned to the residue by bayonets;" but that such a union was not the one constituted is clear and plain.

Equality of the states, therefore, was the fundamental principle of union among the Americans, the one sacred principle, to touch which was profanity, and it was guarded by the instinct of self-preservation, as well as by the organic law.

CHAPTER II.

FEDERAL UNION; REPRESENTATIVE DEMOCRACY.

The Anglican Revolution; descent of power from ruler to people — Aristotle's "constitution" and "government" — Contributions of different colonies to the modern Union — Contributions of the United States to the science of government — Federal Union — Representative Democracy — Three great events in North American history — The most striking physical characteristics of the British colonies in America.

HE who would know the whole extent and character of the great Anglican Revolution, which, beginning in the latter part of the XVIth century, continued its course to the closing decade of the XVIIIth century, should not restrict his observation to the events which occurred in the British Islands, but should embrace in his scrutiny the part taken by the Americans in these colonies which afterwards became the United States. For the story is not complete without the parallel and supplementary chapters furnished by these colonies to the history of the Anglican Revolution.

Down to the reign of William and Mary, we hear little of the "constitution;" after this reign the word meets us on all sides, and by the time that Walpole sought recreation from state-craft by riding to hounds at the county meet, the standing toast among the squires, next to that of "the king," had long been "our glorious constitution!"

The explanation of this fact is, that from the death of Henry the Eighth, power, political power, began to descend from the throne; its movements were erratic and contradictory; sometimes it rushed downward, then retraced its steps, but, taking its whole action together, it has continued its descent from that day to this. Its tumultuous course during the XVIIth century is in marked contrast with the orderly and grave progress it has maintained since the flight of James II. It rapidly sought the people; it ignored the nobles and beheaded the king. The Long Parliament was made up of Presbyterian squires and city lawyers, but Pride's Purge ousted them and brought in the farmers and shopkeepers; Cromwell cast these aside when he had done with them, and when life had done with him, the king had his own again, and the old régime held sway more merrily than ever. But the earnest, convulsive workings of a century could not terminate in such futility as was this mere doubling of tracks. Revolution righted itself and resumed its march. The Stuart dynasty was overthrown, and the results of revolution were stored up in the Exclusion Bill, the Bill of Rights, and the Habeas Corpus Act. The royal prerogative was defined and limited; Parliament was organized, lastingly, fixedly organized, the nobles were cooped up in a House of Lords, and the commons, flown with authority, and with the purse and the sword to maintain it, thronged the lower House. When noses were counted, it was found that the commons meant the squirearchy; the landed interest, the rural gentry, were "in," and there they remained until Chatham sounded the note for their downfall.

When the British people emerged from the revolution of 1688 they had effected that which their ancestors had failed to achieve; they had given their country a constitution, a structural frame of statehood, under which the powers of the sovereign were restricted; the executive and legislative functions were separated; the judiciary was independent of the appointing power, as well as of those who were to be judged, and the citizen's rights and liberties were clearly ascertained and guarded. The forces of government were no longer susceptible to confusion, nor to concentration in one hand. Power was distributed and made accountable, and rights were ascertained and were to be respected. England at last had a constitution. Political power, in its early efforts to get away from the throne, had ignored the great nobles of Simon de Montfort's day; at the accession of William and Mary it established the throne more firmly, but restricted the action of its occupant; it had done a king to death. When its reconstructive work was nearly over, and it was casting about for a resting-place, it remembered the lesson of Pride's Purge; it would descend no farther, and, turning its back upon shopkeepers and shepherds, it took up its abode in the manor-house. One ancient characteristic of this power is lacking since 1688 — irresponsibility; thenceforth political power is accountable. Another century and the merchants and manufacturers were to gain its favor; but, for the time being, the squires had it all to themselves. They discarded brown October for Port, and no wonder they toasted with enthusiasm, "Our glorious constitution."

In surveying the results of the revolution of 1688, it is impossible to come to any other conclusion than that the whole movement was one which had for its aim the lessening of the inequality existing between the constituent members of the state. The throne and the great nobles had been shorn of authority and the commons had waxed in power. The distance between the sovereign and the people had been lessened. This diminution of inequality was a positive gain of equality. England, it is true, emerged from its revolution with the old classes of king, lords, and commons; but the power of the state was in the hands of the people, who were the real rulers, and who retained king and lords for the good they could do the commonwealth. The tables were turned; the state henceforth made for democracy, and with such effect, that the modern assertion, that England is as democratic as the United States are, can be controverted only by pointing to the monarchical and aristocratic *form* of government. All are equal in the courts; power emanates from the people, and monarch and nobles are mere conduits or agents of this power.

The chapters of American history that are parallel to those of the English revolution, those from 1630 to 1688, tell the same story. The conditions under which the forces of society acted in America were very different, but the aim of these forces was the same, and the result was democracy; representative democracy, in politics, and in matters of conscience, absolute freedom. After 1688, the revolution in America continued its course, interrupted by nearly a century of repose and of force-gathering, until 1788, when it terminated, after protracted convulsion and revolt, in giving to the world a form of government unknown until then, but which assumed its place among the governments of the world with an assurance of power and stability that belonged more naturally to one of ancient growth. This form of government is known as a Federal Union. It was the latest form of Anglican freedom. Alliances and leagues, federations and confederations, had existed in numbers, but a government which was the creature of sovereign states that had delegated the sovereign powers necessary to the exercise of its functions, and which, nevertheless, acted directly upon the citizens of these creating states, and which, at the same time, stood in external relation to the rest of the world as a great power, had never before been known to history. These states were founded upon the doctrine that the sovereignty lay in the people, because the people constitute the source whence all state-power emanates. It is true, that where the real power of a state lies, there resides the sovereignty, and that, judged by this standard, the sovereignty of Great Britain must lie in the commons, who are the repository of power; nevertheless, the British people disclaim the notion that the sovereignty reposes anywhere but in the throne; that is to say, they invest the occupant of the throne with the attributes of sovereignty, they make him the repository of sovereign powers, and carry out the principle of personification to the extent of styling him "the sovereign." It is evident that the great Anglican revolution took a step in America farther than it had taken in England; for in America it did not stop until every revolting colony had become a state, built upon the expressed principle that the state is a commonwealth, and that sovereignty lies in the people and nowhere else. It is in accordance with this principle that the chief official of an American state was made the agent merely of sovereign power, and was styled "the Governor," and that, later on, the style of the chief official of the United States was restricted to one almost barren of importance, and was called, "the President."

Aristotle[1] says, that the words "constitution" and "government" have the same meaning, and that government is the supreme authority in states. He also says that when the citizens at large administer the state for the common interest, the government is called by the generic name, a constitution (πολιτεία).[2] Modern publicists, with the rich examples of constitutional states before them, and especially the Anglican commonwealths, will not entertain for a moment the confusion of the term "constitution" with that of "government;" as well confound the soul with the action of the body. Government is the application of the ruling forces of the state; Dahomey has a government, but one would hardly venture to attribute to it a constitution, or even a policy. In its broadest sense, government is the art of governing; in another sense, it is the method and manner of governing a particular country; in another, it is synonymous with the state, and in a still more restricted use of the word, it embraces the great executive officials only who administer the functions of the state. In this last and personifying sense, it has been employed for many generations in the British Islands and dependencies, where we hear of one being "on the side of government;" "government purposes to do this or that;" "what

[1] Politics, III, 7: Jowett's translation. [2] Id. I, 79, 80.

will government have to say?" It is noteworthy that, in the United States, the term "administration" is invariably used to express this personification. This is to be attributed to a substantial distinction between the modes of governmental administration in the two countries. In Great Britain all statutory enactments have their inception in the cabinet; Parliament acts only upon that which is laid before it by the ministers. In the United States, on the other hand, all legislation has its origin in the legislature itself, and the President and cabinet merely administer the laws which have originated in and have been enacted by Congress. It is clear that in Great Britain the cabinet is a governmental body more than it is in the United States, and hence it is that the British people call their ministry "government," and that the Americans speak of the President and his cabinet as "the administration." Nevertheless, the use of the term "the government" is common with the Americans in personification of the governing power; but it is equally noteworthy that, when this is the case, the term is applied to the President and cabinet in the exercise of functions not in compliance with special enactment for the case in hand, but which are general, and dependent more upon the Constitution than upon legislation, or where the legislation is ancient and general, or where the function is one which relates to the President, as the official head of a great power, and is *dehors* legislation altogether. Thus, where a difficulty has occurred between the United States and one of the great powers, the expression, "What action will the administration take?" would grate upon the ear of an American, for he would be aware that there would be no law of Congress to administer. The correct expression would be, "What action will the government take?" for the circumstances present conditions for the exercise of constitutional powers, or those conferred by early legislation, and not of administration merely.

If these examples, sustained by the ancient and common speech of two distinct peoples, of the same race and tongue, illustrate the popular use of the word "government," it is clear that "government" and "constitution" have not the same meaning. The lapse of two thousand years has created a distinction between them. Constitutions now-a-days are written or unwritten. If written, they embrace, among other things, the form of government. We see the different elements defined and described and we see further the lines distinctly marked upon which they are to act. Constitutions contain also, in few but very clear words, something to which everything else contained in them, and the people themselves, must be subordinate without gainsay or contradiction. These expressions are those which, whether they set forth the nature of government or the rights of the citizen, may be styled the utterance of the very soul of the people thus organized into a state.

There is only one way of estimating the constitutional character of a people — by its comformity or nonconformity with its constitution, written or unwritten; for in this constitution will be found the natural expression, and, therefore, the spirit of the people. If the constitution be unwritten, then it is to be collected from certain monumental statutes, judicial opinions, charters, or events; as in England from

Magna Charta, the Habeas Corpus Act of Charles II., and the statutes which marked the course and termination of the revolution of 1688, and others which dot the records of legislation down to the Reform bills of the XIXth century. Where, too, the constitution is unwritten and the form of government is the product of time and tradition, this constitutional form may be ascertained from the visible branches themselves of the government. A constitution, then, embraces the structure of the state, and also manifests the spirit of the state. In it resides the soul which governs the government. So positive has this conception become in later days, that the modern writers are few who do not regard the state as a moral being. This, certainly, is carrying personification to a far point, but we have just seen that the common speech of the English-speaking people sustains the publicists in this position. True it is, that of the Anglican governments the moving spirit is embodied in their constitutions.[1]

Few, then, will question Aristotle's second remark, that when the citizens at large administer the state for the common interest, the government is called by the generic name, a constitution. For, though when strictly analyzed its terms cannot be completely reconciled, it contains this truth, derivable from anglican experience of the last two centuries — that a popular state, when founded in sound principles, conducts its government by certain methods, and that from these princi-

[1] In respect to the moral attributes of a state, the modern writers merely "go back to Aristotle" and to Plato. For the Hellenic notion of this element of state-being, and for the reflection of a people's nature and social conditions by their political constitution, and for the ethical influence of constitutions, see Newman, Politics, I, 209-211, 223 *et passim*. Compare, too, his references to Plato.

ples and methods a constitution can certainly be deduced: πολιτεία cannot bear the interpretation of "constitution," as an English-speaking publicist understands the term, and it requires all the weight of Jowett's name to make it do so. Nevertheless, Aristotle's remark applies with singular force to the experience of modern free governments. For though England unquestionably had a constitution previous to the revolution of 1688, it was an imperfect one, and so confused and ill balanced, and so faulty was it in the distribution of political rights and powers, that, until this revolution had wrought a change, the constitutional history of that state can hardly be deemed to have set in. But the revolution over, we behold two things: the commons have the preponderance of power, that is to say, the citizens at large administer the state for the common interest; and forthwith the government is called a constitutional government.

Thus, though Aristotle doubtless had in mind a government far more democratic than that of Great Britain, the general truth of his remark is sustained by an illustration from the history of England.[1]

[1] It must be borne in mind that Aristotle could not have had the conception of a constitution nor even one of a state, such as dwells in the mind of an English-speaking man of to-day. The only notion of a state that he gives us, is that of the City-state. "Of Empire — of the subordination of several states to one ruling state — he has nothing to tell us; he must have looked on such a form of union as artificial and unnatural, and therefore as beyond the scope of his inquiry. Nor does he treat of federation, or the union of several states under a common government for the common good; to his mind the City-state should need no help from other states, and in combining with them would only be surrendering a part of its own essential vitality." Politics, 1326 B; Fowler's City-state, 62. Aristotle's state was composed of men who lived the highest life, and whose fealty rested on neither fear nor force, but on enthusiastic patriotism and devotion.

It was in Connecticut that the written constitution, if not for the first time exhibited to the world, first appeared as the organizing instrument of a new state; and first became indispensable to the formation of society in British America. The circumstances under which it appeared account for its importance. A few congregations, dissatisfied with the exclusive and overbearing action of the Massachusetts oligarchy (notably the imposition of taxation without representation, though, doubtlesss, there were personal and doctrinal antagonisms also), left the shores of the Charles River and sought those of the Connecticut. Buried in the woods, unknown to the revolutionary government in England and uncared for, these dissenters from dissent organized their society into what eventually proved to be a state, and this they did by a written constitution establishing representative democracy. About the same time, other dissenters from dissent settled the colony of Rhode Island with the avowed purpose of founding a commonwealth where all should be equal and no man should be called to account for matters of conscience. Thus side by side grew up communities, one of which had under its care the fostering of a state founded upon representative democracy and the doctrine that the governor was accountable to the governed for the exercise of his power, and the other had for its object equality of citizenship and the development of absolute freedom of inquiry. Across the line remained Massachusetts, the colony from which the others had departed, where

Such a state would afford scope too restricted for a modern constitution. "The Politics," says Newman, I, 485, "is at once the portraiture of an ideal state and a statesman's manual."

state and church were not so much in conjunction as they were one and the same thing; where freedom of inquiry was regarded as a bane of social life, and where government was merely rule by the few. Intolerance flourished luxuriantly in Massachusetts, and democracy and free inquiry had hard work to keep their footing alongside of her, in Connecticut and Rhode Island. Yet the necessities of those rude days compelled the few handfuls of New England zealots [1] to confederate — the first step towards the Union that was to follow a century and a half later. Thus we behold in this remote spot, written constitutional government, and the shoots of representative democracy, accountability of the governing power, free inquiry, and union, taking root at the same time. In the South we find the conservatism of the landed classes, and, in the middle colonies, at a later period, the free inquiry, and, strange to say, the equality of citzenship of Pennsylvania and New Jersey, although under a government almost purely palatine.

It was these things which entered into the political life of the several colonies, which found voice in the state constitutions, and which, at a later day, were stored up in the federal Constitution. In them lie our vital forces, and in them consists the real federal Union — that plant of slowest growth, but of completest maturity known to our institutional race.

The most noteworthy contributions of the United States to the science of government, have been the elements of union between separate states and repre-

[1] With the exception of rejected Rhode Island and the disdained settlers along the north coast.

sentative democracy. Federations there had been long before this government was organized, and representation was of high antiquity; but representative democracy had its inception in this land, and here it is, also, that the principle of federation for the first time assumed the character of that which is now known as "the American Union." Union, in this sense, means a combination of sovereign states, wherein a central power, created by the members, acts for all combined into one whole in its external relations, and, in their inter-relations and internal administration, has jurisdiction of such matters only as are prescribed by the constitution creating this power. In America it is essential to the notion of federal union, that the central government should possess sovereignty as far as it is delegated; that it act upon the individual citizens alike in all the states; that it should act upon the states; that it have the three great divisions of political power, to wit, executive, legislative, and judicial; that its legislature, in the popular branch, should represent the people of each and every state; and that its upper house should consist of the representatives of the states themselves; that the constitutionality of any law of such legislature, or Congress, should be determined by the courts, and that the chief executive officer should not be clothed with so much as a vestige of sovereignty, though he is to execute the powers of government. This Union, like each of the states composing it, rests upon the principle that sovereignty lies in the people.

Such, in a few words, is the notion of a federal union conceived of in America. It is the principle of federation carried to the latest stage of development

— to the stage where it is in combination and in equilibrium with the principle of nationality. First in historical order comes the grouping of neighborhoods, no matter how formless, as were the Connecticut towns. Next is the combination of political bodies, no matter how loose, so long as the parties to the combination act as political units, are unrestricted, and do declare the purposes of combination, which purposes are purely political; this is confederation, such as that of the United Colonies of New England in 1643, and that of the United States of America in 1781: so far, however, we see no central body or government embracing the three functions of government, and none which can compel the compliance of individual citizens; but next, and lastly, such a body or government does appear; the citizen owes obedience in two jurisdictions, and that which an American calls "a Union" exists. The principle of federation, in the course of its development, has finally assumed the characteristics and the attitude of a power, whose chief function in internal affairs is to preserve in harmony the conflicting principles of localism and nationalism. Historically, the former precedes, and nationalism in the United States may be called the offspring of localism, for the United States constitute a group of peoples, each of which is autonomous and inhabits a particular locality.

There is, likewise, another product of localism, and that is the representative democracy, which is indigenous to this country. When the colonists came here they brought their institutions along with them, and they were unfettered in the task of planting these institutions and of adapting them to the new conditions which invested them. Moreover, in the northern colonies, the colonists were of one class; political development did not have to contend with distinctions of classes. Neither was there disparity of wealth sufficient to make itself felt adversely to the principle of equality; and the ruling colonists being of one speech and of the same manners, democracy may be said to have come with them and to have taken possession of the country unopposed. The colonists, too, north and south, were familiar with the idea of representation in government, and the parliamentary struggle going on in England during the infancy of the colonies was their struggle as much as it was that of those who were waging it abroad. The township soon appeared in the northern colonies, and by the beginning of the XVIIIth century had attained the height of its effectiveness. The township is the neighborhood, and the neighborhoods constituted the General Assembly, being represented there by members of their own choice. In the south, where the parish existed, and was not the neighborhood, the neighborhood, nevertheless, ruled, and there, too, it constituted the legislature. This principle and form of representation is a natural characteristic of us as a people, and, being natural, its growth has been constant, silent, resistless, full.

Three great events have influenced the course of civilization in North America: the Conquest of New France by the British, the achievement of Independence by the Thirteen Colonies, and the subversion of the slave power in the United States.

The Conquest of New France, by assuring British

supremacy, secured to this quarter of the globe predominance of the notions and principles contained in the word "anglican;" that is to say, the assertion of individuality in matters of conscience, and the assertion of individuality in matters of government. Both of these principles had been evolved from the ages by Free Inquiry, which, on one side, took the form of religious liberty, and, on the other, of representative government and accountability of the governing power.

The second event, the American Revolution, was not a struggle between races, but was one between members of a race-family, and was a conflict of principles, which, though not unknown to the most of Western Europe, had made for generations the British islands their peculiar field of strife. In England, this struggle terminated with the Revolution of 1688, when constitutional limitations were at last placed upon authority, which had been wont to hold itself free from accountability, and when certain rights of the individual received constitutional guaranty. This Revolution, however, did not extend to these shores, and, in the course of time, it became necessary to fight the battle over again upon the soil of America. The Revolution of 1776 accomplished this, and, advancing still further than the Revolution of 1688, transferred the sovereignty from the throne to the people. From that time to this the Americans have ascribed to government a different origin and a different object from those which had been previously accepted. The source of authority is now said to lie, not in the governor, but in the governed, and all political power to emanate from and return to the people;[1] every administrative force is held to be delegated and accountable, and to have for its purpose the greatest good of the greatest number. These doctrines have been steadily approached in England by the slower and less direct processes resulting from the Revolution of 1688, but, in this country, the operation of our independence was direct and speedy, and the citizen was regarded at once as a different being from what he ever had been before. By this transformation of the governor into an agent, and the governed into principals, is meant the transfer of sovereignty from the throne to the people, and this transfer was Revolution.[2]

The third event, the American Civil War, was a logical sequence of the American Revolution. Starting with the assumption that sovereignty lay in the people, it answered the inquiry, What constitutes the people? by sweeping away the restrictions upon citizenship, which had been imposed by race, color and previous condition of servitude. It converted on the spot four millions of slaves into as many free men,

1 "All power henceforth reverts to the people." Constitution of New York, 1777. "All power is vested in and consequently derived from the people." Declaration of Rights, Virginia, 1776; and see state constitutions of revolutionary epoch.

2 "Sovereignty is the right to govern; a nation or State-sovereign is the person or persons in whom that resides. In Europe the sovereignty is generally ascribed to the Prince; here it rests with the people; there, the sovereign actually administers the Government; here, never in a single instance; our Governors are the agents of the people, and at most stand in the same relation to their sovereign in which regents in Europe stand to their sovereigns. Their princes have *personal* powers, dignities, and preëminences, our rulers have none but *official;* nor do they partake in the sovereignty otherwise, or in any other capacity, than as private citizens." Chisholm *v.* Georgia, 2 Dallas, 472; Jay, C. J. (1793).

and is the latest constitutional assertion of individualism, and the latest effort of Free Inquiry known to us in constitutional history.

If we look at the map of North America during the later colonial epoch, but still previous to the conquest of New France, we shall see that the British colonies occupied a long strip of seacoast and backlying uplands, upon a line which was unbroken from the Savannah to the Penobscot. The first thing to strike the eye is, that these colonies were contiguous, and that they extended from a warm to a cold climate, but that all lay within the temperate zone. It is further to be remarked that, while nothing opposed the westward march of the British into the valley of the Mississippi, no other European race could enter it, without proceeding by way of the St. Lawrence river, which is closed by ice for many months in the year, or by taking a circuitous and irksome route southwardly through the Gulf of Mexico. Thus, the natural expansion and advance of the British in America would be on shorter lines and through more temperate climes than could be enjoyed by any other people; deep bays and navigable rivers facilitated access to the interior, and the front of seacoast secured direct and open communication with Europe. Such physical conditions could not be otherwise than favorable to colonial development.

The second striking characteristic is the predominance of the anglican element. There was great diversity of race, tongue, and religion in the middle colonies; the Dutch were uppermost along the Hudson, and the Huguenot French were conspicuous in

South Carolina, but these races, tongues, and religions were so assimilative with those of the character-giving localities, New England and Virginia, that, even where assimilation stopped short, political conformity became complete. The English are not assimilative, therefore their exaction of the eradication of foreign institutions, or the conformity of these with their own, is inexorable; and, as time invariably rewards fixity of purpose, these communities, from one end of the country to the other, at last presented unmistakably the appearance of English colonies. Looking at the colonies comprised in one view, the forms of religion are those peculiar to England, the universal language is English, the governments are such as can spring from anglican sources only, the physical appearance of the people, their accent, manners, habits, and modes of living, all are English. Though nearly every tongue of Western Europe was spoken within their limits, so predominating and absorbing was this single element, that no one could mistake these settlements for anything else than English colonies, nor deny their possessing a remarkable degree of political uniformity.[1] It is true that, in respect to homogeneity, they did not equal the French colonies in Canada, nor has account been taken of the African contingent; nevertheless, the more complete homogeneity of the French, to all appearance, had no greater effect on the political structure of New France than the approximate homogeneity

[1] "Providence has been pleased to give this one connected country to one united people; a people descended from the same ancestors, speaking the same language, professing the same religion, attached to the same principles of government, very similar in their manners and customs. . . . This country and this people seem to have been made for each other." The Federalist, II (Jay).

of the English had on the British colonies. New England was as English as Canada was French, and the southern colonies were more so than Mexico was Spanish. In Pennsylvania, upper New Jersey, and New York only could this characteristic be said to be modified in any great degree, and everywhere the Scotch and Irish were in such harmony with the English population around them, and were in such constant process of assimilation, that the general condition of homogeneity remained intact. The whole population, north and south, presented an unbroken appearance of anglican civilization, and the governments, if not struck from the same die, were unmistakably products of the same mint.

No great cities appear. There is Boston in the far north, New York at the mouth of the Hudson, and Philadelphia, the largest of the three, on the Delaware.[1] Flourishing as these are, they cannot be called great; south of Philadelphia, there is no city whatever. There is no such thing anywhere as a common capital, and, to explain the lack of so impressive a feature, we must turn from the map and betake ourselves to a consideration of the political constitution of the colonies.

[1] As late as 1790, when the first census was taken, Philadelphia, then the largest and by far the most important city in the Union, had 42,520 inhabitants only; New York had 33,131; Boston had 18,038; and Baltimore, 13,503 souls. These were the most populous cities, and they are taken in order of numbers. Between Baltimore and Providence, in this list, are no other towns or cities, and yet Providence had 6,380 people only.

CHAPTER III.

POLITICAL SEPARATENESS OF THE BRITISH COLONIES.

Causes of segregation — Lack of the sentiment of union — What was a British colony? — Political nature of a colony, and the relations of a colonist to the crown and to his colony — Political corporations — Allegiance — Social and economical effects of separateness; its advantages and disadvantages — Extremities to which spirit of exclusion reached — Colonial individuality — Colonial development due to self-government: colonies were creatures of growth and development — Separateness due to natural causes.

POLITICAL separateness is the most striking characteristic that greets the observer. Though the colonies are contiguous, and, in New England, homogeneous, they are disunited: they have no common constitution. This condition of segregation is attributable to several causes: 1. They were planted at different times, from different motives, with different objects, under different circumstances, and by settlers of different characteristics. 2. Diverse topographical and climatic conditions were unfavorable to consolidation, or to anything like oneness among them all. 3. Race instinct, as well as reasons of convenience and prudence, imposed limitations upon aggregations which might become unwieldy, which might jeopardize the enjoyment of self-government, or compel too great a sacrifice of individual freedom to the exactions of the community. To establish the verity of this proposition, it needs the mention only of the hundred, the parish, the township, the shire, and the county, as illustrating natural race precincts. Were anything wanting to exemplify other motives for segregation, the migrations from Massachusetts to Connecticut and from the Carolinas to Tennessee would fully set forth the fact that sense of restraint, restlessness, jealousy, or fear of absorption by encroaching neighborhoods, clashing doctrines, adverse legislation, in a word, the thousand personal influences to which independent men are subject, have proved quite as effective in restricting social aggregation and causing disjunction, as have motives of mere convenience and social order. Historical, social, political, topographical, and personal reasons, then, explain the diversity that appears in the components of this assemblage, as well as the political separateness of the colonies, and to climatic influences, difference of soil, and qualification of homogeneity, must be ascribed the contrast of social constitution, whereby concentration distinguishes population in the north, and dispersion population in the south.

4. To these reasons must be added another, that it was not to the interest of the home government, or central power, to suffer consolidation of separate communities upon their own motion, in a distant land, where the conditions were exceedingly favorable to the development and expansion of power. These colonies were regarded as dependencies, but consolidation or even union, by revealing strength, is more suggestive of independence than it is conducive to the maintenance of dependence. While, then, united effort of several colonies might be tolerated for special and temporary purposes, such tolerance was purely an act of grace or necessity and not the concession of a right.

As for consolidation on the motion of the colonies themselves, it was out of the question; the interest of the crown then manifestly lay in maintaining the disjunction of these dependencies.[1]

So deeply impressed upon colonial life was this condition of separateness, that, for generations after the occupation of the Atlantic coast by the British, no effort was made towards a permanent union of the colonies, nor of any considerable part of them.[2] There was coöperation, but never union. Such combinations as occurred were provoked by considerations other than those of social development, and were not political and voluntary, but were physical and compulsory; such as defence against the aborigines, attack of the French, and the like. These operations were of a temporary nature, were accomplished under the spur of impending destruction, and ceased as soon as the necessity was removed. For instance, the combination of the New England colonies for military purposes was dissolved by the reduction of the hostile tribes of Indians, and, at a later day, the coöperation of New York and New England came to an end with the retirement of the French from the border. There is no instance of a general union of the colonies in arms until the Revolution, nor is there an instance of general and spontaneous union for any purpose before the Stamp Act. Supplies of men and money granted

[1] "The British government, not choosing to permit the union of the colonies as proposed at Albany, and to trust that union with their defense, lest they should thereby grow too military and feel their own strength," etc. Works of Franklin (Bigelow), i, 249; ii, 343 *et seq.* See, also, Life and Works of John Adams, ix, 591, 592.

[2] To this the confederation of the New England colonies in the seventeenth century may be considered a qualified exception. It certainly did not contemplate political union.

upon requisition of the king are not significant of union, nor were they spontaneous and general; spontaneous assuredly they were not, as they were occasioned by the requisition of a superior, nor can that be called general and united which was not imposed upon all the colonies, nor complied with by all, and which, when discharged, was the particular contribution of each individual colony. No action of all the colonies collectively, either of their own motion or of that of the home government, ever occurred. The sentiment of union was entirely wanting for four generations,[1] and it is difficult to see how such a sentiment could develop under the colonial system; for a common ground of their own was needful to union, and this the colonies did not possess; and reciprocal ties were requisite to bind men together in unity, but of these there could be none so long as the only ties permissible were those that attached dependents to their superior. In fact, there was nothing political in common between a colonist of New Hampshire and a colonist of Georgia; the allegiance that they swore to one and the same person made them subjects of the same lord, but nothing more. It was not until subversion of the liberties each colony possessed was threatened by the spirit which prompted the Stamp Act legislation, that there was any general and spontaneous action. Then, for the first time, a common sentiment pervaded the land; for the first time a common interest was awakened; and, for the first time, what was

[1] "It is a significant and curious fact," says Bigelow, speaking of the Albany Conference of 1754, "that, with the exception of those from Massachusetts, none of the delegates had any instructions to discuss the question of a union of the colonies for mutual defence, or for any other purpose." Works of Franklin, ii, 344.

styled a Congress of the Colonies met together; though, even then, four of the thirteen colonies remained at home. This was the first indication that such a thing as a general sentiment of union existed in British America.

This characteristic of separateness in the colonies was such a radical feature of their structure, and has had such a far-reaching and lasting effect upon the states into which they have since developed, and upon the Union which was formed from them, that close study of it, and thorough appreciation of its force as a condition precedent to union, and as a political element in our constitution, is essential to a correct understanding of the history of the United States. We have seen already, that, apart from known physical and moral causes, this trait had political reasons for its being, and was influenced by the relations which existed between the crown and the colonies. It may be well, therefore, to inquire what a colony, in the political sense, was; what its relations to the crown were; and what the relations of the colonist to the crown and to his colony.

A British colony was a dominion beyond seas, of which the sovereign of Great Britain was lord. This dominion was integral; that is, it was a corporation comprising in itself the powers and performing the functions of a body politic, independently of the world, except in the single respect, that it was bound unto its lord; he was its head, and was represented by a Governor.[1] This dominion was self-governed; it

[1] In the charter colonies at the outset of the Revolution, viz., Massachusetts, Connecticut, and Rhode Island, the Governors and assemblies were elected by the people.

had a parliament, whose statutes were subject to revision by the king only, and, when these were not disallowed, they became the law of the land.[1] Thus it was autonomous, it was independent of the other dominions, and it was subject to no other control than its lord's. The frame of a colony's political structure, it is seen, differs in no respect from that of England itself, where the three most prominent features are, likewise, king, parliament, and subjects. If, for illustration, we take any one of the American colonies, we behold, first, the king in the person of the Governor; next, the law-making power in the shape of the provincial legislature; and, finally, the body of the people, who are subjects. These last were freemen, and they were so by birthright of British subjects; their liberties, which were numerous and great, were theirs by prescription, or by royal grant of franchises. The Governor was a symbol; the only military power was the militia, which the colonists themselves composed; the judiciary was their own, and they paid no taxes which were not laid by themselves. Such was the political constitution of every colony whose people were British, either by birth or descent. King, legislature, free people; these were the invariable and unmistakable components of anglican constitution the world over.[2]

[1] In Maryland, Connecticut, and Rhode Island, the laws were not required to be sent to the king for his approval; it was otherwise with the rest of the colonies. Chalm. Annals, 203, 295; 1 Doug. Summ. 207, 208; Story, Constitution, Book I, ch. xvii, § 171. The Maryland charter was the first by which the Proprietor and the freemen were authorized to legislate free from the negative of the crown.

[2] The governments of Rhode Island and Connecticut were so republican in constitution, that when the colonies became states they retained their charters as the organic law. A number of the states,

To the assertion that no power intervened between the lord and his dominions, there are two seeming contradictions, the Board of Lords of Trade and Plantations, and the claim of right in the British Parliament, or, what amounts to the same thing, the British people, to legislate for the colonies. As to the first, it may be said that, so long as the colonies were small and the magnitude of their business was not too great, the administration of colonial affairs was conducted solely by the king in Privy Council; but that, as they waxed in size and numbers, it was deemed necessary for the facilitation of business to commit a great part of purely administrative matters, and particularly those relating to trade and commerce, to a body created for the purpose, and styled the Board of Lords of Trade and Plantations. This body did not escape the detraction that invariably opposes everything novel, nor could it avoid the insinuations that attributed its creation to motives not altogether in the interest of remote and unfriended communities. Nevertheless, as the ground assigned for its formation was a reasonable one, this board was accepted, especially as the right of appeal to the king in council was left unimpaired, and, though narrowly watched, it was regarded by the colonists as a mere instrument of the sovereign for the administration of colonial affairs, and, hence, was no intervening third power.

The act of Navigation, which regulated colonial commerce and restricted trade with foreign powers, and the acts of Trade, which, so far as colonial manu-

also, in adopting new constitutions, made their ancient charters the foundation of them, and, indeed, may be said to have merely adapted the charters to the new conditions.

factures were concerned, were chiefly of a prohibitory nature, were enactments of the British Parliament; distinctively a third party and an intervening one. It has been a matter of surprise, that the colonies remained submissive to this legislation. Docility, however, was not in every case a matter of course; for Massachusetts, in order to assert her independence as an autonomy, made the Navigation act her own, by enacting it in her legislature, and Virginia, declaring that, under her charter, she was not bound by it, acknowledged it only as a matter of bargain and compact with the Commonwealth.[1] Nevertheless, it was accepted generally, though reluctantly, and this acquiescence in what, at first glance, seems interfering and meddlesome, is readily accounted for, when it is considered, that, to the one who owned the navy must be committed the task of maintaining open communication between the different members of the anglican family, and of affording them protection on the high seas, and that it did this at its own cost and charges. Acquiescence, then, in this legislation, whereby great profits were diverted to the commercial classes of England, was regarded by the colonists in the light of compensation for benefits rendered; it was a matter of compact. It is true, moreover, that the British Parliament, from time to time, asserted legislative authority over the colonies, and that, in this persistent conduct, it finally had the passive, if not the active sympathy of the king, and it is further true that a notion existed, even among the colonists themselves, that the parent parliament must be something greater than their own puny legislatures; a central sun, around which the

[1] Life and Works of John Adams, iv, 48.

lesser orbs revolved. But this notion, more easily accounted for by sentimental than by political reasons, was eventually rejected by those who entertained it, and as they at last took up arms against what they styled the usurpations and encroachments of this body, it can be asserted, that, at least, one of the parties to the question refused to recognize the intervention of this power between the dominions and their sovereign. The claim of the British Parliament to legislate for the colonies, though asserted to this day,[1] thus finds no support worthy of consideration in the history of these dominions.

The fact, then, remains, that a colony was a dominion; that its people were subjects; that these subjects had for their lord and sovereign the person who was likewise sovereign of Great Britain; and that they

1 "The legislative authority of Parliament extends over the United Kingdom, and all its colonies and foreign possessions, and there are no other limits to its power of making laws for the whole empire, than those which are incident to all sovereign authority — the willingness of the people to obey, or their power to resist. Unlike the legislatures of many other countries, it is bound by no fundamental charter or constitution; but has itself the sole constitutional right of establishing and altering the laws and government of the empire. . . . The power of imposing taxes upon colonies for the support of the parent state, though not now enforced, was exercised by Parliament in the case of the provinces of North America; and, as is but too well known, was the immediate occasion of the severance of that great country from our own. But whatever may be urged against colonial taxation on grounds of justice or expediency, the legal right of Parliament to impose taxes upon all persons within the British dominions is unquestionable." May's Laws, etc., of Parliament, 36 *et seq.* But see Lord Glenelg: "Parliamentary legislation on any subject of exclusively internal concern to any British colony possessing a representative assembly, is, as a general rule, unconstitutional. It is a right, of which the exercise is reserved for extreme cases, in which necessity at once creates and justifies the exception." Parl. Pap. (118), 7.

were entitled to make their own laws free from the intervention of any other people. That this view of their political structure was general throughout the colonies became apparent during the discussion that followed the Stamp Act, and it was to preserve the integrity of this structure, that the colonists finally embarked upon what proved to be revolution. Had not such been really the political fabric, the rising of the colonies could not have been justified, and it is to be presumed, therefore, that it would not have occurred. That it was the true one, is sustained by the facts, that the original grant by which every colony was established issued from the king as sovereign lord of the territory occupied; that he granted the lands as of himself alone;[1] and that none of them, in the course of its existence, was ever annexed to a realm. Thus the colonies were derived immediately from the king, and depended immediately upon him, and, not being annexed to any realm, or conjoined with any other dominion, were separate dominions and independent of each other. The course of royal administration confirms this view, for colonial business was always transacted by the sovereign and his assistants directly with each colony, and never with the colonies collectively, and thus it is clear that both of the only parties in interest regarded each colony as a distinct and separate body, and free from the intervention of any other power.

Allegiance had no effect to augment, diminish, or qualify the characteristic of separateness. It certainly

[1] "Every acre of land in this country was then held mediately or immediately by grants from the crown." Chisholm *v.* Georgia, 2 Dallas, 470.

did not lessen the disjunction; for, as a matter of fact, as the sentiment of union gained strength, loyalty waned. Allegiance had no lateral power of conjunction; it did not bind subject to subject, but subject to lord; it was individual and personal, not collective nor sworn to an abstract, intangible object like the commonwealth. It was sworn, not to the crown, which represents the political capacity of the king, but to the king's person, or to the king in his natural capacity. It was due from the subject wherever he might be, and it was due to the sovereign wherever he might be, though he were a prisoner in the midst of an enemy's territory, and restrained from acting in his political capacity. It was, therefore, a matter existing solely between lord and man, and what binding or uniting effect it had between subjects was social and moral, not political.

These relations, then, which existed between the king and his dominions, endued, as they were, with every principle of Anglican constitution, had the effect of making each one self-contained and exclusive of the rest of the world. They were, in fact, separate and distinct bodies in separate and distinct territories. Each held the title to its territory by a grant separate and distinct from its neighbors, and, as allegiance was an act of the person and related only to the natural capacity of the king, there could be little political in common between them. The colony of Massachusetts was as distinct from the colony of Pennsylvania, as it was from the colony of Jamaica. As far as their relations to the king were concerned, the people of each owed individual allegiance; and the king, in return, afforded protection and tranquil enjoyment of granted franchises, without the slightest reference to any other colony. Had the people of Virginia owed allegiance to the king of France, and those of Maryland allegiance to the king of Spain, they could not have been more distinct and separate bodies politic, in relation to each other, than they were when both bore allegiance to the king of Great Britain. A British subject, indeed, residing in one of these colonies, would have certain rights within the territory of the other, had he chosen to transfer his residence thither and exercise them, and some did he not so choose: as the right to own property there, to inherit lands, and the like. But this he had from no unity of the colonies, express or implied, but merely from the force of the allegiance which constituted him a subject; a fact which gave him these rights in whatever part of the British possessions they might fall — as well in the Bermudas or Bengal, as in New York or Barbadoes. In a word, they were separate and distinct autonomies, of which the citizens of one, from the fact of bearing allegiance to the same person, were not aliens to the citizens of the others.[1]

It follows from this, that the citizens of each colony formed a political corporation[2] created by the king, to whom they owed particular and sole allegiance; that they were bound by no laws which they did not make, and were bound only by those which they made with the assent of this king when this assent was specifically required; that they possessed common political interests, were subject to common duties and obliga-

[1] Development of Constitutional Liberty, 36, 37.

[2] "All states whatever are corporations or bodies politic." Chisholm v. Georgia, 2 Dallas, 468.

tions, and were entitled to common political benefits; that their government was administered for the purposes of each whole, but for no others; and that, consequently, the colonists of each colony constituted a people. It follows further, that none of these colonies was bound nor was affected in any way by the laws of another; that no one possessed political interests in nor was subject to the political duties and obligations of another, nor was entitled to share in another's political benefits; that there was no government whose administration was for the purposes of all the colonies taken collectively, and that, therefore, there was no one people throughout the colonies, but that there were as many separate and distinct peoples as there were colonies, and that these peoples were autonomous. Thus it was, that they had no common capital, and no common army, judiciary, treasury, or governor, and thus it was that they had no common ground whereon to meet, nor mode of common action.

This political separateness had its effect likewise, economically and socially. No common ground afforded room for honorable rivalry or for strife of interests; nor could there be commercial competition between the two great producing sections, since the peculiar productions of each, though flowing to the same marts, met with different demand. The North produced roots and cereals, the South plants and vines. Philadelphia, from its position and extent of trade, was the largest and most influential city, yet it cannot be said, that there was any one great commercial or social centre; the commercial classes of England controlled colonial trade, and London and its court set the fashion to colonial society. The difficulty of intercommunication strengthened the tendency to adhere to the standard of manners maintained in the old country, and to reject any which might be set up in the provinces; for, similarity of manners depends upon intercourse, and this upon facility of locomotion, an advantage unknown to the colonists. The perils of coast navigation being peculiarly great, communication was mainly confined to land travel, which, from the length and badness of roads, made a voyage to London and back a much less serious affair than a journey from Charleston to Philadelphia. Thus, the intercourse which most directly affects the manners of the upper classes, (and in those times it was the wealthy or the trading classes only that travelled,) was restricted to almost nothing, while on the other hand, it maintained with great persistence its accustomed course to the capital of Great Britain. There was too little variety of social features to tempt the colonist from his home, and, when a grand tour was resolved upon, he was not long in choosing between the splendors of London and those of Philadelphia. It is easy to see from this, why trans-Atlantic travel remained the mode; its perils were less and its attractions greater. The known and fixed standard of social life abroad was ready at hand, and, first in possession, kept the field against any innovation at home. The rusticity of colonial life could not prevail against the polish and elegance of the court; the contrast presented was too unfavorable to the former, and distaste, not to say contempt, of anything that savored of the provincial, was engendered. Separate by political constitution, with their external relations centring in a distant prince, with their manners regulated by those of a foreign court, and with their trade controlled by trans-Atlantic marts, it is no wonder that they looked to other peoples than their own for their standard of social life. Here the affairs of one were not the affairs of another, intercourse between remote colonies was well-nigh impossible, and no interest existed of binding force sufficient to overcome the feeling of exclusion and indifference; and thus the political and commercial separateness of the colonies extended to their social life and manners.[1]

This state of feeling had its disadvantages as well as advantages, for it is evident that the tendency of exclusion is to place society upon a narrow and shallow basis; its action is selfish. Men cannot shut themselves up from extraneous influences, and become broader and more humane; on the contrary, they become narrow, and this effect was manifested in more than one passage of our colonial history. It is not the lack of cohesion that affects us unfavorably in surveying the annals of the colonies, for cohesion is not expected in a system characterized by disjunction, and, moreover, in itself it does not partake of the nature of a virtue: it is the apparent indifference for each other that grates upon our feelings, and the absence of common interest and sympathy. This spirit of exclusion kept the colonist, for generations, from being more than a mere provincial, and it was not until the upheaval of the Stamp Act that he began to style himself an American.

Though such was a disadvantage of an exclusive

[1] In 1760 Franklin maintained that union of the colonies against England would be impossible, since all loved the mother country more than they loved each other. Works (Sparks), iv, 42.

and restrictive system, it cannot be denied, that separateness had its advantages; it was, for instance, highly favorable to the development of local self-government. The race is an energetic one, and is distinguished by its capacity for making the most of the means in hand. A system, therefore, which, by making no account of neighborly sympathy and good-will, might have discouraged a people of sociability but of feeble temper, lent force to the development of this people. For, as remoteness of the sovereign, and persistence in a *laissez-faire* policy of administration, afforded no diversion from the home governments, every energy and every force of the colonist was given to the administration of his own colony, and these energies and forces acquired all the more vigor from the very fact that they were pent up and had but a single outlet. The stage of culture had not yet been reached when this energy takes the form of literature, so that destitute of this means of expression, what had the colonist to do, but to talk law, philosophy, and politics,[1] and to administer government directly or indirectly? That he did this to good purpose, is shown by the burst of admiration with which Chatham directed the gaze of Parliament to the little senates in these woods, for the colonist attained such skill in administration as to remain to this day the highest example we have ever produced of mastery of the art of government.[2] No being was more firmly attached to the soil. He

[1] The autobiographies and diaries of the leading men of the Revolution afford many instances of the habitual discussion of these subjects, especially by young lawyers. They would meet regularly for this purpose. Sir Henry S. Maine notices how prevailing was the influence of Montesquieu.

[2] See *post*, pp. 129, 131–133.

loved it as the abiding-place of everything dear to him: out of its dust had he been made and to it he expected to return.[1] His province was to him what Laconia was to the Spartan; his cradle, his home, his citadel, his country, his grave. He was eager to develop its resources, to maintain its dignity, to assert its rights or to resent its wrongs, and he was exceedingly jealous of anything that affected unfavorably its individuality. He stayed not on the threshold, but met the offender more than half way, and, next to actual invasion of its rights, he feared committing himself to any position that might compromise them. Hence this jealousy of interference, and this sensitiveness to anything like intermeddling, which constantly betrays itself in our colonial history, and hence, too, one main reason for the lack of a sentiment of union, and for persistent exclusiveness.

To such an extent was the spirit of exclusion carried, that one is startled at meeting it under circumstances and at times in which, to modern notions, its appearance is incomprehensible. Thus, the pages of our annals teem with instances of what the historians style apathy, when neighboring colonies are in the presence of great danger. Mere apathy, however, is not sufficient to explain insensibility to danger, which, to-day their neighbor's, to-morrow may be their own. It has an explanation, and this, too, is to be found in the separateness of the colonies. For, being separate, what concerned one colony did not concern the rest, and, therefore, from the standpoint of the colonist, he might with equal justice be called upon to assist an

[1] Observe, *inter alia*, the pathetic and oft-repeated utterances of Hutchinson. See Diary and Letters, *sparsim*.

East Indian colony from an attack of Sikhs, as a neighboring colony from an attack of Algonquins. So long as the security of his own province was not at stake, the affair was no concern of his; it was the concern only of the colony whose border had been assailed.[1] It was not until the impending danger involved his own security, that he dared to take a step upon his neighbor's territory, for unless called upon for aid, he would have to account to the colony upon whose territory he had trespassed, and, in any event, he would have to justify his infraction of the known and determined policy of his sovereign. Gratuitous assistance might, in one case, be construed as intermeddling, and, in the other, a violation of a settled principle of government. Hence, it was a matter not of feeling, but of politics. That this was the view generally taken, is shown by the fact, that no apathy whatever appears in the case of colonies who made ready to respond to a call for aid, or who united promptly when the danger of one border affected the security of the others: but it took the impulse of self-preservation to justify and effect such union, and, as has been already observed, the danger over, the constituents resolved forthwith into their normal condition of separateness. It was not, then, lack of public spirit, nor jealousy alone, nor insensibility to distress, nor apathy itself, which made the colonists slow to move at the spectacle of a neighbor's distress, but it was the inefficacy of the constitution of the colonial system, and of a governmental policy loath to exonerate

[1] See an interesting note, entitled "Military Inefficiency of the British Colonies," in Parkman's Count Frontenac and New France, 408. Also Works of Franklin (Bigelow), ii, 351, 352.

infraction of its rules: this withheld the means of effecting union, that inspired the fear of setting precedents which might lead to political complications thereafter. Thus, when, even on motion of the sovereign and not of the colonies, colonial forces were concentrated at Albany to resist or attack the French, the troops were drawn only from New York and New England, the parts immediately affected; and when Braddock's column advanced to the subjection of the enemy which threatened the borders of Pennsylvania and Virginia, the contingent of Provincials was composed of Pennsylvanians and Virginians only.

It is evident, from what has been said, that the individuality of a colony had strong retroactive support from the condition of separateness. This attribute was strengthened by the moral effect lent by the diversity of character existing between the colonies. If their virtues were alike, their prejudices were dissimilar and conflicting, and each one had those peculiar to itself. The aristocratic colonies regarded the democracies as inferior communities, and the democratic colonies congratulated themselves upon being free from the old-world delusions of the aristocracies. Where the Church of England was uppermost, it scorned the theocracies as oligarchies, and these, on their part, thanked God that they were not as the others were. The regions where society was concentrated, looked upon those in which it was dispersed as examples of a false conception of social constitution; an opinion which was returned in kind. Degrees of latitude were equivalent to degrees of variance in character, and each colony, satisfied with itself, sought to cultivate its own notions and to exclude those of its neighbors.[1]

Such was the structural condition of the colonies during the colonial epoch. It was emphatically a condition of separateness, and one which was favored by the policy of disjunction maintained by the sovereign. One cannot but feel, that a condition existing so long without any significant disturbance, must have had its foundation in the nature itself of the people. No artificial structure, and no mere administrative policy, can account for the tenacity with which the colonies maintained their individuality. Natural causes alone account for a characteristic, which, in its political relations, is to be described as an absorbing love of local self-government. Those who see in the separateness of the colonies the effects of a mere *divide et impera*

[1] In treating of the separateness of the colonies, their points of dissimilarity have been indirectly revealed. It may be well to give the points in which all the colonies were alike, as they are set forth by one so accomplished in political analysis as Bluntschli: —

"(*a*) English law, without either landlords or feudal tenure: free property in the soil was the basis of the economic system. (*b*) Essential equality of position and rights, and the absence of any aristocracy like that which still held power in England. This equality was, however, broken by marked differences of race [such as those of the Indians and the negroes]. . . . (*c*) The constant habit of self-reliance in contrast to State-aid. . . . (*d*) The general education of the people by means of national schools. . . . (*e*) A free constitution of the villages, and independent administration of the colonies. (*f*) The small number of officials. . . . (*g*) Hardly any standing troops, their place being taken by the militia. (*h*) The existence of a House of Representatives, elected in each colony by the free men, which acted with the Senate in making laws, but by itself granted taxes and controlled the administration. (*i*) The custom of short tenure of offices, so as to provide for frequent changes. (*k*) Lastly, the gradual development of a free press and freedom of combination." Allgemeine Statslehre, or The Theory of the State, b. vi, chap. xxii (Engl. ed., 1885).

policy, attribute to colonial docility more than belongs to it; and much more than the other members of the anglican family have shown, even when under conditions more favorable to its exercise than those which surrounded the American colonies. And those who attribute to provincial self-importance a characteristic so general, and which appears so natural on the face of things, fall short of the true explanation, which, as has been observed, is to be found in the race-nature of the colonist. Thanks to the conditions of colonial existence which permitted these colonies to develop themselves, they came to be natural and complete exponents of the most powerful forces of their being; of inherent, spontaneous, irresistible individuality in government, and of abiding love of the soil. Without these traits they would have become mere factories of British commerce, but, with these, they became autonomies, each of which was as rich in institutions and in personal liberty, as England herself was.

A comparison of the British colonies with those of France or of Spain, which bordered them, will show them to be creatures of growth and development, and that this growth and development is to be attributed to their self-government. So well was this understood at Whitehall, that the fixed and wise maxim of administration concerning them was, Let them alone: a maxim recognized by George II., when he said: "I do not understand the colonies; I wish their prosperity. They appear to be happy at present, and I will not consent to any innovations, the consequences of which I cannot foresee." [1]

[1] "Solomon in all his glory," said John Adams, "could not have said a wiser thing." Life and Works, x, 347.

CHAPTER IV.

SEPARATENESS OF THE BRITISH COLONIES — CONTINUED.

Separateness during the Stamp Act period; during the Congressional period — Congresses of 1774 and 1775 — The Declaration of Independence — Local self-government.

How dominating and persistent this principle of local self-government was, is shown by its manifestations during the Revolutionary period, which extended from the agitation of the Stamp Act to the adoption of the Constitution of the United States. This period may be divided into three subdivisions, as follows: the time intervening between the beginning of the Stamp Act agitation and the Congress of 1774; that between the meeting of such Congress and the adoption of the Articles of Confederation, and that which ensued until terminated by the adoption of the Constitution.

It needs little more than to recall the expressions of public feeling during the Stamp Act period — the speech of Otis concerning the writs of assistance, the addresses of the committees of correspondence and congresses, and the like — to see that the underlying principle maintained by the colonies, was the integrity and independence of their local legislatures and the sanctity of their personal freedom. Resistance to encroachment by the British Parliament was the cry, and for the reason, that, not being represented therein, such parliament was not their own, and, therefore, had no right to legislate for them. They had their own parliaments, and, to the minds of the colonists, their local self-government being menaced, to prevent its violation they united in taking up arms.

As affairs neared the vortex of actual hostilities, one might suppose that the gravity of the situation would compel a union of all the governmental forces possessed by the colonies. Surely, in the face of the overawing danger without and of the perilous distraction within, the instinct of self-preservation should prompt a complete and harmonious union. Nothing of the sort occurred; it was still mere combination, and one which was restricted, incomplete, and inharmonious. This condition can be accounted for — the sentiment of union, which had been growing for ten years past, had been too lately awakened to become presently an active and willing force; its character was not yet well enough understood, it was not altogether above suspicion; it exacted too much of those who never had been called upon to share their liberties with their neighbors, and, in a word, it was still a sentiment, strong enough to effect a combination of arms, it is true, but was not strong enough to act the part of a binding, cohesive force. It could induce a combination which promised immediate and visible results, but when it came to exacting the surrender of liberties to a power yet to be created, and for results that could not be forecast, it was impotent. A colonist of Rhode Island, for example, knew nothing of colonial relations, except those existing between Rhode Island and the crown; to him there were none else, and all the opinion that he could entertain upon the present troubles was, that his own colony and its fellows were in a bad plight together, and that, as the conditions were similar, common counsel and common effort were better than individual action. Further than this he did not go; as for a common colonial parliament with governmental powers, his mind had never suggested, much less entertained, such a notion, and, had it been broached, he would have rejected it, if on no other ground than that it would be turning over to a new and untried creation in America powers which he was then denying to an ancient and venerated institution in England; he would be yielding to equals the very thing he denied to those who asserted that they were his superiors, and who he half-believed were his superiors. Accordingly, the Congress in which he consented to appear, was a body that met merely for counsel and not for government.

But, even had this sentiment been strong enough to sustain union, the capacity to effect it was wanting; for, so long as the colonies remained dependencies, they were confined within the limitations of dependencies; and such organizations, as we have seen, had no power to unite. Union of governmental forces in the face of administrative prohibition, would be rebellion, and they abhorred and repudiated the thought of rebellion. No man can serve two masters, and, so long as they held to their allegiance to the king, they could serve no one else; any other position would be a contradiction of their assertion that they would suffer interference in their affairs from none except their natural lord, the king. They might counsel together, but they could not act as one power; and that this was the view taken by them of their position, is clear from an examination of the credentials [1] by which they empowered their delegates to meet in Congress. One and all set forth these things: 1, that the delegates were to consult and advise with those from the other colonies respecting the present troubles; 2, that Congress should define and describe the rights of Americans with certainty; 3, that it should devise a plan of maintaining, upon constitutional principles, the ancient union with the mother country; 4, that this general plan, suggested by Virginia and Maryland, should operate on the commercial connection of the colonies with Great Britain; and, 5, that, when agreed upon, the plan should be recommended to all who were interested. Thus, the effect of united action would result from the simultaneous but individual action of the thirteen colonies.

There is not a word in these credentials, nor any internal evidence, leading to the supposition that new relations with anybody were contemplated, nor that anything was sought for but such a modification of the old relations with the crown as would give the effect of a constitutional guaranty to their liberties — such a guaranty as the English themselves enjoyed under the Bill of Rights and kindred securities. Nor is there to be found in these documents any expression that had the appearance of a colony arrogating to itself the attributes of sovereignty. It will be observed, that, in constituting the Continental Congress of 1774, the colonies acted in their individual capacity, without reference to each other, and that they made common cause from no political association, but only because

[1] Journal of Congress, I. See Appendix A.

the principles at stake affected every one alike, and because the object sought was the same in every case; that each colony appointed its own delegates, instructing them according to its notions of right and policy, but making no pretence of conferring power and authority, which, as a dependency, it did not possess, and that, therefore, no colony gave any power or authority, except for deliberation and advisement only, i. e., to ascertain what should be done, not to do; that the purposes set forth were, not to establish a new government, but, upon constitutional principles, to preserve the old one; and that this Congress was organized by the colonies as colonies, and with a careful regard to their separate and independent rights and powers; for it was restricted to declaring what the hitherto undefined rights of Americans were, to devising a plan of reconciliation by operating on their commercial character as feeders to British commerce, and to ending its deliberations with a recommendation of the course agreed upon.

That the Congress confined itself within the limitations thus set upon it, and recognized its subordination to its creators, is evident from its own action. In accordance with the instructions to the delegates to settle the undetermined position of the colonist, in respect to the crown and to Parliament, the Congress, upon report of a committee composed of two from each province, made a Declaration of Colonial Rights. This Declaration was in the nature of a Bill of Rights, and was intended to perform the same office for America that the English Bill of Rights had done for England; the latter, of course, not extending to this country or any of the dependencies, inasmuch as its extent was limited to the territory of England. The instruction to "operate on the commercial connection," the one most vital to the interests of Great Britain, was obeyed by adopting the "Articles of Association," or the non-intercourse, non-importation, and non-consumption pledges. The instruction to devise a plan for maintaining, upon constitutional principles, the ancient union with the mother-country, was fulfilled by a grave and dignified "Address to the People of Great Britain," together with "A Petition to the King."[1] Thus, having advised and consulted together and set forth their plan, and having obeyed their instructions without exceeding them, Congress dissolved, and the delegates returned home to report to their colonies, through their Assemblies, what they had done.

There is nothing in our history more clear and certain than this: that the Congress of 1774, as far as its functions are concerned, was nothing more than a council. Except in respect to discussion, it had no features of a parliament. It was not a legislature; it neither legislated nor did it pretend to legislative power. It entertained no bills, it passed no acts, it left behind it no statutes. It resolved merely, nor did its resolutions have any greater force than that which was lent them by their own importance, or by the character of the delegates who made them; for, the resolutions, once taken, had no motion of their own, but only such as was given by the recommendation of the Congress. They carried with them no authority, but depended for their efficacy upon the will of those to

[1] The Address was drafted by Jay, and the Petition to the king by Dickinson.

whom they were addressed; for each colony was at perfect liberty to accept or reject them. Thus, Congress could resolve, but not enact: it could recommend, but not enjoin. Organized for the sole purposes of ascertaining and declaring colonial rights with precision, and of devising and recommending proper measures for the redress of grievances and the security of rights, (which, having the force of custom, nevertheless lacked the sanctity of constitutional guaranty), when these purposes were accomplished its work was done, it was *functus officio*, and, destitute of the power of prolonging its existence, it did not adjourn, but it dissolved and disappeared forever.

One thing clearly appears: the Congress of 1774 was not a revolutionary body.

The character of this assembly is indicated by its name; it was a congress or body of delegates for the transaction of matters between parties independent of each other. It is clear, that it was constituted by the concurrent action of as many peoples as were represented in it, and that each of these peoples asserted its individuality by casting one vote, irrespective of the number of its delegates; and it is equally clear, that, as it was not the creation of one people, neither did its organization make these people one. The colonies, being dependencies, and having the intention of remaining such, as their instructions to the delegates testify, had not the political capacity to effect union. For, to effect union requires parties who are as independent of the world as they are of each other, and who have, of themselves, the governmental powers, executive, legislative, and judicial, necessary to the creation of a new body politic which is to be the visible and tangible form of their union. These powers the colonists did not possess in entirety. What of them they enjoyed, they enjoyed in a union already existing with their sovereign but not with each other, and this union could not be changed, nor these powers assumed in entirety, without severance from that sovereign. But the Congress was convened for the express purpose of maintaining the ancient union. An intention to supplant the old régime by a new one, an act implying the assumption of entire governmental powers and a thoroughly revolutionary act, cannot, surely, be deduced from the assemblage of a body which made no pretence to the possession of the executive, legislative, or judicial powers necessary to accomplish such an end. The colonies, therefore, in convening this Congress, took no governmental action whatever, and any conclusion whereby their political conduct as one people is inferred, or that they exercised sovereign powers, must be wrong. *First*, then, no governmental action being taken, neither the surrender nor the acquisition of constitutional rights and powers, by one or by any, could be possible. *Secondly*, the Congress was constituted by the concurrent action of a number of peoples, none of whom had cast off their allegiance to the king; so that there was no nation *de facto*. *Thirdly*, the Congress itself, endued with no element of permanence (an essential governmental element), and destitute of governmental powers of every description, save that of deliberation and discussion, was not a body politic, and, therefore, could not be the expression of anything like sovereignty, nor could its mere existence confer on its creators, one or many, the attributes of sovereignty. *Fourthly*, the parties to this Congress made no compact of any kind.

From all this, it is evident that the creation of a new sovereignty, or assumption of an old one, cannot be inferred.

The Congress of 1775, an entirely new and distinct body, came, like that of 1774, fresh from the hands of the colonial Assemblies; being created for specific purposes, and with no greater scope and powers than those of its predecessor. An examination of the credentials of the delegates displays the same purposes of deliberation and advisement, the same limitations upon functions, and the same lack of power and authority.[1] There is the same want of the essential element in constitutional government, permanency.[2] It, too, was created by as many peoples as were represented in it; these peoples expressed themselves, each by one vote irrespective of the numerical proportion of its delegation, and each delegation had to report the proceedings to its colony, as an agent reports his transactions to his principal. This Congress, like its predecessor, exercised no authority, either *de facto* or *de jure*. The only original powers it possessed were those of deliberation and advisement; it sat as an assembly of the delegated agents of the colonies, representing in no one thing either a people or a sovereign, and could claim no quality of sovereignty, either directly or by implication, inasmuch as it was not a constitutional body, but one wholly without govern-

[1] See Appendix A.

[2] Massachusetts and South Carolina limited the exercise of their delegates' power to the year.

mental qualities or features. In all its doings it referred only to the colonies, and never to a people or a sovereign.

The true nature and constitution of this Congress at its inception, should be kept steadily in view, inasmuch as confusion may result from the fact, that its scope and course of action, though not its nature, were completely changed in consequence of revolutionary events. The conduct of the war fell upon its shoulders; for the affair at Lexington[1] was the signal for active hostilities, and thenceforth the character of this body conformed to the necessities of revolution. Instead of remaining a merely deliberative assembly, the Congress became an active body, exercising powers with which it never had been endowed,[2] and performing functions which never had been prescribed. It became, in fact, a revolutionary body, a Committee of Public Safety; and, assuming powers which had not been granted, it committed acts, the validity of which depended absolutely upon the acquiescence and approval of its creators. A government *de facto*, it never became one *de jure*, but maintained its position solely by virtue of the necessities of war and the convenience of the colonies. Concert of action was the first need of the times, and to this end it was made use of as an instrument which was ready at hand. Fortunately, its assumption of powers could be safely tolerated, inasmuch as the causes which provoked it were temporary and peculiar, and devoid of the qualities which would make such precedent a dangerous

[1] Lexington, 19 April; 2d Congress, May 10, 1775. With the exception of New York, all the delegates were chosen previously to the affair at Lexington.

[2] Journals, i, 81, 82; 162; 112; 118. etc.

one; but that which particularly ensured the public safety was, that the colonies could at any moment correct abuse of these powers by recalling their delegates, and thus at once put an end to usurpation and usurpers. As a matter of fact, however, the colonies had nothing to complain of Congress in this respect, even had they been disposed to criticize censoriously the measures taken in their behalf; for these measures do not appear to have been adverse to the principle that the new states were sovereign and independent. It is apparent that Congress strictly maintained its character as a deliberative body as long as possible, and that it did not assume powers not belonging to it, until the pressure of hostilities compelled it to do so. Even then, it never for a moment lost sight of its real nature and its real relations to the colonies; it continued to resolve, but not enact; to recommend, but not command.[1] The colonies were still the principals, the delegates were still their agents, and never by a single act did Congress betray the notion, that it was accountable for the exercise of power to one people instead of to thirteen peoples, or that there existed a general government representing a single sovereignty.

After the Declaration of Independence, by the force of which paramount authority was held to exist in the people of each state, Congress, now a Revolutionary Committee entrusted with the public safety, assumed powers exercised by sovereigns, as far as external relations were concerned; such as the right to declare war and to make peace, to authorize captures, to institute appellate prize-courts, to direct and control the

[1] "Congress is properly a deliberative corps, and it forgets itself when it attempts to play the executive." Hamilton to Duane, 1780.

military and naval operations, to form alliances and make treaties, to contract debts and issue bills of credit on the public account, and, in general, such powers, in the external relations of the country, as were necessary to insure the efficacy arising from concert of action. But the exercise of these powers was not inconsistent with the federal character now borne by the lately separate colonies. Many of them could not in practice be exerted conveniently by single colonies, and none were ever considered, either by Congress or by the states, to be exclusive of the latter's right to exercise them. On the contrary, different colonies exercised these powers contemporaneously with Congress, by raising troops on their own account, by carrying on military operations, and by commissioning vessels of war; thus asserting their sovereignty, and this without a word of objection.[1] Troops required by Congress were raised by the states, and the commissions of the officers were countersigned by the governors, who typified the paramount authority. Congress issued bills of credit, but had no power to make them a legal tender, nor even to punish counterfeiters; nor could they bind the states to redeem their bills, nor, of themselves, raise the funds necessary for redemption. Congress could not extend to foreign envoys the protection they receive from every nation. In June, 1776, Congress recommended the enactment of laws defining and punishing treason, and it is very clear that it made no pretensions to sovereignty, for it takes the ground that the crime shall be deemed as

1 "Every state in the Union, both while a colony and after becoming independent, had been in the practice of issuing paper money." Sturgess *v.* Crowninshield. 4 Wheaton, 203; Marshall, C. J. Some states supported what they styled navies; as witness Pennsylvania.

committed against the colony individually, and not against the colonies collectively or federative. Evidently, there was no sovereignty in this body, however governmental it came to be; whatever was done, was efficacious only as far as it was acquiesced in by the states, as their refusal of an embargo, requested by Congress, shows.[1]

Thus, even after the Declaration of Independence, the relations of Congress to the colonies remained unchanged. Its subordination was complete and unmistakable; its assumption of powers was acquiesced in as a matter of expediency, or act of grace, but not as of right. Moreover, these powers, when exercised, were not regarded as resting exclusively in Congress, but as exerted exceptionally and temporarily by the only body, happening to exist, which could express the general will and wield the combined strength of so many different peoples whose purposes were alike. All its functions were exercised upon the external relations of the colonies, or upon those common affairs presented by the peculiar exigencies of war. As for the internal life of the colonies or states, Congress never meddled with it in the slightest degree. In regard to this, it never resolved, nor recommended. It, indeed, recommended "to the respective assemblies and conventions of the united colonies, where no government sufficient to the exigencies of their affairs had been established, to adopt such a government as should, in the opinion of the representatives of the people, best conduce to the happiness and safety of

[1] A striking instance is the law enacted by Pennsylvania, indemnifying those who acted in obedience to this resolution of Congress. 2 Dall. Col. L. of Pa., 3.

their constituents in particular, and of America in general,"[1] but it needs no argument to prove that a recommendation to establish a government is not meddling with one; on the contrary, a recommendation to others to perform each an act of sovereignty is a recognition of sovereignty in these others, and of these others there were thirteen individuals.

It is evident, then, that after the Declaration of Independence, there was nothing in the states from which the existence of one common, general people could be inferred, nothing to indicate a nation *de facto*. So far, the union of the colonies or states was exceedingly imperfect; a combination, a partnership, there may have been, but of a union of governmental powers there was little. If there were any, it must have lain in Congress, but, as we have seen, this was a body merely deliberative in its inception, and, though assuming governmental powers to a limited extent, it

[1] 10th May, 1776. 1 Elliot's Debates, 80, 83. New Hampshire, South Carolina, Virginia, and New Jersey adopted state constitutions before independence was declared, in compliance with a special recommendation to them by Congress to do so, made in 1775. Pennsylvania, Delaware, Maryland, and North Carolina adopted constitutions in 1776; Georgia and New York in 1777; and Massachusetts in 1780.

One effect of the organization of state governments was the withdrawal from Congress of many of the leading men, who returned home to take part in the transformation of their ancient colonial constitutions to new state forms. This withdrawal, the assignment of others to civil positions which were incompatible with service in Congress, and the transfer of others still to the army, materially weakened this body, and delayed the adoption of the Articles of Confederation. The absence of such men as John Adams, Benjamin Franklin, Thomas Jefferson, Robert Treat Paine, Francis Hopkinson, Benjamin Rush, Samuel Chase, George Wythe, Benjamin Harrison, Cæsar Rodney, Edward Rutledge, Arthur Middleton, and William Hooper, could not fail to make itself felt detrimentally. Hamilton to Clinton, February 13, 1778.

never reached a stage of development which implied the exercise of executive, legislative, and judicial functions, nor ever exceeded the subordination to its creators which they had impressed upon it from the beginning.

Much has been said and written, to convey the idea that the Declaration of Independence was the act of one people, instead of thirteen bodies politic, and that it implied the existence of a nation *de facto*. The attempt has proved a vain one, and has been made in defiance of adverse historical facts, and of the known constitution of the body that promulgated it. An expression of certain peoples, now fairly united in sentiment, but still without political union, except of the crudest description, it was; but not of one people. The fact that several parties unite in a certain act, does not, *per se*, make them one. Such a fact might, under peculiar circumstances, be accepted as evidence of oneness, if corroborated by extrinsic evidence, but the corroboration must be complete and irresistible. In this case, however, there is no ground for inference, for the evidence, far from being corroborative, is, in every respect, contradictory to the notion. The political structure of the colonies, the vicarious character of Congress, the circumstances under which the instrument was produced and its plain terms, all rebut the presumption that the Declaration of Independence was the act of the people of the colonies taken together as one, by the instrumentality of their representatives, and demonstrate conclusively that it was the joint expression of the several colonies, by the instrumentality of their delegates acting in concert.

In their condition as dependencies of the crown, it

has been seen that the colonies were separate and distinct from each other. The sovereignty to which they were subject was in this crown; each held separately of the crown, was individually dependent from it, and the sovereignty, consequently, was over each but not jointly over all. The effect of the Declaration of Independence was to break off the allegiance of the colonist, and to cast off the dependence of the colony upon the crown. As sovereignty, according to the accepted doctrine, cannot be in abeyance, it must have existed somewhere the instant after the declaration, as it existed somewhere the instant before, and as there was no other body or bodies politic wherein it could reside, the conclusion is natural that it resided in the colonies, now, by the mere force of the assumption of sovereignty, transformed into states. But, as this sovereignty had not been joint over all but separate over each, so could it not vest altogether in one or more, but in each. For, there was no one people to receive it, but thirteen peoples, and therefore each took that sovereignty to itself to which it had been subject when it resided in the crown; or, to speak more objectively, each of the thirteen peoples became sovereign, and each of the thirteen colonies became a state. This is the character with which they have invested themselves in the Declaration itself, and in this character they were recognized by foreign nations, as witness the treaty of alliance with France in 1778, the treaty of amity and commerce with the Netherlands in 1782, the treaty with Sweden in 1783, as well as the provisional articles with Great Britain herself in 1782.

The ancient separateness of the colonies proved so

persistent, that, though modified in various ways, it survived the shock of civil discord, and remained the most characteristic feature of these communities. As the relations of the colonies became closer, this separateness became less and less significant, until we find it giving way to a broader and truer form of expression, and we recognize the term *local self-government* as the one best defining the radical principle of their being. Separateness is a term inconsistent with union, yet the fundamental principle which characterized separateness, was, nevertheless, the one which provoked our Revolution, and which, emerging from the storm unshaken, became at last the dominating force of union; this principle was local self-government. It nurtured the colonies when mere settlements, and continued its care until it had reared them into states; it had brooded over the waters, and, henceforth, was to be the ruling spirit of the new creation.

CHAPTER V.

THE ARTICLES OF CONFEDERATION.

The Articles of Confederation expressive of segregation, and also of union — Old School and New School — The government designedly a weak one; elimination of the "ruler" element — Confederation suggested by the New England Confederation of 1643 — Slight effect of the Revolution upon the colonial governments — Growth of union — Defects of the Articles of Confederation as a governmental structure set forth by Hamilton.

THAT this individuality was the all-compelling impulse of the new states, as it had been of the old colonies, is manifest from an examination of the Articles of Confederation. These Articles have always been regarded from the historical point of view, with great interest, inasmuch as they set forth the notion of union at that time entertained by the colonies: and being the first definite and solemn enunciation of that principle, we see not only what it was, but, knowing its antecedents, we can definitely ascertain its growth and development. Equally interesting is it from the political standpoint; for it discloses with certainty the bounds and limits beyond which the colonies would not go in their effort to create a new government common to them all. The first glance shows that the old condition of separateness had left behind it its qualities and traditions; everywhere indisposition to yield independence of action is manifest, and, where yielded, the authority to decide on appeal is retained. The parties to this compact call themselves the United States; but, were they so? The Articles undoubtedly testify to one thing of profound significance, that the sentiment of union had become at last an active political force. But it must be borne in mind, that combination is not union, and that even partial union is not such union as satisfies the notion of unity which has prevailed among us since the adoption of the present Constitution. Concert of action, as displayed by the continental army and by the contribution of funds needful to carry on war and manage the business of external relations, does not constitute the union now exacted by American publicists. In order to a complete and perfect union of independent parties, *there must be a compact between sovereigns by virtue of which a body politic is created, central and common to the contracting parties, itself sovereign to the extent of its delegated powers and no further, which acts directly upon the citizens of each contracting sovereignty and which contains in itself executive, legislative, and judicial powers in such integrity and with such freedom of action, that the purposes of its being may be subserved as promptly and effectually as if it had been a sovereign power from time immemorial.* Nothing short of this now satisfies what may be styled the American notion of union, nor will the term be applied for a moment to anything inferior to this in constitution. But, where in the Articles of Confederation is the evidence of such a union? where the body politic containing in itself the combination of governmental powers which are needful to subserve readily the purposes of its being? where are executive, legislative, and judicial powers complete, entire, and in harmonious combination? Nothing is clearer from this instrument, than that separateness had yielded to union, and that local self-government was more than ever the radical and dominating principle; but nothing, too, is clearer, than that the union then defined was an incomplete one, a union scarcely worthy of the name, according to modern notions, and that the principle of local self-government, still distrustful of its ground, could not bring itself to creating a representative government with any power in completeness heretofore exercised by the sovereign only. The states existed as they exist to-day, but not so the Union.

A slight scrutiny will prove the truth of the foregoing remarks. The first article, announcing merely the style of the Confederation, viz: the United States of America, is immediately followed by the declaration, that "each state retains its sovereignty, freedom and independence, and every Power, Jurisdiction and right, which is not by this confederation expressly delegated to the united states, in congress assembled." This clause, in the highest degree prudential, hardly bears out the construction sometimes put upon it, that it is, in itself, evidence that the parties to it intended no union; on the contrary, it implies a union of the powers that are contributed, and further implies that the parties to the compact are sovereign and equal. It, and the article following, taken together, strongly imply that there shall be no consolidation; but they as strongly imply also, what is clearly stated in the preamble, that there shall be union of some kind. But, again the question recurs, what kind of union? The second clause, just quoted, answers, "confederation" —

an incomplete and inchoate union, and that there may be no doubt concerning the degree of unity, the third clause specifies the nature of this confederation and the purposes of its creation, as follows: "the said states hereby severally enter into a firm *league of friendship* with each other for their common defence, the security of their Liberties, and their mutual and general welfare, binding themselves to assist each other, against all force offered to, or attacks made upon them, or any of them, on account of religion, sovereignty, trade, or any other pretence whatever." It will be observed how clearly and unmistakably the notion of individuality is conveyed — the said states "severally" confederate with each other; and how precisely the nature of the confederation is set forth — it is to be merely "a league of friendship." Such a thing as contribution of full governmental powers, that is to say, a complete union, is not so much as hinted at. The states act as sovereigns, but as reluctant sovereigns, who are more disposed to retain than to impart.

Thus each state retained what was not expressly delegated, or, as it would be expressed now-a-days, each state not only retained what was not expressly delegated, but, in retaining, forbade the exercise of implied powers, and the establishment of powers by construction; and thus protected and guarded in their local governments, the states solemnly made together — a mere league of friendship, and for the purpose of effecting the ends prescribed, and nothing more. These purposes or objects by no means involved the creation of a central and directly-acting government, and thus this instrument is to be regarded as being merely what it says it is, a league of friendship for the attainment of certain and specified objects. Inasmuch as it was the first step to the existing constitution, it has been styled "the First Constitution of the United States," a designation at which no one should cavil, for crude and rudimental though it be, it is, nevertheless, a constitution, and worthy of earnest study. One thing respecting it is very clear; that it is more valuable to the historian in showing the growth and development of the sentiment of union, than it is to the politician as an expression of what the American notion of union has been since the adoption of the present Constitution.

Diversity of opinion regarding the nature of government and the relations of the citizen, had assumed in the course of time two forms, which are not adequately defined by the modern names of Conservative and Liberal, but to which may be applied those of Old School and New School. Whatever the separateness of the colonies, there had been no bounds to the expansion of political inquiry, which now, in greater or less vigor, overspread the land. The class of colonists which was content with the British constitution as it stood, and which was ready to abide by it without question; the class which scouted the application of philosophical inquiry to so practical a subject as that of government and was determined to adhere to the empire, right or wrong, was to be found mostly among the loyalists. When those comprising it had been silenced, expelled, or had taken voluntarily their places in the opposing ranks, their influence was gone, and no further attention need be bestowed upon them. The Whigs, or Patriots, remained masters of the field, but there was anything but unanimity among them, and beside the conservatives, who regarded the British constitution purged of its obnoxious qualities as well as of those features which were not adapted to a youthful and isolated people, as the best model for an anglican community, there were the radicals who would take advantage of the *tabula rasa* presented by the revolt, to put the most daring theories in practice. Although the war repressed the formation of these differing schools into opposing parties, it is certain, that, during the conflict, thought was none the less busy, and it is apparent, that upon the return of peace, these schools would assert themselves more positively than they were then doing. Sentiments had been uttered in the first enthusiasm of rebellion, which were not sustained by the sober second thought of the speakers. The "brotherhood of man" was a notion altogether foreign to the colonists, and one which the young enthusiasts of a much later date were the only ones to welcome; for in 1777, when the plan of Confederation was first submitted, it is very clear that our ancestors were not ready for brotherhood of any kind; a league of friendship was all that they would assent to, and even to this reluctantly. The single body representing the states and the qualified union of the colonies under Articles of Confederation were wrung from unwilling hands, and they whose comprehension of present need and of future development led them to advocate a positive union which should be manifested by a single and responsible executive head, found themselves in a woful minority. To part with the very powers which they had taken up arms to preserve, had not been contemplated by them, and at once the great mass of public opinion arrayed itself in opposition to this notion.

The Articles of Confederation were presented to the states for ratification in 1778. It had taken more than three years of rebellion and strife, three years of distress within and of hostility without, to effect something which after all turned out to be coalition rather than union. Even then it was not accepted until it had danced attendance in the ante-chambers of the state legislatures for three years longer. It is evident that the ancient separateness of the colonies still made itself felt in the prevailing sentiment of the country, and that the sanctity of the local self-governments and the supremacy of the individual were considerations against which even destruction threatening at the hands of their enemies, could not prevail. These were the all powerful motives of political conduct, and to these must be referred every constitutional act committed by the new states. Twelve years afterwards, when parties assumed definite shape, this was the ground upon which opposition to the administration took its stand ; for the questions upon which the people divided were, How much power shall be entrusted to the central government, and to what extent shall it be endowed with the attributes of sovereignty? Is government made for the individual, or is the individual made for the government? The Confederation proved to be a weak government, and great has been the obloquy for being so, which it has encountered at the hands of latter-day publicists. One would suppose in turning over the pages of writers of to-day, that this "First Constitution" was an attempt of a parcel of school boys at government-making, and that at best it serves only for an example to be shunned. It should be remembered, nevertheless, that many of the men who constructed the Constitution of 1788, had a hand, directly or indirectly, in the Articles of Confederation, and it is incredible that the skill manifest in the former should be the growth of only half-a-dozen years. [1] There is a plain and substantial reason for the government of the Confederation being a weak one, and this is, because it was intended by its makers to be weak.

Why was this creature fashioned without a head? The answer is, to prevent its becoming dictatorial. Why a mere league, instead of a union? The answer is, through fear of a government of full powers becoming greater than its creators. The framers of the Articles of Confederation reasoned after this wise: No central government can be created without the powers necessary to its being, and as such government implies perpetuity, the delegation of these powers runs the risk of becoming a perpetual abnegation of them by the states from whom they must be derived. Furthermore, the tendency of central authority is to absorb powers, and this, likewise, can occur only at the expense of the states, and this absorption will proceed until all the powers of the creators are concentrated in the creature, and the states be subjected to the central government, and thus will ensue the evil of entrusting power to a single hand. Accordingly the framers saw to it, that the central government should not have capacity to absorb the states' powers.

[1] The Articles of Confederation did not receive the requisite ratification of all the states until 1781; the present Constitution was submitted to the states in 1787.

A strong government was an abomination in the sight of the members of the Confederation, and they took care that there should not be such a one. To them strong government meant weak people, and weak government meant strong people. They had good reason for thinking so, for such was the lesson taught them by the annals of their own race. To cite the instance most frequently referred to at the time; when, in 1625, the people of England entered upon their contest with absolutism, they were weak and the ruler was strong, but when they emerged from the struggle, in 1688, the ruler was weak and the people were strong. This lesson was not lost upon the men who were now in the third year of a like contest, and they shrank from stultifying themselves in their first essay at government, by creating the very thing against which they were then in arms, viz: too strong a central government. Therefore, with their eyes open and with a full comprehension of what they were doing, they made their central government a weak one. They were determined to eliminate, as far as in them lay, the notion of "rule" from government in the United States, and to show that in the system of their creating there was no place for a "ruler." Had the Articles of Confederation no other claim upon our consideration, this should render them imperishable.

With the return of peace, this "government of supplication" proved inadequate to the task of restoring prosperity and of enforcing respect at home and abroad. The framers of the Articles had overdone their work; they had made the government too weak, and speedily it became obvious, that the sustaining vigor which had been imparted by the war spirit, must now be drawn from other sources. Whence could it be derived except from the powers of the states? Nevertheless, to show that the failure of the Confederation was not deemed to have impugned the principle which had regulated its creation, and that the abhorrence of strong governments should prevail over other considerations, the resolution to convoke the constitutional Convention made no mention of a new Constitution, nor did it refer to any other than the one already existing, but provided for the revision and alteration merely of the Articles themselves. Thus, with failure upon their hands, the states could not bring themselves to the point of creating a strong or "ruler" government, but were willing to accept improvement only of that which they then had. The Convention, however, turned its back upon the limitations set by Congress, and gave to the country an altogether new and different instrument. This arrogation of powers came near causing the rejection of the present Constitution.

Such was the political reason for this inefficient government; there is, furthermore, a historical reason for making it a mere league. Never had there been a form of government which united in a completely developed system the state and national elements. Our ancestors, therefore, had no such example before them, and never before had they reached the stage where such a form was to be evolved as a natural product of their conditions. They had no other models than the numerous leagues and confederations of foreign or of ancient states. Their aversion to entrusting power in a single hand, whether it were the hand of a person or of a corporation, forbade their adopting any of the examples of modern confederation, and disposed them to regard more favorably the leagues or confederations of ancient times. There had been, however, an instance of confederation, imperfect though it was, among a portion of these very colonies, which was not without its effect. The New England Confederation of 1643 had fairly subserved the purposes of its organization, and had lasted for nearly two generations; and this, though destitute of mandatory power, and without an executive chief or headship. Why, then, should not the purposes of the new states be accomplished by a like combination? The foremost duty of the moment was the successful conduct of the war: this war had been conducted so far with reasonable success by a Congress, or Committee of Public Safety: if a Congress without ascertained and defined powers could do so well, a Congress with such powers could do still better: a bridge over the troubles of the present was all that was needed, and such a bridge would a confederation without headship be.

The Articles of Confederation, manifestly, were the outcome of civil commotion and confusion. The Congress had been acting the part of a Committee of Public Safety, and, accepting it as it stood, the Articles merely constitutionalized its action. The experience of several years of warfare had shown what course was to be pursued, what needs should be relieved, and what purposes subserved. The Congress was a body which had long outlasted the period it was intended to endure, and the recollection of a Long Parliament was an ever present one. A revolutionary body exercising governmental functions, might, by the provocation of circumstances, if not by the mere force of time, arrogate to itself power which would disdain the acquiescence of its creators to establish its validity; and the feeling grew that it was high time to place constitutional limitations upon a servant capable of becoming greater than the master, and high time to define constitutionally the limits of the union *de facto* which already existed. Accordingly, Articles of Confederation were proposed, and, after a delay which brought the war almost to the closing scenes of active operations, they were adopted. Congress was not so much empowered, as it was recognized; that is, a termination was put to its existence as a revolutionary body or Committee of Safety, and henceforth its proceedings were to be invested with constitutionality. It had been exercising governmental functions all along, it is true; but, while powers were now solemnly conferred, they were also definitely ascertained and described, and, by the same instrument, the retention of undelegated powers in the states and the limitation of the delegate's term to one year, afforded security against abuse of authority. A more cautious, suspicious, grudging compact was never penned. However prodigal the colonists might be of their blood, they were miserly of their powers: and justly so, for the lessons of history were so many warnings against free peoples parting with their independence; and, certainly, if ever there is a period of weakness when advantage can be taken, it is in the moment of transformation, when putting off an ancient character they are not yet invested with the new.

One great advance in the jurisdiction of Congress was made by the Articles of Confederation: it became a legislative body, so far as the subjects allotted to it were concerned. As to these matters, it could pass ordinances; but as to those not submitted expressly to its action, it remained deliberative and advisory, and it could resolve and recommend only, but not enact. Thus, its legislative power was yet incomplete and restricted;[1] and it is a striking illustration how feeble was the influence of the Articles of Confederation, and how little they contributed to representative government and to the transformation of union from a sentiment into a governmental force, that the war was virtually fought, treaties made, and confederation organized, without them. This of itself shows, that the union which carried the states through the war, was not political union, but was mere cohesion induced by the coercive pressure of hostile forces. The successful result of the revolt may be pointed to in support of the conclusion, that the government, under the Articles of Confederation, must have been reasonably complete, inasmuch as, through its direc-

[1] Hildreth says, vol. iii, 402: "Instead of increasing the authority of Congress, the Articles of Confederation tended rather to limit it. Sessions for the future were to be annual; the delegates to be appointed for a year, but liable at any time to be recalled, and incapacitated to serve more than three years in six, or to hold any federal office of emolument. On all important points, the assent of nine states was required. What added to the embarrassment, and proved a serious detriment to the dispatch of business, no state was to be considered as voting unless represented by at least two delegates. In relation to peace and war, Congress possessed, under the Articles of Confederation, most of the powers now exercised by the federal government, but without any means of raising a revenue independently of state action except by paper issues and loans. . . . Congress might make requisitions on the states; but as it had no means to enforce them, the oftener they were made the less they were heeded. The only substantial addition made by the Articles of Confederation to the powers of Congress, consisted in the authority to pass ordinances on the subjects within its control."

tion, our institutions survived with remarkable integrity the convulsions of civil war. But, the fact is, that Congress, which was almost the only subject of the Articles, had little more to do with the political than it had with the social institutions of the country. Like all revolutionary bodies, its immediate concern was the progress of the strife, and it accomplished its purpose, which was a specific one, and one which was obviously extraneous to the inner political life of the colonies. This Confederation had nothing to do with the internal administration of the colonies: colonial life had gone on uninterruptedly before it was ever heard of, and went on regularly during its existence, and as the Assemblies, though disturbed, were not impaired by the military operations, they survived in entirety.[1] The Confederation had no direct action upon the colonies and represented nothing that had. The war, on the part of the colonies, was waged principally to preserve these local governments, and the office of the federal government was to stand between them and their foes. This it did; the Assemblies consequently preserved their integrity, and, had the war terminated adversely, would have emerged from it in much the same condition as they did when it terminated favorably. The vitality of colonial life lay in the different peoples and was expressed through their local Assemblies: Congress represented the external action and the defensive force of these combined peo-

[1] During the whole war the British were unable to erect and sustain any civil government whatever: the colonial assemblies maintained possession of the field without effort. For consequences of this, from a military point of view. see paper drawn up by Benedict Arnold for the information of the king, in 1782. Arnold's Life of Benedict Arnold, Appendix, 421.

ples.[1] It must not be forgotten, that the war was more than half over and the most important part of the work of achieving independence accomplished, before the Confederate government had any existence. Inasmuch as most of the states had signed the Articles when presented to them, and the expectation was general that those declining to do so would eventually give in their adhesion, they doubtless afforded a standard by which Congress regulated its action: but this is presumptive only, not historical, and the fact remains, that as, to be valid, the signatures of all the states were required, so long as any of these declined to sign, the Articles were not a constitution, and the federal government was not a body politic. The necessity of acceding to the Articles could not be very pressing upon states whose leisurely action is shown by one of them not signing until 1779, another until 1780, and the last not until 1781: yet, all this time, the local governments pursued their natural course, and, hence, it is evident, that the unimpaired vitality of these governments was not dependent upon so tardy and so inchoate an instrument as the Articles of Confederation.[2]

[1] "The powers delegated by the proposed constitution to the federal government, are few and defined. Those which are to remain in the state governments, are numerous and indefinite. The former will be exercised principally on external objects, as war, peace, negotiation and foreign commerce. The powers reserved to the several states will extend to all the objects, which, in the ordinary course of affairs, concern the lives, liberties and properties of the people; and the internal order, improvement, and prosperity of the state." The Federalist, XLV (Madison).

[2] "The state governments may be regarded as constituent and essential parts of the federal government; whilst the latter is nowise essential to the operation or organization of the former." The Federalist, XLV (Madison).

The American Revolution had little of the character of a civil war. It was really waged against a distant and external power, and for nothing that was before the eyes and could be seen, but for the preservation of a principle or set of principles. The colonial governments, in the course of time, had grown to be so republican, that the repudiation of monarchy had little effect upon them: they remained, in principle, as they had been before.[1] So with the social constitution: there were no classes to be uprooted, banished, or slaughtered, no local institutions to change, none to destroy. There was nothing which war-for-preservation-of-principle could affect, and, consequently, when the storm had passed over, the local governments and society emerged unscathed, and more fresh and vigorous than ever. Unless it was to adapt old forms to novel conditions, or to paint an eagle in the place of a crown over the Speaker's chair, or to write the word "people" instead of "king," there was really nothing to be done in any of the state capitals. Why should there be? What changes of political constitution had there been? None that were vital: the war had been fought to prevent change and to preserve integrity, and, these ends effected, there was nothing to memorialize, nothing to commemorate.[2]

Down to the time, then, that we became an independent power, separateness of colonial constitution, restricted intercourse between the colonies, and espe-

[1] See note 2, *antea*, pp. 48, 49.

[2] "The Revolution of 1776 did not subvert government in all its forms. It did not subvert local laws and local administrations." Webster, Works, iii, 460.

cially the relegation of every element of political life that smacked of sovereignty, to the control of a central and distant power, prevented community of sentiment or even effective concert of action. Massachusetts could not be influenced by the social constitution of Virginia, where all were either owners or owned, and therefore Massachusetts took no interest in Virginia. She was not accountable in any way for Virginia's social structure or for her political acts: to the king in Privy Council alone belonged the right of interference. As the colonies were not united but were separate, there could be no one people common to them, and, therefore, the inhabitants of each constituted a people by themselves. It is plain, too, that, there being no union, there was no common ground upon which all the sisterhood could stand as one, nor any upon which repugnant colonies could interfere with each other. It was a political impossibility, therefore, for colonies of different notions and habits to intermeddle, and there was little incentive for conflicting ideas to express themselves, and less opportunity for one set of notions to assert itself at the expense of another. With the union of the colonies, incomplete as it was, under a central and common government created by themselves and existing on their own soil, all this was changed. The sense of restraint by a superior was gone. It is not enough to say, that, under the new order of things, that which affected one colony affected all; we must go further, and recognize as the most positive result of union, that what was the political and social constitution of one colony affected vitally all the rest.[1] Be the union what it may, com-

[1] "Who can predict, what effect a despotism, established in Massa-

plete or incomplete, one of original or of delegated powers, a federation or a consolidation, the constitution of a single element of the body affected all the other elements, morally if not politically. All the diverse interests now held relation to the common weal; they now had a common ground whereon to meet, and for many such interests, indeed, there was no other field of action. The accessibility of this central government invited reciprocal criticism, rivalry, and interference, and thus an ever present incentive to discord rose among the states.[1]

It is the perfect comprehension of the changed condition of their political relations to each other, that explains the creation of so weak and futile a power as the one which had for its constitution the Articles of Confederation. Men were reluctant to hazard the real independence they had enjoyed as colonists; for more benign relations never existed than were those which had been maintained for generations between the crown and the American colonies. It cannot be too often insisted upon, that the colonists took up arms against the mother-country, not to gain more than they already had, for their political condition was almost Utopian, but, to preserve what they already had. Nay, they hardly hoped so much, for the books are full of the utterances of the leaders in rebellion, all going to show that they had no expectation of the future being a continuation of the happy past known

chusetts, would have upon the liberties of New Hampshire or Rhode Island; of Connecticut or New York?" The Federalist, XXI (Hamilton).

[1] For condition of the country after the war, resulting from the impotence of the general government, see Marshall's Life of Washington, vol. ii, chap. iv. The Federalist, XV.

to them and their fathers. The Grenville, Townshend, and Lord North administrations had brought them reluctantly to the conclusion, that this well-nigh ideal condition was gone forever, and that the future was to be as dark as the past had been bright. To save what they could of this free life, was the motive of their rebellion. This successfully accomplished, they had to face the necessity of creating a central power. But, if the ancient royal authority, with its might and orderly administration, had failed them, what was to be expected of a novel and feeble creature of no higher origin than themselves, and without the imposing effect of tradition and history? If the ties of blood had failed to keep mother and child together, would they hold brethren to each other? If conflicting commercial interests had brought upon them the hostility of the home government, would they not likewise place the weak states at the mercy of the strong? Did not the ancient local prejudices which had been harmless from want of a common field of action, and the diversity of social constitution, hitherto unfelt, now offer new motives of dissension? Community of interest was the only tie, yet community of interest was defined and restricted, while contrariety of interest was undefined and limitless. Indeed, one element of community of interest, and the most powerful one, would be eliminated by the very achievement of independence — they would no longer be bound together by the coercive force of external pressure.

Thus it was, that, distrustful of their own ability, and suspicious of each other, they dallied over the work of providing a federal constitution, and that, when completed, they afforded the spectacle of a government, if such it may be styled, without a permanent head, the executive functions being feebly performed by a committee; of a Congress consisting of a single house, for there was not even a council; and of a judiciary without a bench of judges. There was no general power to lay or to compel the payment of taxes, to collect revenue, to raise troops, or to build a lighthouse. The states retained in reality every direct administrative function, for it was in the power of a small minority to block the wheels of government itself.[1] Congress was neither simply executive, legislative, or judicial, but an inchoate and confused composition of these three governmental elements. It need hardly be said, that it augmented rather than diminished the confusion of revolutionary times; and that success resulted in spite of, rather than by reason of it. The explanation of this abortive production, is partly to be found in the jealousy which shrank from lending to any one member of the federation the preponderating influence which might be derived from the fact of the executive being chosen from it, and in the dread each had of weakening itself by undue contributions of men and material. The small colonies feared the great, who, in turn, were jealous of each other, and thus ensued an organization which has been well denominated a rope of sand. It is evident, that

[1] "Congress, from the non-attendance of a few states, has been frequently in the situation of a Polish diet, where a single veto has been sufficient to put a stop to all their movements." The Federalist, XXII (Hamilton).

Where states failed to comply with the requisition, they could undoubtedly be compelled to do so by the other members of the Confederation, according to the laws of nations: but it is very evident, that the mere application of force would end in the dissolution of the Confederation, and that the remedy would defeat itself.

the sentiment of union was not yet strong enough to overcome the ancient condition of separateness, and that the notion of nationality had no allurements persuasive enough to effect relinquishment of powers. Sooner than remedy these evils by the creation of a central government at the expense of rights and franchises, the states endured them for eleven years, before coming together not to create a new power but to reform the old one.[1]

"The great and radical vice, in the construction of the Confederation," says Hamilton,[2] "is in the principle of legislation for states or governments, in their corporate or collective capacities, and as contradistinguished from the individuals of whom they consist." In other words, the defect of government under the Articles of Confederation was, that it was a mere league of states, and that it exercised no direct action upon the citizen. Though this principle, which he styles the parent of anarchy, does not run through all the powers delegated to the Union; yet it pervades and governs those on which the efficacy of the rest depends. We have already clearly seen, however, that such government was not the result of ignorance so much as it was of intention; the notion of any government requiring cession of powers being repugnant to the states,[3] and a mere league being the utmost to which they were disposed to assent. What he means,

[1] "This government of supplication cried aloud for its own reform." Randolph, Atty. Genl., *arg.*, Chisholm *v.* Georgia, 2 Dallas, 423.

[2] The Federalist, XV.

[3] "They [the states] have a mortal reluctance to divest themselves of the smallest attribute of independent separate sovereignties." Humphries to Washington, Jan. 20, 1787.

then, by "the great and radical vice," is, that a league was a form of government inadequate to the changed conditions of the new states. He enumerates its defects[1] as follows: 1. The total want of a sanction, i. e. penalty, to its laws; whereby it resulted, that the United States had no power to exact obedience or punish disobedience to their resolutions, either by pecuniary mulcts, by a suspension or divestiture of privileges, or by any other constitutional means. There was no express delegation of authority to them to use force against delinquent members. 2. The want of a mutual guaranty of the state governments; without which they were bereft of assistance in repelling domestic dangers. 3. The principle of regulating the contributions of the states to the common treasury and to the army by quotas; whereby glaring inequality and extreme oppression ensued, the system of quotas and requisitions, whether applied to men or money, being a system of imbecility and of inequality and injustice. 4. The want of a power to regulate commerce; which operated as a bar to the formation of beneficial treaties with foreign powers, and gave occasions of dissatisfaction between the states. 5. The interfering regulations of some of the states; which caused umbrage and complaint to others. 6. The right of casting the vote of a delegation regardless of its numerical proportion to the others; whereby every idea of proportion, and every rule of fair representation, was condemned; contradiction given to the fundamental maxim of republican government, which requires that the sense of the majority should prevail, and opportunity afforded to foreign corruption as well

[1] The Federalist, XXI, XXII.

as to domestic faction. 7. The want of a judiciary power; to avoid the confusion which unavoidably results from the contradictory decisions of a number of independent judicatories, and this is the more necessary where the frame of government is so compounded, that the laws of the whole are in danger of being contravened by the laws of the parts. 8. The organization of Congress in a single assembly; being itself inadequate for the exercise of those powers which are necessary to be deposited in the union. 9. That the Articles of Confederation never had a ratification by the people, but had rested on no better foundation than the consent of the legislatures. Owing its ratification to the law of a state, it had been contended that the same authority might repeal the law by which it had been ratified. However gross a heresy it may be to maintain, that a *party* to a *compact* has a right to revoke that compact, the doctrine itself has had respectable advocates. The possibility of a question of this nature, proved the necessity of laying the foundations of our national government deeper than in the mere sanction of delegated authority.[1]

[1] See also Madison's specification of "the vices of the Political system of the United States," still further enlarged upon and in greater detail than Hamilton's enumeration. Works, vol. i, p. 320: and see Edmund Randolph's exposition of the weakness and lack of powers of the Confederation, in convention. Elliot's Deb. i.

CHAPTER VI.

THE CONSTITUTION.

The Constitution a necessity — It guarantees the integrity of the state governments — Its inherent conservatism — In it the sentiment of union has become a dominating political force — The Constitution terminates the Revolution and hands down its gains — Federation and popular representation — Apportionment of taxation and representation; a compromise between the North and the South — The guaranty of a republican form of government.

THE coercive pressure which had bound the new states together, ceased with the cessation of hostilities, and the general distress and confusion which ensued, compelled them to betake themselves to the repulsive task of creating a power strong enough to enforce respect without and to maintain order within. In the absence of apposite examples [1] nothing could be predicted of such a power. They approached this task, then, with fear and trembling, and if there was one sentiment common to them all, it was, that their ancient independence of each other should not be compromised by undue contributions of rights and franchises or by undue contributions of men and material.[2] One thing, however, stared them in the face; the necessity of cre-

[1] See review of historical illustrations: The Federalist, XVII, XVIII, XIX, XX.

[2] "Why should we do more in proportion than those who are embarked with us in the same political voyage? Why should we consent to bear more than our proper share of the common burthen?" The Federalist, XV.

ating a substitute for the late imperial government, for, under the Articles of Confederation, they had no common head, no common army, no common judiciary, and, at last, no common credit.[1] Were it merely to evoke and maintain internal order, the work could be performed by supplying the now known defects of the Articles, but it was clear, that a union of thirteen states required something more than provisions for domestic tranquillity. Such a combination could not exist without taking upon itself the character of a national power, for it was a mere question of time when the federation would be regarded by the world as one of the great powers. Already its advent had involved treaties of alliance and of commerce, and it was impossible to ignore the fact, that the act of independence, by inducing recognition of the combined powers of the colonies, had thrown upon it also the responsibilities inhering in any member of the family of nations. But, to maintain such a character, required the exercise of sovereignty, and it was necessary, therefore, to invest the new government with sovereign powers.[2] How uncongenial the creation of

1 "We may indeed, with propriety, be said to have reached almost the last stage of national humiliation. . . . We have neither troops, nor treasury, nor government. . . . We seem to have abandoned its cause [that of public credit] as desperate and irretrievable. . . . That most useful kind which relates to borrowing and lending [private credit], is reduced within the narrowest limits, and this still more from an opinion of insecurity than from a scarcity of money." The Federalist, XV (Hamilton), which see for description of the country's condition in 1787.

2 "The ground-work being laid, the great objects which presented themselves were: 1. To unite a proper energy in the Executive, and a proper stability in the Legislative departments, with the essential characters of Republican Government. 2. To draw a line of demarcation which would give to the General Government every power requi-

a new power was to men fresh from the subversion of the old, and how repugnant the substitution of the unknown and untried for the known and tried, must be left to the imagination. We have seen, that, when the first congresses came together, there was nothing in the credentials of the delegates or in their action, that betrayed a suggestion even of the colonies creating a new and strange government. Later on, when, in the rapid course of events, independence assumed portentous form, and actually declared itself, there is still nothing to indicate that the formation of a great power had entered the minds of the colonists. It is safe to say, that, when the colonies resorted to arms, no colony regarded the combination with its fellows as committing it in any sense to further conjunction after the troubles were over ; redress of grievances was the only object sought. The combination, forced upon the new states by outside pressure, was of the barest prudential nature, and was merely a war measure. As the need of concert of action became more and more apparent, it dawned upon the public mind, that, should the independence lately declared ever be established, some sort of combination might

site for general purposes and leave to the states every power which might be most beneficially administered by them. 3. To provide for the different interests of different parts of the Union. 4. To adjust the clashing pretensions of the large and small States. . . . The due partition of power between the General and local Governments, was perhaps, of all the most nice and difficult. A few contended for an entire abolition of the States ; some for indefinite power of Legislation in the Congress, with a negative on the laws of the States ; some for such a power without a negative ; some, for a limited power of legislation, with such a negative ; the majority, finally, for a limited power, without the negative. The question with regard to the negative, underwent repeated discussions, and was finally rejected by a bare majority." Madison to Jefferson, Oct. 24, 1787.

be advantageous even in times of peace; a league perhaps, or an Amphyctionic Council: but we have positive evidence, in the written words of the Articles of Confederation, that, as late as 1781, the colonies had entertained no further political connection than that which is contained in the least responsible of all combinations, "a league of friendship." Even this slight tie had been submitted to tardily and reluctantly, and had been borne with a grace so ill, that it was contemptuously ignored the moment that peace brought to the new sovereigns the exhilarating sensations of independence.

But, though peace had brought its illusions, it bore, too, its disillusions. Primarily among these was the realization, that, in permitting the common government, called the Congress, to act for the common benefit, the states had incurred responsibility that was common. Treaties in the name of all together had been ratified, and, worse than this, indebtedness contracted by all together, bound them to foreign powers as well as to their own people. The fatal first step had been taken;[1] and a colonist, who, at the outset, had flattered himself with visions of complete independence of the world, and the spectacle of his colony,

[1] "Prior to the date of the Constitution, the United States had, by taking a place among the nations of the earth, become amenable to the laws of nations; and it was their interest as well as duty to provide, that those laws should be respected and obeyed; in their national character and capacity, the United States were responsible to foreign nations for the conduct of each State, relative to the laws of nations, and the performance of treaties. . . . While *all* the States were bound to protect *each*, and the citizens of *each*, it was highly proper and reasonable, that they should be in a capacity not only to cause justice to be done *to* each, and the citizens of each; but also to cause justice to be done *by* each and the citizens of each." Chisholm *v.* Georgia, 2 Dallas, 474; Jay, C. J.

not only irresponsible to a superior, but free from entangling alliances of any sort, now realized that the necessity of self-preservation had already betrayed him into something more serious than a temporary alliance or even league. He had thrown off the known for the unknown; he had turned his back on the past, only to face a forbidding and menacing future, and had severed himself from a limited sovereignty only to incur subjection to one which might prove despotic. The fears that had prompted him to resist encroachment upon his self-government, now returned with tenfold force as he fancied its very existence at stake. As his illusions were dissipated, and the realization of the necessity of creating a central government took their place, one question absorbed his thoughts: How should his state retain its sovereignty, and yet create a central government which should be a body politic and exercise sovereign powers? History refused to come to his aid.

Nevertheless, he answered the question; [1] the work was done, and done so well, that it has been a marvel ever since then. The chief significance of the Articles of Confederation, in the historical sense, is, as has been seen, that, primarily, they represent a serious and earnest effort to effect constitutional concert of action between parties which were constitutionally separate; and next, that this separateness was so strong and stubborn, that it consented to yield but little ground to the necessities imposed by the combined

[1] The Constitution was presented to the people, September 17, 1787: the day appointed for the meeting of this Convention was the 14th of May, but such was the dilatoriness, that it was not until the 25th that Washington took the chair as President, and then seven states only had appeared.

forces of a foreign war and of internal distraction. The most striking feature of the adoption of the present Constitution, in the same historical sense, is, that the development of the sentiment of union had succeeded in overcoming the ancient condition of separateness, and the ancient repugnance to part with powers,[1] to such an extent, that states relinquished to an untried body of their own creation, powers and jurisdictions for which they had lately given their blood, and the exercise of which they had denied to a government which was ancient, known, and which had been handed down to them by their fathers.

The notion, that, these powers and jurisdictions once yielded, the colonist submitted as to the inevitable, and took no more thought of them, must not be harbored for a moment. Nothing was further from their thoughts, than that, in parting with the exercise of these rights, they were surrendering their property in them. So far from it, they regarded them as subject to the same conditions as franchises are when granted by a sovereign, that is, that though these powers had been delegated in perpetuity, the exercise of them was strictly subordinate to the object for the

1 "Whatever power is deposited with the Union by the people for their own necessary security, is so far a curtailing of the power and prerogatives of States. This is, as it were, a self evident proposition: at least, it cannot be contested." Chisholm *v.* Georgia, 468; Cushing, J. And: "Every state in the Union, in every instance where its sovereignty has not been delegated to the United States, I consider to be as completely sovereign, as the United States are in respect to the powers surrendered. The United States are sovereign as to all the powers of government actually surrendered: each state in the Union is sovereign as to all the powers reserved. It must necessarily be so, because the United States have no claim to any authority, but such as the states have surrendered to them: of course the part not surrendered must remain as it did before." Id. 435, Iredell, J.

attainment of which they had been parted with; and, to add meaning to this construction, as well as to secure what had not been parted with, the assertion in the Articles of Confederation, that the powers not expressly *delegated* were retained, is repeated in substance. No one can view the Constitution of the United States, without receiving the impression, that it was the work of men whose object was not to claim greater liberty than they had all along possessed, but to preserve as much of this ancient liberty as they could; that it was the work of men in whom tenacity of ancient institutions and of ancient individuality was the most deeply rooted characteristic belonging to them, and that these men strove to create a power whose first purpose was to preserve and guarantee the undisturbed existence of these institutions and this individuality. In making the constitution, they never lost sight of the real, underlying ground of their war for independence; the fact that their liberties and institutions had been lacking in the constitutional guaranty which those of the mother-country had enjoyed since the Revolution of 1688, and that it was essential to their welfare that they should possess such stable safeguards. It was to secure this guaranty; it was to place their liberties on a like constitutional foundation with those of Great Britain, that was the main object of the war which had been lately fought. In the creation of a central power, then, that was to take the place of the old one, of which the king had been the exponent, the uppermost thought was, first, to establish this guaranty beyond peradventure, and, secondly, to retain, as far as possible, the same benign and mild features which had characterized the displaced government. The outcry raised at the omission of a Declaration of Rights[1] was so speedily followed by the amendments embodying the provisions, that they have been regarded in the common view as parts of the original instrument, and the objection thus made, indicates how important the people considered the expression of such guaranty. To reconcile the relinquishment of power with the retention of sovereignty, limitation of the exercise of powers to the point of administrative efficacy, and no further, was the obvious course, and this according with the race reluctance to part with franchises, was the mode adopted. But, inasmuch as the abolition of monarchical rule left the colonial governments such as they really ever had been, republics, the republican principle prevailed against that of substituting one king for another, and a republican form of government was adopted. Apart from this there was no change. The colonial governments had been pure exponents of anglican liberty; pure exponents of anglican liberty they remained when they became states, and such they exist to-day.

[1] "The most considerable of the remaining objections is, that the plan of the convention contains no bill of rights. . . . I answer, that the constitution offered by the convention contains a number of such provisions:" and refers to Art. I, section 3, clause 7; id., section 9, clause 2; id., clause 3; id., id., clause 7; Art. III, section 2, clause 3; id., section 3; id., id., clause 3: "I go further, and affirm, that bills of rights, in the sense and to the extent they are contended for, are not only unnecessary in the proposed constitution, but would even be dangerous. They would contain various exceptions to powers not granted; and on this very account, would afford a colorable pretext to claim more than were granted." The Federalist, LXXXIV (Hamilton). "The truth is, that the constitution is itself, in every rational sense, and to every useful purpose, a Bill of Rights." Id. For Madison's view of this particular omission, and of Declarations or Bills of Rights in general, see his letter to Jefferson, Oct. 17, 1788. And see Lee's reasons, Elliot's Deb. iii, 186; and others, id., *sparsim*.

The achievement of independence did not alter one jot or tittle of their character in this respect. In these governments the world had beheld the natural, the instinctive development of race notions of personal liberty and of government under novel conditions. The adoption of the federal constitution, far from changing or affecting their character, expressly guarantees the integrity of these governments. In respect to the local governments, then, the federal constitution found them anglo-american, left them anglo-american, and guarantees, that anglo-american, they, and all they represent, shall remain.

A character has sometimes been attributed to the makers of this constitution which is not sustained by their work; the character of those whose boldness and audacity have been crowned with success. Nothing is farther from the truth: they did not meet to air new doctrines, but to embalm the old; [1] they were cautious to timidity about anything which savored of the novel in governmental principle, and their stormy episodes arose only with the suspicion, that, what was known and settled was not finding its clear and unmistakable expression, that old rights were not having their due, or that too much was required of their local self-government. To restrict, not to expand; to bind, not to dissolve, was the work in hand, and there exists not a crumb of comfort, within the four corners of the federal Constitution, for the restless, vague democracy whose end seems to be the subversion of that which is. The democracy which appears, was the representative democracy of which first the colonial and afterwards

[1] In fact, the Constitution of the United States has proved a successful attempt to set government to ancient landmarks.

the state governments were and have since remained such striking examples, and of which, from their nature as immediate exponents of the different peoples, they must be the principal conservators: all that the federal Constitution did, was to recognize such democracy, and to abide by it. What representative government owes to America, it owes more to the thirteen colonies than to the United States. In short, the federal Constitution recognizes a preëxisting condition of representative democracy animate in thirteen states, and conforms itself to its laws as the creature naturally subjects itself to its creator: it expresses this principle in every paragraph,[1] not as a dogma, but as every living organism expresses the real, the very principle of its being. The word "democracy" does not occur in the Constitution, nor does any other word indicative of political principle, unless it be the word "republican" which is here expressive rather of the form than the principle of government. What it asserts, nevertheless, is, that the sovereignty resides in the people, that the states are distinct and separate autonomies,[2] and that it, itself, is the work of their hands.

[1] Even in the provision for the election of President and Vice-President.

[2] "There is no doubt that the several states of the United States are foreign to each other; for, though in the aggregate they form a confederated government, yet the several states retain (theoretically), *sic*, their individual sovereignties, and, with respect to their municipal regulations, are foreign to each other." Note to Buckner *v.* Finley *et al.*, 2 Pet. 586, revised ed., citing Warder *v.* Arrell, 2 Wash. (Va.) 298; Brown *v.* Ferguson, 4 Leigh, 37; Lonsdale *v.* Brown, 4 Wash. C. C. 86, 153; 2 Pet. 688; Chenowith *v.* Chamberlin, 6 B. Mon. 60; Duncan *v.* Course, 3 Const. R. (So. Car.) 100; Cape Fear Bank *v.* Stinemetz, 1 Hill, 44; State Bank *v.* Hayes, 3 Ind. 400; Warren *v.* Coombs, 20 Me. 302; Daniel Neg. Instr. sec. 9; Phœnix Bank *v.* Hussey, 12 Pick.

In this Constitution, we find the first appearance of union as a dominating political force in the history of the United States; and its transformation from a sentiment into a principle had been radical. First, there existed separateness of the colonies; then, at a late period in their annals, and stimulated by external encroachment upon colonial autonomy, arose a sentiment of union, which, however, was effective only in ensuring concert of action, not altogether complete; then ensued a further advance towards union under the Articles of Confederation, which, nevertheless, did not evince anything like complete union, but rather that the ancient separateness had yielded to the less disjunctive but still intensely individual principle of local self-government, and, finally, under the pressure of public distress and the inefficacy of a government without powers, such as that of the Confederation, we see a central authority evoked, which, for the first time exhibited a complete political union. The government of the United States, as presented by the Constitution, displays complete development and individuality of all the governmental elements, viz: the executive, legislative, and judicial, and all these acting in harmony.[1]

483; Carter *v.* Burley, 9 N. H. 558; Wells *v.* Whitehead, 15 Wend. 527; Amner *v.* Clark, 2 Cromp., M. & R. 468; Dickens *v.* Beal, 10 Pet. 572; Bank of U. S. *v.* Daniel, 12 Pet. 32. *Contra:* Miller *v.* Hackley, 5 John. 375. The foregoing references, which comprise but a partial list of the authorities, not only prove the states to be foreign to each other, where not declared by the Constitution to be united, but prove, likewise, that the several states retain actually, and not theoretically only, their individual sovereignties.

[1] "The departments of the government are legislative, executive and judicial. They are coördinate in degree to the extent of the powers delegated to each of them. Each in the exercise of its powers is independent of the others, but all rightfully done by either is binding upon the others." Dodge *v.* Woolsey, 18 Howard, 347; Mississippi *v.* Andrew Johnson, 4 Wallace, 500.

The approach to complete political union had been slow, reluctant, and characterized by caution which savored of timidity, and the general joy at its consummation was more expressive of hope than of confidence. The distress of the country was become intolerable, and the Constitution had to content itself with the reception given to anything which promises relief. Though its supporters were sufficiently in the majority to secure its adoption, it met with strong opposition. Even of those who had taken part in its formation, there were men who put little faith in their work, and who, to say the least, were not satisfied with it;[1] and there were vast numbers throughout the country, who saw in it the downfall of their fond and persistent hopes for the absolute individuality of their states. These men had fought in order to render their colonies independent of a great power, and to them the Constitution threatened renewed subjection: at best it meant surrender, not independence. All distrusted the giant they had called into being, and eyed askance their own progeny. It never gained the full confidence of the generation which produced it, and thousands of the men who had borne the brunt of the war for independence, went down into their graves believing that they had left behind them a monster, whose avidity would not be satisfied until it had swallowed up the last right of the states, and had effected in itself consolidation of the local governments in the place of union.[2] It need hardly be said, however, that

[1] Madison Papers, iii, 1593, 1594, 1595, 1600, 1601; ii, 1542. There can be little doubt that, had there been a second Convention, it would have rejected the present constitution. Washington to Chas. Carter, Dec. 14, 1787.

[2] For objections to the Constitution, see them collected and com-

time and experience wrought a change of sentiment. The Constitution won its way into the public confidence as familiarity with its scope and principles increased, and as the beneficence of its operation became manifest, until, at last, this confidence was supplemented by general admiration. Nevertheless, the fears of the founders of our government were prudential fears, and the possibility of centralization of power, at the expense of local self-government still remains the chief source of apprehension to the lover of anglican liberty.

The characteristics of colonial separateness and local self-government have been dwelt upon at length, because, without thorough understanding of these primitive and radical elements of our constitutional existence it is impossible to comprehend or to account for the events that flowed from them, or for the growth of the union of which they were the forerunners. The sources of all political events are to be found in constitutional principles, and if we are to account for union, disunion, or reconstruction, we must seek their causes in the underlying principles most likely to produce them. It is natural, then, that we should study the governing principles of our ancestors in the days of their simplicity, and turn our eyes upon their first essays at constitution-making until we come to the Constitutional Convention of 1787 and its final result, the Constitution under which we now live. For, certainly, if the determining forces of the Constitution are to be found anywhere, they are to be discovered in

mented upon in Story's Constitution, Book III, chap. ii; The Federalist, XXXVIII (Madison).

the deliberations and utterances of a body called together for the express purpose of discussing and enunciating constitutional principles. The Convention of 1787 presents the desired opportunity in a peculiarly favorable aspect, not only from the remarkable ability and character of the men who composed it, but from the circumstances which called it into being. It completed the Revolution; its purpose was to hand down the gains of this historical event, and to embody in the clauses of the Constitution the results of the political upheaval then terminated, and these results were comprehended in the Union of the States. Henceforth the people of these states were to refer their political events to this Revolution, because without it they would not be what they are, and therefore everything occurring since that event, has reference to the charter which summarizes and directs the political forces defined within its corners.

There are several features of the Constitution of 1788, which bear so forcibly upon the Civil War and its results, that specific mention must be made of them.

We have seen the condition of colonial separateness give way to the "federal" principle of the states. This principle was manifested in the Articles of Confederation, which set forth a compact between sovereign states only, and this constitution, like every compact between equals who are without appeal to a higher power, rested solely on the good faith of the parties; no compulsory power save that of war, could be invoked against delinquents. There was no popular representation, for there was no people; nor were there any means by which the general body could act upon individual citizens. There was, consequently, nothing "national" about this government, nor anything which embodied the power of the combined and united peoples in respect to the general purposes this government was intended to effect.

When the Confederation had had its day, the principle of "federalism" was compelled to accept a yokefellow, and it had to act henceforth in conjunction with the principle of "popular representation." There was a conjunction in the same frame of government of the federal principle and of the national principle, and these two principles were intended to work for the same end — the good of the whole and the good of all. It is the conjunction of the several states under these conjoined principles which forms the Federal Union. The term "federal" applies to the conjunction of the state sovereignties, and the term "Union" applies to the conjunction of the peoples; and in an ethical view, the states convey the notion of *natural growth* and the federal government that of *fabrication.* Thus the features of the Union were, that the parties to it were not only sovereign states and governments, but also that the peoples were represented in the general government by citizens of their respective states, chosen by themselves at the polls, and that these respective states had representation by citizens chosen by the legislatures of the several states. This representation of the peoples was proportionate in the House, and thus the number of representatives varied with the populations, while the representation of the states in the Senate, being founded upon the equality of the sovereignties, was fixed and immutable; each state having no more nor less than two senators. Therefore, while the federal principle held its own in the Senate, as an indispensable principle of government, popular representation, the antithesis of federalism, held sway in the House of Representatives, and the general legislature embraced the two elements of states and peoples.

From the adoption of the Constitution to this day, the equipoise of these principles has been regarded as constituting the highest condition of safety for the government, and it was the irrepressible conflict between these principles that brought on the Civil War between the states.

The questions, what constituted an equitable ratio of suffrage, and how should representation be apportioned, were embarrassing ones, and they engrossed much of the time of the Convention. The contest between property and persons, between values and numbers, waxed warm: but whether slaves were to be considered property or persons, it was conceded, that this general element was to be represented in Congress. The efforts of the Convention became concentrated upon a combination of numbers and wealth as a basis of representation — "an expedient to prevent the balance of power from passing to the western from the Atlantic states."[1] The objections to this, on the part of the great slave-holding states, were, that "it left the question wholly undetermined whether the slaves were to be regarded as persons or as property, and therefore left that question to be settled by the legislature at every revision of the system. Moreover, although this rule might enable the Atlantic

[1] Curtis, i, 409.

states to retain the predominating influence in the government against the western interests, it might also enable the northern to retain the control as against the southern states, after the former had lost and the latter had gained a majority of population."[1] Thus the South, from Maryland to Georgia, would be in a minority from the outset, and in a minority whose influence would become less and less with each recurring census.

The Convention was forced eventually to abandon the task of combining wealth and numbers in a basis for representation and taxation; the South insisting that their slaves should be regarded as persons, and the North contending that they should be regarded as property. A compromise was at last effected on the principle of assuming, that representation should be proportioned to direct taxation; that an actual enumeration of the free inhabitants and three-fifths of all other persons (excluding Indians not taxed) should be periodically made, and that direct taxes should be apportioned among the several states, according to their respective numbers so ascertained.[2] All the southern states, except South Carolina, voted for this basis of taxation and of the House of Representatives.

It was not the first time that this question had come before the country. In 1776 it was discussed in relation to the quotas of contribution prescribed in the Articles of Confederation, and in that instance, the North insisted, as it did in this one, that slaves should not be a subject of federal taxation; a position which was resisted by the South, on the ground that this left the North to be taxed on numbers only, while

[1] Id.: id.

[2] Article i, sec. 2.

the South would be taxed on numbers and wealth conjointly, inasmuch as slaves were property as well as persons. The inability to come to a satisfactory adjustment, drove the Congress of 1776 to adopt land as a measure of wealth — a measure which was found to be impracticable, and in 1783 Congress reverted to the basis of numbers, and it was then that the proportion of three-fifths was established for the slave population.[1]

Thus, the very first efforts of the newly-born states to unite, were met by the question: What is to be done with the slave? It is true, that what is now known as "the slavery question" did not then appear, for the question, What shall be done with the slave? was general, not sectional (slavery then prevailing throughout the country), and it was purely political, for it related to representation and taxation only, the ethics of the question having no place in a contest in which each side was striving in order that it should not be overreached by the other. Nevertheless, this question was full of gravity, and no one can peruse the remarks of Randolph and of Mason in the Convention without seeing how alive Virginia was to its bearings on her future. It is apparent that, even then, the South regarded the North as the growing section of the country; that she looked upon herself as destined to be passed in the race, and that she was then concerned more about guarantees for the future, than about the gains of the present.

This basis of popular representation and of taxation was a compromise between the North and the South, and this equality of state representation and

[1] Curtis, 415; Madison's notes, Elliot, v, 78–80, 81, 82; Journals of Congress, viii, 188.

vote in the Senate, was a compromise between the small and the great states and between the national and federal parties in the Convention. The latter compromise has been styled "the great compromise." The Constitution itself has been considered as a compromise between sections and interests, and indeed the spirit of compromise throughout it is evident. Concession had to be made on all sides and by all parties before it was reduced to its present form.

There is a word in the Constitution of 1788 which is not to be found in the Articles of Confederation; it is the word "republican," and it occurs in Article IV, section 4, where it is said that, "the United States shall guarantee to every state in this Union a republican form of government." What was the notion of a republican form of government entertained by the makers of the Constitution? The answer is, that, in reference to the Constitution solely, it was the form of government then prevailing in the thirteen states: that is to say, a government consisting of an executive, a representative-legislative, and a judicial branch, each distinct from the other branches, and one, the judicial, independent of them: and a government which rested upon the principle, that it derived its powers from the governed, and that the sovereignty lay in the people of the state, or in the words of James Wilson, that the supreme, absolute, and uncontrollable authority *remains* in the people.[1] Such were

[1] Wilson before the Ratification Convention of Pennsylvania, 1787. He says further: "His (Mr. Findlay's) position is, that the supreme power resides in the states as governments; and mine is, that it resides in the people as the fountain of government; that the people have not — that the people meant not — and that the people ought not, to part with it to any government whatsoever." — Elliot's Debates, II, 418, *et seq.*

the forms and principles of the governments of the states that met in Convention, and of the two states, Rhode Island and North Carolina, which afterwards joined the makers of the Constitution in their adoption of this instrument. They were popular, representative, and defined governments acting as agents and representatives of the body of the people to whom they were strictly accountable.

That these existing forms were the only ones in contemplation of the Convention, is shown by the debates, the correspondence of the members, the essays of the Federalist, and the journals of the day, and by the requirements of the Constitution itself; for the frame of the general government was such as was adapted only to the particular governments that embodied such forms and such principles, and the object of this clause was to prevent the admission to the Union of any government not in harmony with the existing constituents, and to maintain by the combined forces of these constituents, the integrity and stability of each of the existing governments. It need hardly be said, that future accessions to the Union were required to accept this clause, and that the government of the United States, like the governments of its constituents, was a republican form of government.

It will not fail to be observed, that the requisite went no farther than the *form* of government; all that was required was, that the government should be "republican" in form. This left everything else to the pleasure of the state, and the Union took no account of its domestic institutions. It might have a Senate, the terms of whose members were for one year or for life; its electoral vote for President might be cast by the legislatures or through electors chosen by the people at large or in districts; it might impose a property qualification for the exercise of the voting franchise, or suffrage might be free; it might maintain or abolish slavery, which was then general; in a word, it might govern itself as it pleased, so long as its form of government complied with the Constitution: when this was done, the United States guaranteed the maintenance of this form, and protection against foreign and domestic violence.

The action of the United States is limited to a guarantee of this form of government: this form therefore is a prerequisite without which there can be no action of the government. Nor can the United States compel a people to accept such a form, nor bestow it upon them; much less can they abolish or even alter such a form, for a guarantee implies maintenance of existing conditions. The people of a state may change or alter its constitution at pleasure, but so long as it preserves a republican form of government and remains a member of the Union, the United States are bound to recognize this form and to maintain it against the world.

CHAPTER VII.

THE FORMATION OF PARTIES.

The evolution of parties in free governments — The colonial epoch, the brooding epoch; fondness of colonists for politics, and practical part universally taken by them in governing — No general parties during colonial period — Parties generated during the revolutionary epoch — Change of colonial character — Constituents of the Federalists.

ALTHOUGH parties appeared so abruptly upon the field after the adoption of the Constitution of 1788, as to convey the impression that they owed their existence to circumstance merely, such was not the case. They were the outcome of time, and they owed to circumstance the acknowledgment which is due to opportunity only. They did not appear unheralded, nor had they failed to pass through the regular stages of development: but the final stage of their generation was accomplished so speedily, and their organization was effected so rapidly, that before Washington's first term had ended, they were confronting each other in full vigor. They exhibited the earnestness that is to be attributed to the advocacy of principles which have been handed down from father to son, and they were manifesting the skill which springs ordinarily from protracted and thorough discipline alone. The principles which actuated these parties, had been inherited by one generation from another from the remote period which had beheld the rise of anglican liberty; but the skill was all their own.

Knowledge of the formation of parties in the United States is essential to a right understanding of our constitutional history. We seek in vain to know the nature of anything political in a people, unless we can refer it to the character impressed upon their politics from the beginning. The characters of states are born with them; their politics are expressions and exponents of these characters, and as in representative governments especially, everything, sooner or later, speaks through or is reflected by the government, politics comprehend the historical motives and acts of the people. There is nothing more certain in the history of representative governments, than that every political event is to be explained by the constitutional character of the people, and it is equally certain that this constitutional character is best ascertained at the period of its inception. It is when a people chooses a form of government and creates a system by which its public affairs are to be administered, that it discloses its true nature most simply; it is really making choice of the best mode of living, and in doing so it acts naturally. We must revert, then, to the events and to the principles which actuated it at the period of its formation, in order to determine its constitutional being. When such a people reaches the point of actually writing out in fixed phrase the conditions and principles of its political life, the moment of its doing so is the only one when the circumstances and conditions existed which produced this authoritative expression. The rule holds good, even though the constitution be the original and single act of one people: but where it is a compact between peoples, the rule is all the more applicable, inasmuch as the intention, which is the binding force of all contracts, can be ascertained only at the moment of institution.

Among representative governments, the present stage of growth and development of a people's character relates back to the latest revolution, be this revolution violent and sudden, or peaceful and of the operation of time. The peoples under such governments afford ample facilities for ascertaining their motives of constitution, by reason of their free speech. Hardly is their legislature organized, when two schools differing in their notions of the nature of government and the manner of administering public affairs, reveal themselves, and these soon develop into two great parties which henceforth wage an incessant contest for the possession of the government. These parties are not only the agents whereby the opposing sets of ideas assert their claims to supremacy, but they are the constant expositors of these ideas and principles, and thus become the natural exponents of the governing ideas and of the political nature of a people. The history of parties, therefore, in free governments, may be said to constitute the political history of the people to whom they belong, and, as has been observed of constitutions and of political compacts, the principles actuating these parties are to be found most distinctly expressed at their formation. No matter how immediate and direct their action of to-day may be; no matter how temporary and fleeting their action of the moment or how apparently inconsistent their course, the fundamental principle of their action is to be found in their notions of the nature of government in general, of the nature of the government under which they are acting and of the mode of administering this government; and these notions, as we have seen, are expressed or implied in the written constitution, or, at least, asserted to reside in it. Parties profess to be the interpreters as well as the agents of the constitution; they become, in consequence, the active, practical exponents of the principles of government and of administration entertained by a people, and as to a just knowledge of this people's political character, we must seek the earliest expressions of it, so too, we must go back to the formation of parties in order to ascertain the true character of the principles they enunciate and to comprehend even the latest events which have marked their ceaseless strife.

The necessity of such a course in everything relating to the domestic politics of the United States, is peculiarly great. The government of our country, has a legislature composed of two houses, one of which represents the states and the other the people, and the spirit which has animated our countrymen from the beginning of their constitutional history, has been that of democracy, and therefore the government should be deemed a representative-democratic government. In its form of federation it was novel, and it becomes essential, therefore, to a proper comprehension of it, to betake ourselves to the times when it was inaugurated and to the men by whom it was produced, and whose conflicting notions of the nature of government and mode of administration impressed upon our politics the two great classes of principles which still contend for mastery.

The colonial epoch was the deliberative, the ruminative, the generative epoch of American life: it was the brooding period of our politics. The most amazing thing that caught the eye of Chatham during the Revolutionary period, was the mastery of governmental principles displayed in the provincial legislatures: the most significant thing to the eye of the politician in looking back upon the Constitutional period, is the appearance of the great parties at the outset. Both facts are the products of the brooding, creative period of colonial life, but the immediate origin of these parties is to be found in the active and revolutionary times which followed the Stamp Act. Colonial life previous to the Revolutionary period, was peculiarly favorable to the race predilection for the contemplation and study of everything relating to the subject of government. Never since the days of the ancient Romans, has there been a people so devoted to this study as the English have been, and it is significant that disquisitions concerning government have appeared most, and this subject has been pursued with greatest activity, during the seasons of internal tranquillity, when there has been no exciting cause to provoke their appearance. Whenever the kingdom has been convulsed by civil discord, the parliamentary debates and speeches of popular orators and the ephemeral writings of the day have exhibited such readiness and such comprehension of the subject as can be accounted for only by the fact that protracted and deep reflection had preceded utterance. The men were ready for the event before it happened. So with the Americans; offshoots of British stock, they displayed the same characteristic. The nature of government, whence it came, what it was, and what its end, such was the subject of their speculation. Their philosophical inquiries bore ultimately upon the political relations of man, and in this they followed the English philosophers: not that they blindly accepted either their philosophy or their notions of government (for, as will be seen, there was throughout the country a deep and widespread contrariety to accepted notions), but that, like them, their disposition was to apply philosophical methods to political inquiry and to make the nature of government the subject of philosophical reflection. In no country of the world were works upon this subject, speculative or practical, and from Aristotle to Locke, more closely read than in these colonies. Montesquieu was generally known, possibly more so than in France, and certainly, in proportion to his readers, this publicist was more discussed throughout the colonies than he was in any other country. A rage for discussion and debate respecting the nature of things, and particularly the nature of the citizen and what his relations to his fellows and his superiors were, possessed the land. When we take up the biographies of the leading men of our Revolution, we are struck with the universal disposition of the law students during the middle of the eighteenth century to debate abstract questions relating to government, and to discuss with gravity and earnestness the abstruse propositions set forth by political history. It was the custom, too, in the south, for the young planters to do the same thing, long before Blackstone advised the youthful aristocrats of Great Britain to pave their way to the hereditary administration of their country's affairs by reading its laws, and hundreds studied law, not to practice it, but for the sole purpose of enlarging the knowledge that is essential to the art of governing well. Thus throughout the land, those who were to have a hand in its government, fitted themselves especially for the task. The higher courts invariably contained numbers of men to whom political history and constitutional law were familiar. These facts explain the eager interest and general intelligence shown in the questions which arose respecting the Writs of Assistance. All over the land, north and south, the people seemed to be alive to the subject and to clearly comprehend the questions involved and how they affected personal rights; and this accounts, too, at a later period, for the flood of disquisitions concerning the relations of the colonies to Parliament and kindred subjects. Many of these productions, even at this day, excite interest independent of the circumstances which called them forth, and are still worthy of the earnest study of the publicist. Thus the colonies were rich in men who had read much, and who had reflected deeply upon the nature of government, upon its different forms, and upon its relations to society as set forth by political history. The land had its prophets.

If such were the favorable disposition of colonial life to speculative and theoretical knowledge of what constituted the state, equally conducive was it to familiarity with the practical workings of administration. Parliamentary government was much the same everywhere throughout the English-speaking dominions; the legislatures usually took the form of two chambers, though even were there but one, the procedure was subject to the same principles and to the same rules as was that of the British Parliament. This may be said also of the executive administration by the Governor and his counselors; they represented the King and his cabinet, and government was administered upon the same principles in the smallest dependency as in the greatest, or indeed as it was administered at Westminster. Service in the legislature was not shunned, but was accepted from a sense of the duty owed by the citizen to the commonwealth as well as from motives of ambition. The consequence was, that, during a lifetime, there were few men of ability and integrity who had not filled office of some kind, while at all times there were young men awaiting impatiently their turn at the task of governing. Every man took his trick at the wheel. There were thirteen governments on this coast with their Councils and Houses of Assembly to a number of white male adults which never equalled 500,000, or the population of a first class American city of to-day. The number of men, therefore, who were acquainted with the practical workings of administration and legislation, must have been greater in proportion than that which existed among any other people at or since that time: the art of administration was brought to one's door, and it is no wonder that visitors to these shores carried away the impression, that every American of respectability was a working politician, nor that the world was surprised at the general familiarity with politics.

It is clear from this brief description of the contemplative life of the colonist, and of his active life in practically administering public affairs, that his race predilections for the science and art of government found in this remote quarter of the globe no mean theatre of action. In truth, the colonies afforded as ready and as good schools of representative government as ever were known.

During the colonial period, there had been no general parties whatever; for there was nothing to call them into existence, nor was there any ground for them to act upon. There could be no question affecting the colonists as one people, for they were not one people; and, as there was no union of the colonies, the crown dealt with every one singly and exclusively. What party spirit there might be, concerned itself with the merest of domestic details, and was confined rigidly within the limits of each colony, and being restricted to the subjects presented by the narrow and dull routine of local administration, it had no opportunity to expand. It is true, that throughout the colonies men classed themselves as Whigs or Tories; but these terms had little significance beyond expressing the sympathies of the colonist with one or other of the parties of Great Britain, though sometimes they were adopted in order to distinguish different local opinions. During the Revolutionary period, the terms "Whig" and "Tory" gradually assumed a general character in this respect, that the latter meant one who took the Parliamentary view of the relations of the colonies to the British Parliament and the former meant one who denied the omnipotence of this Parliament in the colonies. At last, when arms had been taken up, "Whig" applied to a colonist of American principles and "Tory" to one of British principles: one was "patriot" and the other was "loyalist," but these were to be found in opposing camps, not on the opposite sides of a legislative chamber. Had there been such an institution as a general colonial legislature, previous to the Revolution, doubtless there would have been two great parties: but while it is apparent that the elements for parties existed, and that the unsettled colonial relations to the British government alone would have afforded subjects for opposition, it is nevertheless clear that, as things were, we cannot speak of general parties in the colonies with anything like precision or truth. The "Government party" meant the "ins," and the opposition in each province, whatever name it assumed, meant merely the "outs."

The necessity of concert of action repressed the formation of parties among the Americans during the times of agitation and conflict. Factions there were in plenty, and we observe the rise of conflicting notions particularly after the emigration of the loyalists had left the field clear; but there was no organization of parties. Nevertheless, it was during this Revolutionary period, that is to say, between 1760 and the adoption of our present constitution, that the great parties were generated. In 1765 the young men of that day were entering upon times to which no other period in our history affords a parallel. The peculiarity which distinguishes this epoch from the others in our annals, is, that it was conspicuously one of constitutional and political development, or, to speak more accurately, it was the period when the constitutional growth and expansion of the British colonies upon the American continent, having completed the work of adapting ancient principles to novel conditions, reached the stage where the state was to cast aside dependence for independence, and the citizen was to consummate his assertion of individuality in matters of government. As far as constitutional government is concerned, the experience of the British people in the XVIIth century is like that of the Americans during their Revolutionary period: it encountered those political conditions where action takes the place of inquiry, and where the long-generating abstraction parts from its progeny of aggressive principles which assert their right to action and hew their way remorselessly to control. Here, as there, one result of revolutions, and perhaps the most beneficent result, was the production of great parties; those popular organizations whereby fixed but clashing principles of government impress themselves upon administration and legislation, to the control and regulation of both. Revolutionary periods form the startling chapters in a people's history; but when the end of the story is reached, the most impressive thing about them is not the succession of events, the popular turbulence, men quaking with fear, or even the picturesque and lively movement of the physical strife in which they terminate, but it is the changed character of the people themselves. These people are the same, yet not the same: their character appears in altogether another light; new objects are set for their attainment, and motives different from those of old inspire their action.

For example, he who takes up the history of the Revolution of 1688 immediately after laying down the history of Elizabeth's reign, cannot fail to be struck with the wondrous change in character which had come over the English. The fixed and constant qualities of the people, it is true, are the same, but their ways of acting, their motives, their political principles, their spirit, are altogether different. The tranquil lapse of time does not account fully for the change which has been going on during the period of turbulence and revolution set down in the annals. These annals do not equivocate, and they disclose, that the people had been repeating the old and endless question, Who are we, where are we, and whither are we going? as they never before had done, and that the attempt to settle these, as far as politics was concerned, had been accompanied by convulsion which had ended in society taking upon itself a character it never before had borne. So, too, the contrast presented by the eager, restless, but determined Americans of 1789 with the passive, contented, and drowsy colonies of 1750. Like the English of the preceding century, the Americans had been passing through a formative period, and had been brought face to face with first principles. They, likewise, had been inquiring into the nature of things, and the questions which had concerned them were, What is the citizen, and what his rights and duties? What is government; whence did it emanate; what its end; and what the constant relations existing between it and the people? What constitutes the people, and wherein lies sovereignty? Such were the impulses, which, when inquiry gave way to action, and this in turn pursued its course to social convulsion, modified popular character. The young men of 1765, then, found themselves confronted at the outset of their careers, with novel conditions which provoked the inquiry that went to the root of their nature as men and as subjects. The war for independence absolved them from the sense of dependence upon a superior power: they could, therefore, look upon their government from a single standpoint. The attainment of independence carried them still further, and, forcing upon them the creation of a central government, brought them to the direct consideration not only of what government was and what it should be, but, above all, what it was in the power of man to make it. The nature of things, the knowledge of the nature of things, and how to use such knowledge for the good of mankind, this it was which had troubled the days and nights of their youthful manhood; and it was this inquiry applied to the experience afforded them by their own colonial governments, which produced the spectacle of a roomful of lawyers and planters giving to their people a constitution, which the world has treated since then as if it were a discovery.

The Articles of Confederation are not of themselves evidence that parties existed at the time they were framed. This instrument was not the outcome of party contention or party compromise; it is indicative merely of the necessity for combination, military and political, then pressing, and of the intentions of its makers. These Articles were not adopted until 1781, and as they were superseded in 1788 by the present constitution, they had an existence of barely seven years. Peace was declared in 1783, and the work of rehabilitation became the need of the moment: divers measures to this end were accordingly brought forward, and every scheme had its advocates who urged its adoption as interest or sentiment dictated. During the Confederation the instances of counteraction had become more and more numerous and significant, and two classes or schools of politicians had begun to assert themselves; those who at any cost would keep the states strong and the agent weak, and those who would have the agent transformed into an authoritative power. The element of union, imperfect though it was, gave rise to a class of men who desired greater union and this class acquired importance with the growing necessities and aspirations of the new republic. These men saw clearly, that the states under the Confederation could not maintain the same security from external foes as they had enjoyed when they had been colonies under the protection of the greatest maritime power in the world, and that, though their remoteness was in itself protection of a high order, they were now very badly off upon the high seas. They would have to take care of themselves; but if they were to influence or command the respect of the great powers, they must be able to exert the force of a great power, and to accomplish this there was nothing to do but to become one. To stand before the world as a great power, and to take a position in the family of nations, was a natural sequence of independence, but in the existing undeveloped condition of the states such a thing was impossible. Again, under the policy of colonial administration, the colonies had been restrained from becoming manufacturing communities, yet to become such was the dream of the extreme northern section; but this was out of the question so long as a portion of the country refused to shut its ports against foreign manufactures, and a central power strong enough to compel uniformity seemed to be a proper result of combination to these men, and therefore they advocated closer union of the states.

There was nothing, in fact, to indicate permanent

organization of the different groups; they were not united by any general and common principle, and the object sought by most of them was temporary and material. There was no leadership, and thus, without general principles, without binding organization, and without guidance or control, they constituted factions rather than parties. It is significant of the lack of general parties, that, at this time, when the common distress of the country called for the greatest energy of Congress, this body dwindled away almost to a nullity. Its intellectual character waned with its declining importance, and it sunk in the esteem of the people. During periods when every member should have been in his seat, days passed without a quorum. It is useless, then, to look for parties in the Congress of the United States, at this time. On the other hand, if we turn our eyes upon the state legislatures, the scene is a different one, and it is apparent that the formative process of parties is in full operation. It is natural, that the first expressions of political notions should be found in the assemblies most closely connected with the daily lives and thoughts of the citizens, and such is found to be the case. The local legislatures and the ratifying Conventions were thronged and debate was active: there was where the great parties generated.

At the peace of 1783, public sentiment had made great advances towards democracy; still, the different parts of the country were not abreast of each other. Republican feeling had had little change to experience in Rhode Island and Connecticut, for their charter governments had been recognitions of the right of self-government, and the governments constituted in accordance with them were of a thoroughly popular nature. There was no reactionary sentiment of any account in either of these states, and, after the emigration of the loyalists, the same may be said of Massachusetts. But, on the other hand, the New England states were the commercial states, and here was the greatest concentration of society. In New York, Pennsylvania, New Jersey, and Maryland, the colonial governments had not been of so popular a character. In Pennsylvania the government had been originally palatine in nature; powers were derived from the crown through the medium of proprietors, and the overshadowing influence of these great landlords had not favored the development of popular notions in government. A class of dependents arose in each, small in number but clothed with an officiality which stood between the proprietor and the people, and which questioned every effort of the latter to acquire power. In New York, the Dutch element planted itself upon immovable conservatism, and the great landowners were virtually an aristocratic class. In Virginia and other southern states, the planters of the seaboard constituted a similar class; they were lords of their plantations and slaves, and they resisted anything that threatened diminution of their importance; they were conservative in the highest degree. The whole frontier, north and south, was republican and democratic.

The privileged classes which had sprung up during the sway of the proprietors and of the royal governments were unquestionably weakened by the loyalist emigration, but they were, too, the classes which had acquired wealth, and this in a new country generally takes the form of land. Many of these persons who possessed estates of which it was impossible to disencumber themselves readily, finding their possessions in danger of confiscation, adopted the course of standing by their wealth and of keeping a civil tongue in their heads. Having made this concession of principle to thrift, it is not surprising that after the adoption of the Constitution, we find them active supporters of him who had announced as one of the objects which he had set before himself to attain, the "restoration of landed property to its due value." They therefore furthered Hamilton's financial measures with their influence.

This element which had been disaffected to the Revolution, it need hardly be said, was in favor, too, of that form of government which most closely resembled the one from which it had been torn. The whilom loyalists were still monarchists at heart, and it is not surprising that they should favor anything which, it was whispered, promised a return to monarchy. An interpretation of the Constitution, which tended to absorption of the rights of the states by the general government would have their support, because it tended to the erection of a central, powerful authority from which a step to a throne would be short and easy to take. It was, doubtless, this class which was most to blame in bringing upon the Federalists the odium of having an intention to restore monarchy.

Another weighty constituent of the Federal party was the commercial interest. This existed chiefly along the seaboard, and was concentrated in the cities. One character which the colonies had borne, had been that of factories for British commerce. Much of the capital which had been employed here, had been British capital, and the connection sustained with Europe by our merchants had been connections with British houses. No sooner had peace been declared, than British commerce sought to regain its American market. To this end goods flowed freely into our reopened ports, and the British Government aided the effort of its merchants to recover our trade, by obstructing us in every continental direction to which we inclined and by facilitating reinstatement of commercial connection with Great Britain. But the depression which followed the peace was attributed in a great degree to the impotence of the Confederation, and the spread of democratic doctrines and the pronounced efforts of the debtor classes to obtain relief by summary processes at the expense of their creditors, alarmed foreign lenders and checked the supply of funds. Domestic trade, equally timorous, shared the alarm. What was wanted by the commercial classes, was a government whose stability would commend it to the foreign lender. It is obvious, that the needs of commerce thus drew to the support of the Constitution the whole commercial interest and threw its weight in favor of a form of government, which, in its division of powers, resembled the British system and promised this stability.

A far different motive enrolled upon the side of the Constitution and of the Federalist administration, the higher grade of officers in the late revolutionary army. Many of these belonged to the wealthy class or had bodies of land which they hoped would attain great value in the course of time. But they were animated also by motives peculiar to themselves: they had tasted the sweets of official and social elevation, and had no sympathy with a democracy which threatened to do away with distinction. The general officers of the late army are consequently to be found prominent among the adherents of a constitution which insured the stability they desired so greatly, and of an administration whose measures were conducive to the subordination of society and to the consolidation of authority.

Finally, it must not be forgotten that men born and brought up under an anglican government, and one which was the outgrowth of race instincts and race experience, should prefer a form of government which resembled the only one of which they had any practical knowledge, and which addressed itself to their race character. The nearer it came to the old government the better, and the Constitution afforded such a government, inasmuch as it was anglican in nature and was free from the features that formerly had become obnoxious to the colonists. Those, therefore, who saw in a government of distributed powers and of powers which checked and balanced each other, the safest form which authority could take, hastened to support the new constitution. Thus the reflective men and those particularly whose avocations led them to consider, more or less, the nature of government, those who having something, deemed the delegation of little felt powers a small price to pay for the security of their possessions, eagerly gave their adhesion to a constitution which promised them this security, and they supported an administration which made enhanced value of these possessions a declared object of its policy. The professional classes, consequently, were largely represented among the Federalists: but the chief support must not be lost sight of, and this was the one which came to the Constitution because it was significant as a race expression, and because the Federalists favored class and the disposition to material aggrandizement.

CHAPTER VIII.

THE FORMATION OF PARTIES — CONTINUED.

Constituents of the Democratic-Republican Party (Anti-Federalists) — Principles prevalent among the people, especially the agriculturists — Errors of the Federalists — Jefferson and Hamilton — The Old School and the New School.

SUCH were the personal and political elements of the Federalists and such the material motives for supporting, first the Constitution and afterward the Washington Administration. As the measures of the Treasury multiplied, divergence of opinion grew, and the different social elements arrayed themselves against each other. It must be kept in mind, that the two great parties had assumed shape in the policy of the administration. He who sees in the opposition to the measures of the Treasury, opposition to the Constitution itself, is wide of the truth. We have already seen, that, though the Constitution was not adopted by such a concurrence of opinion or with such general enthusiasm as to warrant its complete success, the general disposition to give it a fair trial, was unmistakable. This disposition must not be confounded with sullen acquiescence. It was real and hearty, and that it was so, is shown by the rapidity with which the Constitution grew into favor ; and apart from certain localities and interests, there was nothing like hostility to it, but merely the prudential doubt which accompanies every experiment. It is, then, going altogether too far to include opposition to the Constitution itself as an element in the composition of the new party. Those who had opposed the adoption of the Constitution, had been styled anti-Federalists, and as many of the new party had been such, this name clung to them. That it was a misnomer, however, is shown by these facts: 1. That, after the adoption of the Constitution, the anti-Federalists never organized as such; and never re-appeared in any capacity as anti-Federalists. 2. That the name was soon seen to be out of place, and was discarded for others, such as Jeffersonians, Republicans, and, at last, Democrats. 3. That the main cause which brought the new party into existence was to establish a construction of the Constitution which, it asserted, would give this instrument its true effect. This it could not do, had it not already accepted the Constitution and did it not stand pledged to its support.

The elements, then, which the measures of the Treasury drove into opposition to the administration, were as follows: —

1. Those who saw in the federal government a power created for the benefit of the states, and which stood to them as a creature stands to its creator. These were they who believed that the race predilection for local self-government was to be fostered at the cost, if need be, of everything else, except fundamental rule and order. Indeed, in their eyes, there was no social good nor evil that did not flow from obeying or opposing the chief of all race instincts. Self-government was as great a virtue to them in politics as self-control was in ethics, and the right to it

was the highest of rights. It was the one axiomatic political foundation of the race. Argument there might be, concerning this or that element of government, of this or that political force ; but the foundation of free government was beyond doubt or question — it was the inviolability of the governments which had sprung out of local wants and circumstances, and the inviolability of the inalienable right which every citizen had in such governments: concerning this there could be no dispute. In course of time, the accessions to the party which made itself the champion of this "doctrine" became so great as to drive the Federalists off the field. At first it was the fear of compromising this fundamental principle, which produced so weak a government as that of the Confederation and caused many of the most patriotic men to withhold their assent to the adoption of the Constitution. Once adopted, it was these men who led public feeling to the point of giving it a fair trial; and it was these men, who, recognizing its merits and observing its success in the practical working of government, became its staunch adherents and advocated a rule of construction which would ensure the intention of its framers. When they appealed to the instinct of local self-government, the appeal was answered throughout the land, and proved to be the most general, most unsectional, and most popular impulse ever known in our annals.

2. It is not difficult to infer, if the measures of the Treasury tended to the aggrandizement of the moneyed classes, who were the creditors, that the debtors looked for protection to the leaders of the opposition. Now the debtor classes embraced, *a*, the lower grades of

officers and the disbanded rank and file of the late army; *b*, the small traders who were dependent upon the great ones and the money lenders; *c*, the agriculturists, particularly those, who, in the northern states, lay between the rich fields of the seaboard and the frontier. These held small farms which in great part were covered with woods and whose clearings were still encumbered with stumps. Little money circulated among them, and trade was conducted by the unequal method of barter. Their indebtedness though not actually great was relatively so, as every debt is great to him who has not the money wherewith to discharge it. *d*, The merchants without foreign credit, and who were distressed by the enchancement of values in the commodities whose ingress was hampered by the restraints put upon certain species of commerce by Great Britain. Inasmuch as the great depression which followed the peace, produced wide-spread loss, which augmented the waste and destruction of an exhaustive war, there were few localities wherein the debtors did not largely predominate and few which did not supply a contingent to the new party.

3. The southern planters with whom the principle of local self-government was all-powerful, began to change front, and it will be seen that Virginia protested against the assumption of the state debts as a palpable violation of the Constitution. The building up of moneyed classes which could flourish only in that part of the country where society was concentrated, that is the North, augmented sectional feeling, which already had been aroused by the contentions in the convention over the slave trade, the fugitive slave clause, and the representation of slaves in Congress.

Apart from this, the creation of a moneyed class, anywhere, north or south, tended to develop apprehension on the part of the great planters, whose wealth consisted not in money but in land and slaves. Such a class would be a rival to be feared. Alarmed, then, by a policy which ran counter to their interests at every step it took, they ranged themselves with the opposition. Perhaps it was in deference to this general change of sentiment in his state, that Madison took counsel of his fears respecting the encroachment upon the rights of the states, and arrayed himself in open opposition to Hamilton's measures.

Two notions animated the landed or farming classes, for the integrity of which they seemed ready to sacrifice everything material. One of these was, that sovereignty has its source in the people and that the power to exercise it is a power delegated by the people, to whom accountability for such exercise is obligatory. The other was, that there is a tendency in power to concentrate into single hands; that the disposition to abuse power is inherent in the nature of man, and that, therefore, no greater power should be granted than that which is indispensable to the management of public affairs. These two notions had grown up insensibly with the people, and colonial history affords illustration of their development and of their existence as deep, underlying forces of political action. The conditions of colonial life had been favorable to the development of these principles; the history of the people of England, especially that portion of it which embraces the Cromwellian wars and the Revolution of 1688, served to strengthen and confirm them, and when we reached the point where we had to set up a general government for ourselves, they had become so deeply rooted in our nature, as to become all-prevailing political forces. In accounting for the constitutional events of those times, we must never let these principles get out of sight, and they should be as carefully kept in view in observing the formation of parties.

Akin to these sentiments was the dread of standing armies, the aversion to class, and particularly to such distinction as was hereditary. This sentiment had its origin in the democratic nature of society, but it is to be observed that this aversion was not manifested towards such classes only as were hereditary, or of an aristocratic nature. The favoring of any set of people as a class, whether from economical reasons, such as the necessity of stimulating trade, or from political notions, as for instance a class of office holders, was equally obnoxious. The worst of all classes were "the artificial classes." As for the doctrine of "church and state," though fear of its establishment in practice never was general, and, at the period of our Revolution, had long ceased to have any real vitality even in the localities where the church had been established, nevertheless, the apprehension of an intention to impose the establishment upon the colonies, was an important motive of revolt.

Thus the opponents of the administration were composed of those whose attachments to the principle of local self-government led them to contest the mere appearance of encroachment; the great debtor class; and the small agriculturists and traders of the North and the great planters of the South.

It is not to be supposed that sections of the country

or that classes of the community acted in mass. The same anomalies which strike us to-day were apparent then: Madison, the Father of the Constitution, became a leader of the anti-Federalists, as did Hancock, a representative of the commercial and moneyed classes. It is not an anomaly, that Samuel Adams, who had opposed the pretensions of the British Parliament so bitterly, should resist an administrative policy which enroached upon the rights of the states, nor that the mass of the disbanded army which had been moved by the same impulses that actuated this leader, should be found upon the popular side.

When we consider the constituents of the two parties, we cannot but conclude that the opposition had the greater supplies to draw upon, both in votes and in popular principles. In fact, had not the Federalists been especially favored by circumstances, it is safe to say that they never would have obtained possession of the government. They rode into power upon the Constitution, against which anti-federalism had not been generally organized; and the adoption of this instrument was due quite as much to fortuitous circumstances as to its merits. In the first place, such was the public distress and such the necessity of speedy relief, that men were not disposed to judge a reasonable frame of government censoriously, but were ready to accept any good thing which the gods should send them; next there had not been time sufficient for the transformation of the skeptical and halting into active opponents; again, positive opposition was sporadic both in locality and class, while the advocacy of the Constitution, pressed with force and brilliancy, was organized and acting in perfect concert; finally, "Shay's Rebellion" turned the scale in the nick of time. The Constitution thus brought the Federalists as an organization along with it, and had their self-restraint and skill been equal to the situation, no reason is apparent why their possession of the administration should not have continued for a generation. As it was, they were in power for twelve years only, and it is clear that they had not been supported by public sentiment for a number of years previous to their fall. The reason of this is, that, while organizing the government, they neglected to organize public opinion. Long before they reached the point of defying this opinion, they had lost the right to expect its support by a series of measures which manifest anything but skill in popular government or regard for popular sensitiveness. Blame should not be attached to them for the unpopularity of measures which were positively demanded by the needs of government, and yet were exceedingly onerous to be borne; but even the most centralized of governments are not above feeling the public pulse and of conforming themselves to its beats, and this the Federalists did not do. The Constitution having been accepted and inaugurated, they were seized with the impulse to strain its provisions to the utmost, and they rode it to death. The funding of the debt was accompanied by jobbery for which the Treasury was not directly responsible, but by which it was tainted; the assumption of the state debts, which certainly could have been delayed until authorized by a constitutional amendment, was pressed with a rough hand in the teeth of state protest; the incorporation of the Bank was driven to a successful conclusion, though its advocates had failed to prove it "necessary," and in spite of the manifest coolness of the President towards the project; the excise bill occasioned an "insurrection," which, to say the least, did not incur unqualified reprobation in the capital of the state where it occurred, or even among all the colleagues of the Secretary of the Treasury himself. Either the art of governing had not yet become familiar to Hamilton, or it was defied.

In addition to these unpropitious measures, the tone of the Federalists was not assuring to those who considered the Constitution a popular work, and one which had been created for the people, without class or distinction. Irritated by persistent opposition, Hamilton was betrayed more than once into expressing lack of faith in the Constitution, and distrust of public opinion as a governmental force. That men were "reasoning rather than reasonable" beings, was not a novel idea; in fact every government heretofore had been founded upon the assumption that the masses were unequal to the task of self-government, and therefore that the many should be controlled by the few. But, rightly or wrongly, the people believed that they did possess capacity for self-government, that the Constitution expressed this belief, that now or never was the time to put it to trial, and that the administration should not be in the hands of those who were not willing to make the experiment. Thus the reluctance to adopt the Constitution by those who feared its effects upon their local self-government, gave way to a general disposition to give the Constitution a fair trial, and thus the very men who had been lukewarm, became its earnest supporters: as the faith of the Federalists in the Constitution waned, popular faith in it waxed in strength. The people saw the opportunity for testing their capacity for government outside of petty localities and were determined to take advantage of it. How disappointing, not to say alarming, were expressions indicating lack of sympathy with this vital movement, need not be dwelt upon. Nothing facilitated among the people everywhere the formation of a feeling antagonistic to ultra-federalism so much as this tone of distrust and the consciousness of class distinction, and thus the masses became ready for opposition to the administration. It was unfortunate too, that during the first days of Congress it should have been brought into close contact with these sentiments in New York, the former stronghold of Toryism.

Another cause of adverse feeling against the Federalists was, that their notion of the central government was not objective enough to strike the popular eye. A government which is construed into existence evidently exists in the mind only; and a popular government expects too much when it demands fealty to what it cannot present to the senses. Moreover it violates the first maxim of governmental constitution — that though authority should be rather felt than seen, the source of authority must be obvious and apparent and be something upon which hands can be laid. Accordingly when the people were told that, to all intents and purposes, they were a nation before they had reconciled themselves to the idea of becoming one, that this nation was invested with sovereignty, that the whole people of the United States was already a political power distinct from the states, or the people of the states, and "that the residuary sovereignty of each state" was all that remained to the people of this state,[1] they naturally inquired what this "residuary sovereignty of each state" was, and were answered, that, according to the terms of their compact, it was the unenumerated powers, but that by the operation of liberal construction, these had been reduced already, and what would be left in the future, the future only would disclose.

During the early days of Washington's administration, public attention had been concentrated upon the organization of the government and the establishment of a fiscal policy. Domestic affairs had occupied the energies of the country to the exclusion of almost everything else. External affairs, in the meantime, had been steadily assuming a shape which soon called for a definite and stable foreign policy. A new being appearing for the first time within the circle of the great powers, could not long avoid giving an answer to the question, What is to be your attitude towards us, and what the principles upon which you will conduct your foreign affairs? This question had peculiar significance, inasmuch as unfamiliarity with our constitution caused doubt in the minds of foreign powers as to where the ultimate sovereignty of our system lay. This unfamiliar shape needed explanation, and no one could give it but itself. The events then progressing in the old world urged a speedy determination. The

[1] Chisholm *v.* Georgia, 2 Dallas, 471. As to the leading defects of the Constitution, and objections to the Constitution, see Story, Constitution, Book II. chap. iv, sect. 248 *et seq.*, and Book III, chap. ii. Also Address of the minority in the Pennsylvania Convention, 2 Amer. Museum, 536, 543, 544, 545; Address of Virginia, 2 Pitkin, 334.

policy adopted by Great Britain in reference to our navigation and commerce, was daily presenting questions and assuming a tone which could not be ignored, and the French Revolution, fast running a course of which the end and its results could not be prognosticated, added to the complications of the family of nations and increased the perplexity of our department of Foreign Affairs. Were our government completely organized and had our trade beyond seas been recuperated, the task of the Secretary of State would not have proved so difficult. But the government was not yet completely organized, nor was trade upon a sound foundation; a foreign policy should be founded upon fixed domestic conditions, and order and settled principle should be first established at home. Such was not the case, but had it been so and had a definite policy been determined upon, there was nothing wherewith to enforce it; no navy existed to protect our rights upon the high seas, no army had taken the place of that which had been disbanded, and our northern frontier was still occupied by British troops. Thus, without the means of making good a policy, and with a late enemy still keeping a foothold upon the soil, the Secretary of State was not in a position to assert a positive foreign policy. Circumstances, to say the least, were such as were liable to change at any moment, and with them the policy which they supported.

With the assemblage of two national Houses, one of which represented the people themselves, the strife of local interests and of governmental principles, which had manifested itself in the state legislatures, the constitutional Convention, and the ratifying Conventions, was transferred to the First Congress.

Nothing could be more propitious for party development than the composition of the first cabinet. President Washington, alive to the necessity of uniting in his cabinet intelligence in the constructive administration of internal affairs, and skill in the management of foreign affairs such as would steer the young republic safely through thickening complications, had called Alexander Hamilton to the Secretaryship of the Treasury and Thomas Jefferson to that of State. As far as efficiency for their duties is concerned, no better selection could be made, and, doubtless, the President aimed at the moral effect which would be produced by the harmonious coöperation of two men who represented dissimilar notions of government. Everything was yet to be done; the country was not even free from the presence of its late foes, for the northern military posts were still occupied by British garrisons, and the unhappy and distressed people, sunk in poverty and despair, was torn by conflicting factions. It was reasonable to suppose that the spectacle of representatives of different sections and of differing principles uniting their energies in common effort for the general welfare would exert a salutary influence upon the factions, and tend towards calming the popular temper. Whatever the motive of the President, it is now easily to be seen that nothing better could have been devised to effect the evolution of parties. The inevitable course which opposing notions in politics pursue was speedily taken: two sets of doctrines began to define themselves, then to form into systems, and at last to oppose each other.

Public sentiment kept pace with this formative process, and men ranged themselves on one side or the other; so that, when the first presidential term had closed, two great parties had already absorbed the diverse factions, and, confronting each other, were ready to contend for the possession of the national government.

Never did a field offer more important subjects for diversity of sentiment; never were times richer in opportunity; never were leaders better fitted for party organization; and never was a people upon whom the necessity of making choice of principles pressed more heavily, or whose ardor for practical politics exceeded that of the Americans. Time and circumstance combined in affording the opportunity; the character of the leaders and the disposition of the people called every element and quality into play.

The debates in the constitutional Convention had brought out, with startling distinctness, reluctance to innovation and absolute sincerity in the effort to create an enduring polity. Necessity compelled union, and, though the popular majority which decided the adoption of the Constitution was not great enough to assure confidence, the acquiescence which followed revealed the general feeling that, now that the Constitution had been adopted, it should have a fair trial. The administration, consequently, entered upon the task of governmental organization sustained by a sentiment which, if not heartily sympathetic with it, was by no means adverse to the experiment. At all events, there was no organized and effective obstructiveness for it to encounter.

Jefferson, at the outset, was absent from the country, being on his homeward journey from France, where, during the past five years, he had represented the United States as minister. He had left home the year following the peace, and before the illusions which came with it had given way to realities more bitter than the war itself had been. Distant from the depression and distress into which the country had sunk, his knowledge of internal affairs had been obtained only from his official and private correspondence, and from the journalistic reports which were common to all. He had taken no part in the making of the Constitution, and his views of this instrument were unclouded by the agitation which personally affected its framers. The only constitution-making, indeed, with which he had had anything to do had been confined to suggestions offered by him from time to time, on request of various leaders of the French Revolution which was then in progress under his eyes, and with which he heartily sympathized. He could, therefore, consider the Constitution of the United States, not only with the judgment of one who had, all his life, reflected deeply upon the nature and structure of governments, but also with the cool criticism of a bystander. One thing only might affect this judgment unduly, and this was that his predilection for making the rights of the individual the beginning and the end of all government had become extravagant from his sympathy with the French people in their struggle against absolutism. There can be no doubt that Jefferson brought home with him an abhorrence of everything monarchical and aristocratic, and that he was disposed to view any measure which was not altogether popular in its nature as a step towards absolutism. If his interest in the success of the Constitution was devoid of the enthusiasm which naturally appeared in many of the men who had had a hand in its making, hostility to it was not harbored by him. The mental force of the man elevated him above the trivial objections which had been urged against its adoption, and, though it possessed features which did not altogether suit him, he was ready to give it a fair trial. His disposition towards the Constitution, then, may be deemed fairly favorable, and this disposition had been strengthened by no less an advocate than James Madison, who, while keeping him thoroughly informed of its progress, from inception to adoption, had explained away objections, and had advanced arguments in its favor, which his quick and comprehensive mind had readily accepted. The Constitution, therefore, may be said to have successfully passed his scrutiny, and to have been accepted by him, not as a mere relief from present ills, but as an organic structure which was to be perpetual. It may be considered as a substantial advantage that the first administration had among its members one whose character and intellect were of such high order, yet whose judgment of the Constitution was unbiassed by the prejudices of a partisan.[1]

[1] When Jefferson, in the spring of 1790, returned from France, he found that which is now the Democratic Party a body with a code of principles, and active in the performance of its functions. It lacked much of being a fully developed party, for its organization was not complete, its discipline was imperfect, it had no leader, and it was nameless: yet, for all this, it was a party, for what organization it had carried it beyond the mere faction, discipline would certainly come in time, and so would a leader and a name, and, above all, it had principles, — definite, clear, authoritative, and exacting principles; moreover, it had the enthusiasm of the neophyte, and the propagandism which offers to the doubter the choice between the Koran

Hamilton, on the other hand, appeared upon the scene in a quite different character. He came a victor, fresh from a struggle which had riveted upon him the eyes of the whole country, and, from the beginning of what appeared to be a hopeless contest, down to its triumphant conclusion, he had sustained himself with force and brilliancy which have had no parallel in our history since that day. If any single being can be said to have secured the adoption of the Constitution, he was the man. His duties in his state had abridged his action in the Convention; but, no sooner had the Constitution been given to the people, than he began a course of advocacy, which, had there been nothing else to mark his career, would have made him one of the most distinguished men of his generation. He at once took up his pen, and to him, more than to any other, we owe "the Federalist." It was in securing the adoption of the Constitution by his own state that he became, for a time, the most conspicuous man in the land. The opponents of the Constitution might almost be said to have been impregnably entrenched in New York. Few men ever have attained the control of a locality such as George Clinton then had of that state, and his defiance of the Constitution and its advocates was anything but bravado. When, then, in the midst of the discussion, or rather struggle, the leader of the opposition to the Constitution, Melancthon Smith, announced his radical and total conversion to its adoption, great was the

and the bowstring. The party had already been "founded," and was awaiting a leader and a name only, before emerging from immaturity and setting forth upon the career of conquest which was to carry it into power by "the Revolution of 1800."

sensation throughout the country; and greater still the joy of the Federalists, as the friends of the Constitution were styled, when Hamilton presented himself before Congress with the ratification by New York. His appearance in the Cabinet was justly regarded as that of one to whom the inauguration of the Constitution and the care of its fortunes had been especially entrusted. However lukewarm or adverse to it others might be, he was universally regarded as its friend and supporter, and one whose personality was linked with its success or failure. In looking back upon those times, it cannot be denied that the President, in committing its destiny to one so identified with its fate, acted wisely. If the Constitution was worth trying at all, its fortunes should be confided to those who would see that the trial was a fair one; nor can it be regarded as anything but fortunate that the Cabinet should contain two men, one of whom would strain every nerve and encounter every hazard to give the new government an advantage at the outset, while the other would be disposed to let it win its way upon its merits.

The difference in character between these men could hardly fail to impress itself upon their adherents; but it was the difference in their principles which eventually decided the character of the parties they were to lead. It is to be seen already, in the Federalist, that Hamilton had declared the great necessity of the hour to be a government which should act upon the individual citizen, and not solely upon the states in their corporate capacity; and it is also to be seen that it is this characteristic which chiefly distinguishes the Constitution from the Articles of Confederation.[1] Nothing showed the difference between the two leaders more than the views entertained by them in this respect: Hamilton's opinion being that the direct action of the central government upon the citizen was too restricted; Jefferson's, that it went too far. While Hamilton considered government to be the energy of a fully developed body politic acting upon the citizen as a means to an end present to the common will, Jefferson looked at government as the means whereby the end present to the majority of individual wills should be attained. The individual was the political entity to Jefferson; to Hamilton, the state. This state, in Hamilton's eyes, was the central government, the one recently created by the delegation of sovereign powers of the many. In proportion as this waxed, the others waned, and he recognized nothing to be the equal of that in which reposed the powers of greatest magnitude. Number of powers was much to him; magnitude of power was still more. The government which made war and peace, which stood before kings and treated with them, and whose heavy hand was felt to the uttermost parts of the earth, this was the real and superior government. Not so thought Jefferson; to him, that which related to the soil was greatest, and the creature which sprang from its dust was superior to the one which owed its being to the breath of men, and

[1] "The powers of a general government, either of a legislative or executive nature, or which particularly concerns treaties with foreign powers, do for the most part (if not wholly) affect individuals and not states: they require no aid from state authorities. This is the great leading distinction between the old Articles of Confederation and the present Constitution." Chisholm *v.* Georgia, 2 Dallas, 435, Iredell, J. See also, *ante*, pp. 9, 101, 105, 117, 118.

which, almost invisible and intangible, dwelt in the minds of men only and was expressed in the fading characters which were traced on parchment. The end of government was the greater good of man, and what concerned his welfare was the real motive of politics. What was government but the control and regulation of the citizen by himself? and how could this self-control be exercised, but by his possession of the powers natural to him? Why should one man ever rule another; and why should government recognize a condition beyond that which was necessary for the common good? To Jefferson, therefore, the acquisition of power and of security and tranquillity, at the cost of personal liberty, was not only a shocking doctrine, but was an anomaly and contradiction which his mind refused to entertain. What advantageth it the master, that his servant be greater than he? and what the glory of standing before kings, if one stand clothed with powers not his own? The true glory of government lay in its efficacy to develop the individual, not in its display of power. Whatever concerned the individual, this only was the subject of government; whatever concerned his welfare, this only should rouse it to action. The life-work of the citizen lay at home, within sight and sound of his door, and the real object of government was to see that he was let alone. The right to be tried by a jury of his peers, to have his speech free, his person sacred, the thousand rights and powers which cluster around his hearth, these were the true objects of government, and the least of them outweighed the splendor of the greatest combination of forces men were capable of. Thus, the very element which distinguished this Constitution from its predecessor, the direct action of the central government upon the citizen, did not commend itself to him as a feature to be accepted without question, and to be urged without restraint; but it appeared rather as one not exempt from criticism, and as one not to be acted upon, unless it were under the control and mastery of the individual himself. The want of such a principle had demonstrated itself under the Articles of Confederation, and such a governmental force would have to be accepted; but, with Jefferson, acceptance meant toleration; its exercise must be subject to limitations defined and immovably established, and the occasion of its application must be one which was obvious and unmistakable, and against which argument was in vain. When it acted, it should act as a servant acts for its master.

Such being the radical difference between the views of government entertained by these men, it is easy to see that ancient local self-government spoke through Jefferson, and that centralization of powers in a government superior to the local organisms found utterance through Hamilton. Each of these men, in course of time, was wrought to the pitch of believing and averring that his opponent would surely bring about anarchy or despotism;[1] and it can hardly be disputed, if the principles of either should go to an extreme, that the failure of the Articles of Confederation might be repeated, or that such centralization of

[1] The accusations of the Jeffersonians have been regarded as the merest political vituperation. They were not so; they went to an unwarrantable extent, it is true, but they were made earnestly. The Jeffersonians looked on the Hamiltonian policy as setting at naught the goodness in man, and as deliberately substituting for it evil as a principle of government.

power in the general government might ensue, as would terminate at last in the subversion of local self-government and the substitution of irresponsible authority. Though the possibilities of doctrines are never to be lost sight of, few are the Americans of the present generation who could harbor the belief that either of these men was what his opponent fancied him to be: that the man who wrote the Declaration of Independence and insisted on a Declaration of Rights could entertain political principles which were certain to end in anarchy; or, that the man who wrote the Federalist and did so much for the adoption of the Constitution was striving to bring about a consolidation of the states and the establishment of an all-powerful despotism! Nevertheless, the bitterness and prejudices of the day have made themselves felt in government at all times, and their presence cannot be ignored during a period when monarchists in our midst still hoped for the subversion of democracy, and when the youthful "Jacobins" of Philadelphia turned from the men who composed the Federalist, to take their notions of politics from the sans-culottes of the Faubourg St. Antoine.

The doctrines of Jefferson and Hamilton need not be pursued to the extremities which it is improbable that the conservatism of the people will ever suffer them to reach. They have been in active operation for a century; they have controlled the administration and legislation of a country which has multiplied its population many times over; they have demonstrated their power to effect the assimilation of diverse races; they have survived foreign and civil wars, and they are still confronting each other. We are safe, therefore, in accepting them as positive and enduring elements in the history of our politics down to the civil war, and, adopting them as political creeds, we may observe their influence upon the formation of the two great parties in the United States.

The two ways of regarding the end of government had divided the people themselves, and had rapidly assumed the characters of schools.

One of these schools drew its inspiration from the past and rested upon experience. It took the position that political history showed, that the conflict between good and evil in man had been an unceasing one, and that government should recognize it by maintaining from the beginning strength sufficient to overcome the evil; but, inasmuch as this had never yet been thoroughly accomplished, that the evil in man should be so far recognized as to turn it to the advantage of the state. This, they claimed, had been reached by the British system more nearly than by any other government since the days of the Athenian democracy or those of the Roman Republic. The men of this school took the world as they found it; and they pointed to the experience of the British empire, wherein the corruptions of Walpole and his successors had enured more to political stability than had the experiments in constitution-making of the Commonwealth; experiments which had been rejected finally by the British people in favor of the old system with limitations. Therefore, they would confine themselves to tried principles and ancient forms, and would retain the British system, but would have it purged of its corruption and divested of the characteristics and methods which were incompatible with a republic and a federation, and would adapt it to the novel conditions existing in a new country.

Such was the view taken by the Old School: it was the school of experience, of conservatism, of aversion to change, of timidity, and of content.

The New School looked to the future for its inspiration, and placed its hopes upon experiment. It caught at the recognition by the Old School of evil as a governmental force, and insisted that in politics fear of evil had always supplanted faith in goodness, and that, in consequence, the past and the present political systems of the world had not been founded upon the strength but upon the weakness of man and his assumed incapacity to govern himself, and, hence, that each and every government had for its controlling motive the necessity of a *ruler*. This school rejected the doctrine of original sin, and reversed the ancient political creed: it would have for the corner-stone of the new fabric avowed faith in the capacity of man to govern himself, and, presuming that man was more good than bad, and that the development of the good was tantamount to the suppression of evil, it would have the administration of the government act upon the assumption that men were strong and capable. This school extirpated the "ruler" from government; it maintained that government was not a science susceptible neither to new ideas nor to further development, and pigeon-holed as complete, but that the history of the colonies themselves proved that no science had been more generative of new ideas or more productive of new forms. It pointed to the self-government with local representation which Virginia had acquired within twelve years of its foundation; to the representative democracy and written constitution of Connecticut; to the toleration of Maryland and Pennsylvania; to the freedom of conscience and of speech in Rhode Island; and to the reservation of power in the people of New Jersey. All of these innovations, it asserted, had been constituted elements of government; all had been adopted on the assumption that what was good in man was superior as a governmental force to the evil that was in him, and that men were capable of governing themselves, and that all these instances had justified this assumption by their long and sorely-tried experience.

This school asserted, further, that this rich growth of political principles and of governmental forms was due to the fact that the predilection of the colonist for self-government had been unrepressed by the remote principles and forces of Europe; that, left to itself, its expansion had been natural and healthy, and that, the same conditions still existing, new developments would continue to appear. If these things had been done in the green tree, what would be done in the dry? Men of this way of thinking remembered that Oxenstiern had told his son that the world was governed too much, and they were determined that self-government itself should not govern too much. They had seen the colonies rebel, form states, combine and carry to a successful termination a prolonged defence against the greatest of earthly powers, and do this without common headship, without common legislation, and without common courts; and thus, from their own experience, they had proof beyond question that, to a free people, neither "a ruler" nor "a strong government" is necessary, and in fact, scarcely any government. They insisted that the Revolution would prove abortive, were it to stop with a change of forms merely, and without an assertion of the principles acted upon by the colonies, and without a way left open to future development.

It is clear that this school did not reject experience, but that it regarded the experience of its own people as a new dispensation in politics, which it would substitute for the European notions of government henceforth to be discarded. It was radical in its nature; and it was the school of hope, of faith in human nature, of experiment, and of endeavor.

CHAPTER IX.

THE FORMATION OF PARTIES — CONTINUED.

Parties form on Hamilton's measures — Contrary constructions of the Constitution; liberal and strict construction — Madison leads the strict-constructionists in Congress — Personal feeling — Views of Hamilton's financial policy entertained by the Jeffersonians — Hamilton's system favored a plutocracy rather than an aristocracy.

THE inauguration of government under the present Constitution clearly illustrates the normal evolution of parties. So vast was the constructive work to be done that, when Hamilton assumed the Secretaryship of the Treasury, he became, from the force of circumstances, the most important member of the Cabinet. He was, as long as the Secretaryship of the State remained vacant, the head of the administration, and he had the field to himself. Possessed with the notion that the government of the United States, as created, was intended to be supreme in the functions assigned to it, and supreme, too, as a power independent and undelegated, he conceived his first duty to be to invest it as soon as possible with this character. It is true that the powers bestowed upon the new government by the states were few, and that these had been plainly enumerated; but a constitution, from its very nature and for the most sagacious reasons, he conceived to be but a frame of government, a sketch, which legislation and custom are to fill in as circumstances require. The Constitution, therefore, appeared to Hamilton as a text only for construction, and he maintained that this construction should be a liberal one. Within the narrow corners of the instrument lay a world of implied powers, which, dormant, would leave the government limited and restricted, but which, active, might endue it with unqualified and unrestricted sovereignty. It needed but the breath of liberal construction, and internal order would be evoked from chaos, and a great power would be added to the family of nations.

Hamilton took his first step forthwith, and, in spite of opposition from the states which found no warrant for the measure in the Constitution, the federal government assumed the war debts of the several states, consolidated them with the debt of the old government, and funded all in mass. There can be little question that Hamilton's motives in introducing this measure were not restricted to fiscal effects only, but embraced political effects, under the belief that the consolidation of the state debts with those of the general government would exert a cohesive force in favor of the new government, by organizing the public creditors into one body whose interest would be united with that of the administration; perhaps, too, he found in this scheme a wished-for precedent for further advance in liberal construction.

Party lines began to define themselves in the debate which followed the submission of this plan to Congress. On one side, members spoke of "nationality," and were sharply reminded that, before the Constitution had been submitted to the final draft, the word "national" had been in sober second thought significantly erased, and the word "federal" written in its place. The position was taken that, to exceed the powers enumerated in the Constitution, was to exert powers which had not been granted by the states, and which, consequently, were still retained by them, and that this use of powers belonging to other bodies was usurpation. In order, therefore, to resist a tendency to usurpation so manifest, the Constitution should be construed strictly; that is, that the central government should be restricted to the exercise of such powers only as had been enumerated, and that these powers should be deemed to be, what the Constitution expressed them to be, delegated. In this way would the exercise of implied, or, as they were sometimes styled, "incidental" powers, be prevented, and the government be held to its responsibility as an agent in its exercise of enumerated powers. Virginia, through her legislature, protested against the assumption of the state debts on the ground that it was a violation of the Constitution.

The assumption of the debts was followed by a measure which heightened the alarm already taken by the anti-Federalists, as the opponents of the administration were still inaptly styled; this measure was the incorporation of the Bank of the United States in 1780. There were only three banks at that time in the country,[1] and the supply of specie was inadequate to the wants of commerce and the government. Hamilton took advantage of these conditions to advocate

[1] The Bank of North America had been chartered for a term of ten years by the Congress of the Confederation in 1781; but in consequence of the general doubt of the power of Congress to do so, had been chartered also by the legislature of Pennsylvania in 1783; this Pennsylvanian charter was repealed in 1785, but had been renewed in 1787.

the measure on the ground of convenience. He was met in Congress, however, with the objection that the creation of a bank was the creation of a corporation, and that the power to incorporate was not one of the powers which had been enumerated; that what was not enumerated was retained by the states, and that the exercise of such a power on the part of Congress was an encroachment upon one of the reserved rights of the states. In answer to this it was asserted that the Constitution must contain in itself everything necessary to carry on the government, otherwise it would be a nullity, and if these powers were not expressed, it did not follow that they were any less present, or that the duty of bringing them into operation was any less imperative; that the presence of these powers was signified by the provision which bestows capacity "to make all laws which shall be necessary and proper for carrying into execution the foregoing powers, and all other powers vested by this constitution in the government of the United States, or in any department or official thereof:" [1] that a bank is a necessary and proper means to carry on other enumerated powers, and, therefore, that Congress had capacity to incorporate the bank. It was admitted that Congress could not create a bank for merely general accommodation, but it was asserted that it could do so, if the primary object of its incorporation was to subserve the purpose of the government. The opponents of the measure replied that this was too broad; for, supposing that Congress might sanction the means for executing the enumerated powers, the Constitution has expressly restricted

[1] Article I, sect. 8, cl. 17.

these means to such as are "necessary and proper." Let it be granted that a bank is proper, it does not follow that it is necessary; the most that can be said of it is that it is convenient; and the Constitution surely cannot regard mere convenience as a reason for the exercise of doubtful powers.

It is evident that the opposition acquired a great advantage over the Hamiltonians at the outset, for it put them on the defensive. The Hamiltonians had now something more on their hands than mere advocacy of the measure; they had to justify its right to existence, and this wore the air of an apology for presuming to appear. In the end this proved fatal to the Federalists. The Jeffersonians, on the contrary, planted themselves upon the doctrine that, when the states had granted delegated powers which they were careful to enumerate, and had reserved all others in themselves, it was contrary to right reason to construe the existence in the Constitution of any power other than those enumerated; that the powers in question were not among those enumerated, and, holding up the Constitution, they defied their adversaries to point them out. This being an impossibility, the Hamiltonians were driven to make their authority, and this they attempted to do by asserting the right to construe into existence powers which had not been expressed, but which were "incidental" to those enumerated, and which were necessary and proper for the exercise of such powers. The Jeffersonians admitted that Congress was bound to provide the necessary and proper *means* for the exercise of enumerated powers, but, 1, denied the right to establish any powers by construction; declaring that to construe powers into existence was merely a way of making another Constitution, and that this could not be done, inasmuch as Congress was not a Convention; that, 2, the Hamiltonian argument had been reduced to an absurdity because, failing to prove the measure to be such "necessary and proper" means to an enumerated power, the administration had been driven already to the argument *ex convenienti*, and thus that, 3, the states would be at the mercy of any majority in the federal legislature which was disposed to take counsel of convenience. Notwithstanding these objections, the Treasury carried its point. It triumphed, but in doing so it had done a greater thing than it had contemplated: it had given its opponents a bond of union; it had furnished them with the opportunity to define the principle of their opposition; it had supplied them with a reason for being; and it had helped the opposition to organize.

A significant event followed the exhumation of these implied powers: James Madison, whose part in the Convention had won for him the title of "Father of the Constitution," openly left the ranks of the administration and joined the opposition. Madison, hitherto, had supported the administration heartily in its work of establishing the government on a stable foundation under the Constitution, but he was not prepared to establish one over the Constitution, and the illimitable prospect of encroachment by the central government upon the reserved rights of the states aroused his apprehensions. He now ranged himself with those who sought to curb the license which was sure to result from a rule of interpretation which could construe into existence any power desired by a majority of the legislature. His action was taken to signify that the chief framer of the Constitution did not regard it as subject to loose construction, and henceforth the opposition was not compelled to content itself with a leader in the cabinet only, for it had one also on the floor of Congress.

The development of parties is clearly revealed by the assumption of the state debts and the incorporation of the Bank of the United States. Two schools had sprung into existence, and these were distinguished by their modes of construing the Constitution. The necessity of a government which should combine certain powers of thirteen peoples into efficient action had developed the notion that such a government should act directly upon the individual. To do this, it had been necessary that the different sovereignties should part with some of their powers, reserving the rest, and that the peoples, who were thus subjected to diminution of powers, should themselves assent to the procedure. This done, the doctrine arose, and was entertained by a part of the people, that a new and supreme sovereignty had been created, a living, independent organism, endued with the powers as well as charged with the functions of sovereignty; that the Constitution which established it contemplated unrestricted action; that the enumeration of powers was not restrictive but suggestive, and that, consequently, the Constitution actually contained every power necessary to a sovereign; that where there is a power, there is also the duty of exercising it, and, hence, that the true construction should be one which brought these latent powers to the light of day, and thus expanded and strengthened the central government. It is evident that the underlying principle of this doctrine was, that central government in the United States was not federal but single, and that its powers were original and not delegated. The adherents of this principle had one very great advantage over their opponents: when the new government began its operation, they were already organized and they were in power; nevertheless, the doctrinaires could not be said to constitute a party, for the word "party," in its political sense, implies an opponent, and this it could not be said to have. It must, therefore, still be denominated a school.

On the other hand, as circumstances developed opposition, the opponents of the administration, mindful of ancient principles and chafing at the intrusion of new ones. became sensible of the fact that the preservation of their local self-government rested upon denial of illimitable power in the central government, and that the surest way to resist encroachment was to stand upon the very terms of the instrument, and to insist upon a construction which would restrict the government to the powers enumerated, and therefore they adopted the rule of strict-construction. That they constituted a school only, as yet, and not a party, is shown by the discussions of the day, which do not evince the identity of principle and the concert of action now exacted by every party of its constituents, but show that each man still thought and voted for himself with little reference to others. Reflection and discussion at last established the opposition upon a doctrine which did not rely upon argument only, but which drew to its support historical facts and those, too, which were fresh in the recollection. This doctrine maintained that the local governments were creators of the central government, and that logically the creator was superior to the creature; that these local authorities were representatives and conservators of the natural and political rights of the citizens, whereas the central authority, which was altogether an artificial being, represented merely specified powers delegated by its creators and to be exerted only for specific purposes, foremost among which was the preservation of local self-government; that the central government could not be enlarged except at the expense of the states; that, instead of extension of power being conceded to the general government, restriction of power to the terms of the instrument would alone conform to the intention of the framers, which intention was, that these powers were not surrendered, but delegated, and, hence, that the construction of the Constitution should be a strict one. It is evident that the underlying principle of these doctrines was, that government was made for the citizen, and could not be exercised to the furtherance of anything that affected unfavorably his right to local self-government. This principle, henceforth, assumed the character of an active and aggressive political force, to assert which its adherents organized and eventually became a party.

It can hardly be said that the mere coherence of men entertaining similar principles and ideas constituted a party; but circumstances were so productive of opportunity in the early days of the republic, that definition of principles and organization of party proceeded with much greater rapidity than they possibly could do in more settled times. The portfolios of the cabinet teemed with measures, and the spirit of dispute possessed Congress. In those early days, the tyranny of routine and the omnipotence of committees were still unknown, and every measure, as it presented itself, met full and open debate:[1] time was afforded and taken to discuss the plans of government more as subjects of principle than of policy. Apart from Hamilton, it cannot be said that there was any one to urge a distinct or novel policy upon Congress; but then, as far as the internal organization of government was concerned, Hamilton was everything. Members of Congress in time began to conceive of measures in the light of policy as well as of principle, and What would the administration have us to do? came to be a question which presented itself along with the bill. The impulse of resisting an administration measure merely because it was such, it is true, had not yet acquired a footing; but, such was the strong personality of Hamilton, that it impressed itself on friend and foe, and his plans at last met resistance in the feeling that whatever originated from him must run the gauntlet; it may be assumed, too, that the Secretary of the Treasury had often to confront opposition which forebore to encounter the President.

The qualities which inspired the followers of Hamilton with so great enthusiasm, and his adversaries with equally great aversion, must have been singular, indeed. They found their match, nevertheless, in the

[1] It was not until 1799 that the House of Representatives constituted permanent committees; an example which the Senate did not follow until the second session of the Fourteenth Congress, in 1816.

The Senate sat with closed doors until February 20, 1794. Maclay's Journal affords evidence sufficient for the assertion that senatorial discussion was very thorough, practical, and outspoken.

peculiar individuality of his rival, and it must be accepted as a fact that the personal characteristics of the leaders early became positive elements in the formation of the parties they led, and that they stamped impressions which are not wholly obliterated at this day. If, for a time, Congress did not set forth two great parties, it was not long before it displayed two great clans, and it is for this reason that, instead of applying to them names indicative of party organization, during this brief period they came to be aptly styled Hamiltonians and Jeffersonians.

In order to comprehend the feelings, not the principles, which played so important a part in determining the ultimate character of the two great parties, we must look at the measures of the Treasury in the light in which they appeared to the opposition. Such became the virulence of personal feeling, and so discolored by it did party sentiment become, that the effort is not an altogether pleasant one.

Let us consider what Hamilton declared the object of his financial policy to be. It is in these words: "To justify or preserve the confidence of the most enlightened friends of good government; to promote the respectability of the American name; to answer the calls of justice; to restore landed property to its due value; to furnish new resources both to agriculture and commerce; to cement more closely the union of the states; to add to their security against foreign attack; to establish public order on the basis of an upright and liberal policy, — these are the great and invaluable ends to be secured by a proper and adequate provision, at the present period, for the support of the public credit."[1] No one who appreciates the

[1] Report on the Public Credit.

ambition, the earnestness, and the purity of Hamilton's political character, can class this statement of principles with the glittering generalities common to politicians. The plans that flowed from his exhaustless brain, whether to be accepted within or without the Constitution, testify to his persistence in these purposes, and the untiring industry he bestowed upon his measures proves that to him they were real objects of endeavor, and worthy of the utmost efforts of his life to attain. But, to Jefferson and his followers, the funding bill, the assumption of the state debts, the incorporation of the Bank, the excise law, the tariff, all the measures which followed in their train and were initiated by the Secretary of the Treasury, — all these, taken together, assumed the character of a scheme which, changing with circumstances, could have but one result: the subversion of local self-government and the establishment of a general, centralized, consolidated government in its place. To effect this, the fiscal measures proposed by Hamilton had for their object the erection of the capitalists into a controlling class, whose interest it would be to support the present administration, and to keep on extending the power of the central government. Thus, by the operation of the funding bill and by the assumption of the state debts, the public creditors would be organized into a body which would share in the control of the country, through the pressure it brought to bear upon the government, its debtor; by the excise bill, an army of officials, disseminated among the people and clothed with inquisitorial power, would be at the beck of the Secretary of the Treasury; by the incorporation of the Bank, the actual control of the money circulation would fall into the hands of the government, and a party of dependents, who sought office or expected compensation for services rendered, would fill the lobbies, or even organize upon the floor of Congress a party which, holding the balance of power, could determine by their votes the fate of whatever legislation the administration was pleased to favor or condemn ; by a protective tariff, a new class, the class of manufacturers, would be created, and, though this would be but a subdivision of the moneyed class, nevertheless, by its concentration at the commercial centres, it could make itself speedily felt in support of the government which had called it into being, and by whose breath it could be annihilated. This wholly artificial class would play a double part in enriching itself at the cost of the community, particularly of the agricultural portion ; for, at the same time that it brought strength to the central government, the state governments, most of which were founded upon the agricultural interests, would be directly weakened. "His system," said Jefferson, "flowed from principles adverse to liberty, and was calculated to undermine and demolish the republic. . . . The object of all these plans, taken together, is to draw all the powers of the government into the hands of the general legislature; to establish means for corrupting a sufficient corps in that legislature to divide the honest votes, and preponderate their own way the scale which suited, and to have the corps under the command of the Secretary of the Treasury for the purpose of subverting, step by step, the principles of the Constitution, which he has so often declared to be a thing of nothing, which must be changed."[1]

[1] Jefferson's Works, iii, 461, 462.

Such were the views of Hamilton's financial policy which were entertained by the Jeffersonians. They amount to the charge that the Secretary of the Treasury sought to establish a class government; that this government would be founded upon the assumption that men were weak and base, and would recognize corruption as a political, governmental force; and that such a government could not exist unless the present one should be first subverted.

The disciples of Alexander Hamilton have universally assumed that the measures he proposed when a member of Washington's cabinet, and the influence he exerted during Adams' administration, had for their object to impress upon the young republic a certain character which even yet has not been attained: that he did not believe that men had either the capacity or the character for self-government, and that, compelled to forego the establishment of a limited monarchy after the British model, he still nourished in his heart the hope of an aristocratic republic, and bent all his energies and measures to the ultimate attainment of this end.

That Hamilton had no faith in popular self-government we know, and we know, too, his aversion to democracy and his admiration of the British monarchical constitution; but he was a man of great sense, and he realized that the popular abhorrence of monarchy and aristocracy which prevailed among the American people rendered any scheme of the kind out of the question. That, in the absence of a form of government embracing king, lords, and commons, he would be content with one divided into lords and commons, that is to say, an aristocratic republic, may be believed; but, as far as the measures he presented and the influence he exerted went, there is nothing to show that he ever contemplated this republic being an aristocratic one. If he did so, why did he not make use of the materials at hand to constitute such a government? From Mason and Dixon's line southward, no social constitution was ever more aristocratic than the one which existed when he became a member of Washington's cabinet, and which remained so until it was subverted by the civil war of 1861. In this region, society was divided into the owners and the owned, and in his own state, upon the Hudson, the patroons had always constituted an aristocracy. This aristocracy, north and south, was built upon the only foundation which the history of modern civilization indicates as the real basis of aristocracy, land. With these abundant materials at hand, and with the commonalty impoverished and at the mercy of the upper classes whose possessions had not been seriously diminished by the war, why did he not show his hand, if his dearest wish was to found an aristocratic republic? The iron was hot, and then was the time to strike it; but he did not give the blow, nor do any of his measures indicate that such a design was in his mind. On the contrary, everything that he did was so opposed to the landed interest that he was hardly warm in his seat before this class was in array against him. This interest predominated in the anti-Federalist or new party to such an extent that, without it, the opposition would have been of little avail. The reason is clear, — the Hamiltonian measures, one after another, not only struck at the influence of the landed interest, but were directed towards the creation of a class which was to take the place of such interest, and this was the moneyed class. Realty, as a lawyer would say, was to be made subordinate to personalty: the tariff was to build up manufactures, and the bank was to foster a body that dealt in money. Every measure was in the interest of the commercial and money-getting classes, but nothing was done for those who tilled the soil and paid the taxes, and who, at the South and along the Hudson, had for generations maintained the state and habits of a landed aristocracy. Surely, a policy so unfavorable to an aristocracy ready at hand cannot be taken as evidence of a desire to establish an aristocratic republic: rather must it be deemed to have the design of establishing a plutocratic republic. If the Hamiltonian policy had any definite and unmistakable object, it was to subvert the existing aristocracy and to put in its place a plutocracy. This it accomplished; the landed interests became subordinate to the commercial interests; the towns and cities waxed great at the expense of the plantations; the notion of paternalism in government was planted in the minds of the people; a crowd of dependents was fostered and organized into semi-official agents of administration, and before Hamilton went out of office, the character of American society had changed.

Posterity has this charge to make against Hamilton, that when their fathers had by their swords gained a position from which to start the experiment of founding government upon something higher and nobler than the fears and sordidness of human nature, and had the disposition to do so, he threw cold water upon this aspiration, sneered at the notion as visionary, and frustrated the design by starting the young republic upon principles of administration which regarded men, first and last, as base and incapable. To him we owe, more than to any other man, unless it be Madison, the Constitution itself; but to him we owe also the lost opportunity of making the experiment which might have proved that men are not base and incapable, and that government may have a better foundation than the fears and sordidness of human nature. It may be that the notion was a visionary one, but thousands of upright men, whose self-sacrifice had earned for them the right to make the trial, protested ardently against the young republic being invested with a character with which they had not endued it, and earnestly demanded an administration upon far different principles. This opportunity, the only one the anglican race has had since the days of the English Commonwealth, was denied to them and to the world, and the worst form of social constitution known to men, plutocracy, was forced upon the Americans. From Hamilton's time to ours, although more than once strenuously combated, the march of plutocracy has been onward, until to-day nothing opposes its resistless sway except the mutterings of revolution which are ominous of a violent reorganization of society.

The regret at letting this opportunity slip is aggravated by the knowledge we of our day have, that our world was on the eve of the most remarkable expansion of material wealth known to men. Within a few years the force of steam was utilized and the cotton gin invented; and within three generations all the great discoveries and inventions have occurred by which the energies of men in the XIXth century have been concentrated upon material development. To him who regards the Hamiltonian policy as a fortuitous as well as a wise policy, and finds in it the special providence which was to devote this youthful continent to "the spirit of the nineteenth century," nothing can be said. But he who regards man as a creature compounded of good as well as bad, who looks upon government as a science still susceptible to development, and who hopes that every rising sun will bring the world nearer to a time when evil will not be an acknowledged constituent of administration, must bitterly regret that when the opportunity existed, the man to take advantage of it was not in power. It is sad to think that the experiment was handed over to the mobs of the most excitable people, and of the one least subject to self-control since the days of the Athenians: yet, when we see what the French Revolution has done for the human race, what infinite good might have been expected from a fair trial by an anglican representative-democracy! Even had the experiment proved disappointing, our condition could have been no worse than it had been; the resources of a new country, multiplied by invention and discovery, might have mitigated the evils of failure, and men the world over would have been in possession of that rarest and richest political wealth, knowledge of the practical working of a new idea.

CHAPTER X.

CONSTITUTIONAL LEGISLATION.

The Ordinance of 1787 — The Kentucky and Virginia Resolutions — The Missouri Compromise.

MARYLAND instructed her delegates, in 1778, not to agree to the Confederation, unless the northwestern territory "should be considered as a common property, subject to be parceled out by Congress into free, convenient, and independent governments, in such manner and at such times as the wisdom of that assembly shall hereafter direct." Inasmuch as this territory was the subject of divers claims, especially of that of Virginia, which embraced nearly all the land, and the claimants were not disposed to surrender these claims, the Articles of Confederation remained unadopted until the first of March, 1781; upon this day, Maryland ratified the Articles. She did so because New York had resigned her dubious claim in favor of "such of the United States as shall become members of the federal alliance;" Connecticut had resigned her claim; Virginia had offered conditionally to cede the one she had to the territory northwest of the Ohio River; and because Congress had showed itself ready to complete the programme by the declaration that the said territories should be "formed into distinct republican states, which should become members of the Federal Union, and have the same rights of sovereignty, freedom, and independence as the other states." [1]

Pressure had to be brought to bear upon Virginia, whose conditional offer to cede had not been accepted by Congress, but at last she yielded,[2] and the vast regions known as "the Northwest Territory" fell under the disposition of the United States.[3] Jefferson, shortly afterward, as chairman of a special committee, reported a plan for the temporary government of all the western territory including the Northwest, and this was one of the last official acts performed by him before setting sail as minister to France. This plan, which contemplated the future erection of sixteen states, included the following provisions: that "after the year 1800 there shall be neither slavery nor involuntary servitude in any of the said states other than in the punishment of crimes, whereof the party shall have been duly convicted." This prospective prohibition was to cover all the states, as well those south of the Ohio River as those north of it. The six northern states voted for this prohibition: North Carolina was divided; Maryland, Virginia, and South Carolina voted against it, and New Jersey, Delaware, and Georgia were unrepresented. One state more in its favor, and the prohibition of slavery on the eastern slope of the Valley of the Mississippi that was in possession of the United States would have been effected. As it stood, the proviso was lost for lack

[1] October 10, 1780; Journals of Congress, III, 535, 282.

[2] October 20, 1783.

[3] Hening's Statutes, 564–7; Congress accepted, March 1, 1784. Massachusetts ceded, April 19, 1785, and Congress accepted Connecticut's cession, May 26, 1786, but Connecticut held on to the Western Reserve until 1800. South Carolina ceded in 1787.

of the seven votes requisite to a majority. The rest of the report was adopted.

In 1785 Rufus King, of Massachusetts, again presented Jefferson's prohibition, with the omission of the words "after the year 1800," and with a substitution of the words "personally guilty" for "duly convicted." This made the prohibition of slavery immediate instead of prospective. The resolution as amended was sent to a committee, and thence was favorably reported by a vote of eight states to three, but it was not acted upon.

Towards the close of the following year, the government of the territory was again taken up by Congress, but the scope of the committee was limited to the northwestern portion. It was this committee which, with Nathan Dane as Chairman, framed the famous "Ordinance of 1787."[1] Jefferson's prohibition, made immediate instead of prospective, was "agreed to without opposition," says Dane, who expressed his surprise in a letter to King. There were three reasons for this: one was that the prohibition would affect one half only of the territory embraced in Jefferson's proviso, and this half the northern one, which lay in latitudes already demonstrated by experience to be uncongenial to the maintenance of slavery. The South really gave up nothing. Another reason was, the accompaniment of a fugitive slave clause (the first one in our history) to the prohibition. The last reason was one which had a cogent effect upon a Congress which legislated constantly in sight of an empty treasury; it was that the Ohio Land Company stood ready to take five million

[1] Adopted, July 13, 1787.

acres of land in Ohio at a valuation, if it should be organized into a free territory. The bargain was struck, and thus was the Northwest reserved for free states only.[1] The organization of the territory south of the Ohio River was made under an agreement with the ceding states that slavery should not be prohibited within its limits.

The effect of the provisions of this Ordinance in respect to the prohibition of slavery, to freedom of religion, and to the encouragement of education, and the guarantee of the political rights of the individual, and the future membership of the projected states in the Union, was amazing, and makes the most impressive chapter in the political history of the United States. Two distinct forms of civilization and of society grew up alongside of each other, separated only by a thread, the Ohio River, and they were object-lessons ever present to the scrutiny of mankind. They presented the striking contrast between society founded upon free labor and society founded upon slave labor. Two social forms were wide apart, and were hopelessly incompatible with each other.

The Alien and Sedition Laws which were passed by Congress in 1798, during the administration of John Adams, afforded the text upon which the Kentucky and Virginia resolutions were written. These measures were regarded throughout the country as sustaining the constant assertion of Jefferson that, unless the action of Congress was restricted to the powers

[1] For an excellent résumé of the subject, see Alexander Johnson's article, entitled "Ordinance of 1787," in Lalor's Cyclopædia of Political Science, etc.; and for bibliography, see references appended to this article.

enumerated in the Constitution, no protection to personal and civil rights would remain, except that which lay in the reserved powers of the several states. Seizing the opportunity presented by the exasperating execution of these laws, Jefferson and Madison undertook to define, through state legislative action, the nature of the federal government and the relations borne to it by the states, and to point out the exercise of a loose construction of the Constitution as a fit and necessary subject for correction, inasmuch as it would inevitably tend to change the existing constitutional government to something which would be "at best a mixed monarchy."

The attempt to arouse the fears of the states and to call forth a general legislative protest, if not intervention, against the encroachments of the federal government, proved futile, but the resolutions did not fail to excite popular apprehension, and to augment the ranks of the strict-constructionists.

The position taken in the resolutions was: 1. That the general government had its origin in a compact between the several states, under the style and title of a Constitution for the United States; and that to this compact each state acceded as a state, and is an integral party. 2. That these several states had constituted this general government for special purposes only. 3. That they had delegated to that government certain definite powers, reserving, each state to itself, the residuary mass to their own self-government. Therefore, 4, whenever the general government assumes undelegated powers, its acts are unauthoritative, void, and of no force. And, 5, that the general government, created by this compact, was not made the exclusive or final judge of the extent of the powers delegated to itself, since that would have made its discretion, and not the Constitution, the measure of its powers; but that, as in all other cases of compact among parties having no judge, each party has an equal right to judge for itself, as well of infractions as of the mode and measure of redress.

Such were the views of the nature of the federal government and the rights of the individual states set forth in the first of the Kentucky resolutions. The Virginia resolutions took the same view of the origin of the general government, viz.: that it was a result of a compact to which the states alone [1] were parties, and they united with the Kentucky resolutions in deprecation of broad or loose construction of the Constitution, and in censure of the Alien and Sedition Laws. The transmission of copies of these resolutions directly to the governors and legislatures of the other states, as well as to the Virginia senators and representatives in Congress, was enjoined; whereas the Kentucky resolutions directed their transmission merely to the Kentucky senators and representatives for the purpose of securing a repeal of the obnoxious Alien and Sedition Laws.

The Kentucky resolutions had expresssd the hope that "the co-states, recurring to their natural rights not made federal, will concur in declaring these [Alien and Sedition Laws] void and of no force, and will each unite with this commonwealth in requesting their repeal at the next session of Congress." The Virginia

[1] The word "alone" was stricken out, as well as the words "null, void, and of no force or effect." This was done in order to obviate the objection to the resolutions, that they contained declarations "not of opinion but of fact."

resolutions, on their part, declared "that in case of a deliberate, palpable, and dangerous exercise of their powers, not granted by the said compact, the states, which are parties thereto, have the right and are in duty bound to *interpose* for arresting the progress of the evil, and for maintaining, within their respective limits, the authorities, rights, and liberties appertaining to them."

This assertion contains the doctrine, that the states have a right to judge for themselves, whether the exercise of powers not granted by the compact is so deliberate, palpable, and dangerous as to warrant interposition on their part, or no. A resolution, understood to be by a hand other than the one which had written the text of 1798, was added to the Kentucky resolution, in the following year (1799), and this asserted "that the several states which formed that instrument, being sovereign and independent, have the unquestionable right to judge of the infraction; that a nullification, by those sovereignties, of all unauthorized acts, done under color of that instrument, is the rightful remedy; that, although this commonwealth, as a party to the federal compact, will bow to the laws of the Union, yet it does at the same time declare, that it will not now or ever hereafter cease to oppose, in a constitutional manner, every attempt, at what quarter soever offered, to violate that compact, and finally, in order that no pretext or argument may be drawn from a supposed acquiescence in the constitutionality of those laws, and be thereby used as precedents for similar further violations of the federal compact, this commonwealth does now enter against them its solemn protest." In this resolution the right to judge of the infraction is asserted to lie in "the several states," whereas in the first of the resolutions of 1798, it was declared that "each party [to the compact] has an equal right to judge for itself." The wording in the first resolution is not so clear, but in later times it was subjected to the assertion, notably by Webster in 1830, that Jefferson had committed the solecism of making his several states enter into a compact with a government which was a creature of this very compact; but this was a palpable misconstruction of terms.

The passage of these resolutions by the respective legislatures, and their transmission to Congress and to the other states, created a profound impression upon the people everywhere. There was no mistaking their purpose; it was, to formulate a creed for the republican-democratic party, [1] and to place over against the doctrine of incidental, auxiliary, or latent powers the enumerated powers; to meet the assertion of complete sovereignty in the general government with the rejoinder that exercise of powers which were delegated was to be accounted for, and that exercise of powers not specifically enumerated was usurpation. The federal and decentralizing element in the Constitution had turned upon the national and centralizing element, and the two political forces were now arrayed against each other. The general government was declared, once for all, to have had its origin in a compact of equals, above whom there was no superior to whom appeals could be made upon disagreement among

[1] At the time of these resolutions, the "party platform" had not been devised, and as there were no "party conventions" to give authoritative expression to party doctrine, recourse was had in several instances to the resolutions of state legislatures.

themselves; nor upon a question of infraction of delegated power did it behoove the delegate to question the authority of the grant of powers; nor upon a question of the exercise of undelegated powers were there any judges but those in whom the sole right to those powers remained.

Much labor has been expended upon the task of explaining away the word "compact:" but, in view of the fact that the word was made use of in the resolutions only eleven years after the Constitutional Convention had sat; that the author of the Virginia resolutions had been a member of that Convention, and that there is nothing to show that a change in the meaning of so technical and well-defined a word as this is had taken place, it is to be presumed that the word "compact" was used by the authors of the resolutions in 1798 in the same sense in which it had been used by them in 1787. Now, in 1787 and 1788, the term "compact" was in general use in referring to the Constitution, as "The Federalist" and the ratifications themselves of the instrument clearly show; for in the ratification of Massachusetts, the Constitution was said to be "an explicit and solemn compact," and New Hampshire uses the same words. In every one of the debates of the state conventions called to ratify or reject the Constitution, the word was used freely in application to this instrument, and in the same sense as that in which it is employed in the resolutions, and no one was called to account for doing so: and in the correspondence and publications of the friends or the opponents of this frame of government it was applied in the same way, as is to be seen in the letters and other writings of Washington, Madison, Hamilton, Morris, Rufus King, Ellsworth, and Randolph. Edmund Pendleton, President of the Virginia ratifying Convention, went so far as to assert: "This is the only government founded in real compact." Daniel Webster, then, was surely wrong in saying of Calhoun that "he introduces a new word of his own, viz.: Compact, as importing the principal idea, and designed to play the principal part."

Not to dwell upon an interpretation of the word "compact," or upon the objections to it in characterizing the Constitution, the spirit and meaning (so much and so long disputed) of the resolutions themselves are more to the purpose. For, although these tenets failed to call forth the sympathetic response of the various legislatures, they drew to themselves the fealty of the strict-constructionists, who were then on the eve of sweeping the latitudinarians from the political field; and such stupendous consequences have flowed from these resolutions as sources of doctrine, that it is requisite to have as clear a notion of their spirit and meaning as can be gathered from a brief summary of the textual expressions, and of the arguments for and against them made by their advocates and opponents and by contending expounders of the Constitution.

In respect, then, to the spirit and intentions of these resolutions, the question arises, What purpose had their authors in view, when they promulgated them and called upon the other states to make them their own? Did they mean that the states should go to the length of blocking completely the action of the federal government? Did they intend to imply forcible resistance of a state to objectionable laws?

Several ways by which the mass of right residuary in the states could act in case of infraction suggest themselves: 1. By mere protest, or by petition, on the part of the particular governments; in which cases correction of the evil would be left to the action of public opinion. 2. By direct request that Congress repeal the infracting laws. 3. By separate protest of the several states. 4. By separate request of these states for repeal, and, 5, by action of a convention, whose corrective amendments to the Constitution would be ratified by the requisite number of states. The first and third of these methods would be indirect in their action, and would refer the correction of the evil to the sober judgment of the people; they would rely, too, upon the favorable operation of time. The second and fourth methods would be direct and would leave nothing to time; but no one of these four modes of redress would indicate a disposition unfriendly to the general government, for they would be strictly within the provision of the Constitution relating to amendments,[1] and in compliance with the spirit of the article[2] recognizing the right of the people peaceably to assemble and to petition the government for a redress of grievances, and of the article[3] reserving to the states powers not delegated. These methods, then, would be constitutional and therefore unobjectionable, and would accord with the professions of the resolutions, that the state "considers union for specified national purposes to be friendly to the peace, happiness, and prosperity of all the

[1] Article V.

[2] Article VIII.; the first article of the amendments.

[3] Article X.

states;" that, "faithful to the compact, according to the plain intent and meaning in which it was understood and acceded to by the several parties, it is sincerely anxious for its preservation;"[1] that it has "a firm resolution to maintain and defend the Constitution of the United States against every aggression either foreign or domestic, and that it will support the government of the United States in all measures warranted by the [Constitution];" that it "most solemnly declares a warm attachment to the Union of the states, to maintain which it pledges its powers, and that for this end, it is its duty to watch over and oppose every infraction of those principles which constitute the only basis of that Union."[2] The Virginia resolutions took particular pains to assert "the truest anxiety for establishing and perpetuating the union of all, and the most scrupulous fidelity to that Constitution, which is the pledge of mutual friendship and the instrument of mutual happiness," and even the article of 1799 appended to the Kentucky resolutions acknowledges "that this commonwealth, as a party to the federal compact, will bow to the laws of the Union."

Internal evidence certainly displays a right spirit within the resolutions; for they breathe a warm attachment to the Union, the most scrupulous fidelity to the Constitution, and a determination to maintain and defend the government. No fault, then, can be found with the spirit of the resolutions, and none could ever have been found, were it not that, in the eighth article of the Kentucky resolutions, it was declared "that

[1] Kentucky resolutions, article 8.

[2] Virginia resolutions: preamble.

every state has a natural right in cases not within the compact (*casus non fœderis*) to *nullify* of *their* own authority all assumptions of power by others within their limits," and that a "*nullification* by those sovereignties [the several states] of all unauthorized acts, done under color of that instrument [the Constitution of the United States] is the rightful remedy." The word "every" followed by the word "their" threw a shade of ambiguity over this clause sufficient to draw upon it the reproach of maintaining that a *single* state had the right to nullify the common laws of all. But the Virginia resolutions, on their part, made use of the plural term "states," and as the rule of the majority is inherent in the federal system, the conclusion is irresistible that Virginia intended the interposition which she recommended to be that of a majority of the states: and, further, inasmuch as the Constitution provides for its own amendment on the application of two thirds of the states, it is most probable that this constitutional method of "arresting the progress of the evil" was the only one she had in view. Such being the case, an appeal to public opinion with the design of uniting three fourths of the states in ratification of an effective amendment to the Constitution was all that was intended by Virginia.[1] The facts that the Virginia resolutions do not contain the words "nullify," "nullification," or any of their equivalents; that the state confines herself to expressing the confidence that her sister states will concur with her in "*declaring*" that the acts complained of were unconstitutional; that "the necessary and proper

[1] Rives, of Virginia, during the debate in 1833 on Calhoun's nullification resolutions.

measures will be taken by each for coöperating with [her], in maintaining unimpaired the authorities, rights, and liberties, reserved to the states respectively or to the people;" and that, in the mean time, she contents herself with transmitting copies of the resolutions to the executive authority of each of the other states, with a request that the same may be communicated to the legislature thereof, and that a copy be furnished to each of her senators and representatives in Congress, — all these facts are in clear support of this conclusion. These resolutions were expressly *declaratory*, and proceeding from the legislature only, which was not even a party to the Constitution, could be declaratory of opinion only.[1] Nowhere was the right set forth in the resolutions, nor broached in the debates of which they were the subject, that a state might resist the operation of the federal laws in any case in which it might deem an act to exceed the limits of the Constitution; force is not hinted, nor is there a suspicion of nullification.

The same remarks may be made of the Kentucky resolutions of 1798; for the clause asserting the right of "every" state to nullify obnoxious acts of the general government, and prescribing "nullification" as the rightful remedy, does not belong to the resolutions of 1798, but to the addition made in 1799.[2] Thomas Jefferson was the author of the former, and, said Madison in 1831, "that he ever asserted a right in a single state to arrest the execution of an act of Congress — the arrest to be valid and permanent, unless reversed by three fourths of the states — is

[1] Madison to Robertson, March 27, 1831.
[2] Madison to Cabell, May 31, 1830.

countenanced by nothing known to have been said or done by him. In his letter to Major Cartwright, he refers to a convention as a peaceable remedy for conflicting claims of power in our compound government; but whether he alluded to a convention as prescribed by the Constitution, or brought about by any other mode, his respect for the will of the majorities, as the vital principle of republican government, makes it certain that he could not have meant a convention in which a minority was to prevail either in amending or expounding the Constitution."[1] Directly to the point, moreover, is Jefferson's own testimony in a letter to Madison,[2] in 1825, which suggests the passage by the Virginia legislature of a new set of resolutions, having for its subject the unconstitutionality of the federal government meddling with internal improvements. Regarding opposition as futile, the author seeks safety in flying before the storm, and in constitutionalizing by an amendment "the acts which we have declared to be usurpations;" but he promises for the state, and enjoins upon its citizens, acquiescence "until the legislature of the United States shall otherwise and ultimately decide."

Thus do the terms themselves of the Kentucky and Virginia resolutions of 1798 forbid the inference that force, on the part of the states or of any of

[1] Madison to Townsend, December 18, 1831; and see Benton, Thirty Years' View, I, chap. lxxxvii, pp. 347–360, for extracts of debate on the resolutions in the legislature of Virginia, and for Madison's explanations. See also Madison's Report to the Virginia Legislature of 1799–1800, commonly called "the Report of 1800;" Elliot's Debates, 528 *et seq.;* 2 Benton's Debates of Congress, 373; Nicolson's Debates in the Virginia Assembly of 1798; Stephens' War between the states, 441 *et seq.;* Story's Commentaries, sect. 1289 n.

[2] December 24, 1825.

them, to abrogate a law of the United States, or to nullify its operation, was within their purview. The right of revolution, even, was not referred to nor hinted at; but this right, which is a sacred one and which is not to be gainsaid, is presumably ever in contemplation of the freeman, and it is referred to here as something which might well have been alluded to under stress of the circumstances which provoked the resolutions. In short, to adopt the succinct summary of Benton,[1] their intention was: 1. By a solemn declaration of opinion, calculated to operate on public sentiment, to induce the coöperation of other states in like declarations. 2. To make a direct representation to Congress, with a view to obtain a repeal of the acts complained of. 3. To represent to their respective senators their wish that two thirds thereof would propose an explanatory amendment to the Constitution. 4. By the concurrence of two thirds of the states, to cause Congress to call a convention for the same object.

It was the abuse of the resolutions of 1798 which led to after-woes of the republic; or rather, it was the use of that bird of ill-omen, the Kentucky resolution of 1799, whereby misconstruction was put upon all the resolutions, and they were made to appear as sources of false doctrine. Inasmuch as the nullification ordinance of South Carolina in 1832 is to be attributed to this abuse, and in the great debate which followed, the term "compact," and the principles underlying the Constitution and the resolutions, received exposition at the hands of such expounders as Calhoun and Webster, it may be well to anticipate

[1] Thirty Years' View, i, 353.

a stage of history, and ascertain what view the generation succeeding that of Madison and Jefferson took of the resolutions. Both of the great parties involved in the discussion laid the doctrine of nullification at the doors of the Kentucky and Virginia legislatures; one of these parties asserting that the truth was not in them, and the other affirming that the truth, as ascertained by itself, was there to be found. The judgment of the third generation is, unquestionably, that both of these assertions are untrue: that the resolutions of 1798 cannot be held accountable for the doctrines of nullification and of secession, nor that they presented a false (though not unbiassed) exposition of the rights of the states.

The doctrines enunciated in these resolutions became the creed of what in later days was known as the Democratic party, and were at once universally accepted throughout the South or state-rights section of the United States.

The element of nationality introduced into the Constitution of 1788 became aggressive as soon as the new government went into operation, and its consolidating tendency called forth the resistance of the strict-constructionists in defence of the states whose rights it threatened to absorb. The state-rights party was the antitype of the national party, and it sought to preserve the equilibrium between the states and the general government. To do this, it insisted that the term "state" meant the people composing the thirteen political societies, in their highest sovereign capacity, because in this sense the Constitution was submitted to the "states," in this sense the "states" ratified it, and in this sense of the term "states" they are consequently parties to the compact from which the powers of the federal government result: that the compact ought to have the interpretation plainly intended by the parties to it, and that it ought to have the execution and effect intended by them; for, if the powers granted be valid, it is solely because they are granted, and if the granted powers are valid, because granted, all other powers not granted must not be valid. The states, then, being parties to the constitutional compact and in their sovereign capacity, it follows of necessity that there can be no tribunal above their authority, to decide in the last resort whether the compact made by them be violated; and, consequently, that, as the parties to it, they must themselves decide in the last resort such questions as may be of sufficient magnitude to require their interposition. In the case of an intimate and constitutional union, like that of the United States, it is evident that the interposition of the parties, in their sovereign capacity, can be called for by occasions only, deeply and essentially affecting the vital principles of their political system.[1]

Madison, in expressing these views, wished that the perfection of language admitted less diversity in the signification of the word "states," but took comfort in the thought that little inconvenience was produced by it, where the true sense can be collected with certainty from the different applications. In this instance, it was clear to him that the parties to the compact meant, by the word "state," the people composing that political society. The commentator of today must regret that the plural term "peoples" was neither in general nor special use by English-speaking

[1] Madison's Report on the Virginia Resolutions.

writers of that period, for, if the term "states" meant the people of the several states, much of the confusion resulting from the attempt to ascertain who the parties to the compact were, would have been obviated by the employment of the term "peoples." The contention itself, for example, over the construction of the expression in the preamble of the Constitution, "We the people of the United States," would not have occurred, for if "people" here meant "peoples," the interpretation that derives the Constitution from the act of a nation would have had no foundation, and therefore could not have taken place.

Contemporaneous evidence of intention by the parties themselves is the strongest external evidence possible for a compact, and this evidence is to be found in the ratifications of the Constitution by the several states. These ratifications were all made by the "delegates" or "deputies" of each state, "in the name of the people" of that state, except in the cases of Georgia and Delaware, by whom the equivalent, "for and in behalf of ourselves and our constituents," was used, and in the instance of North Carolina, which employed the particularizing term, "in behalf of the freemen, citizens and inhabitants of North Carolina:" so that there can be no question that the people of each of these "political societies" ratified the Constitution, and was a several party to that instrument. Nor can it be doubted that, when grouped together in one term, they were thirteen peoples.

That this fact was recognized universally at the time of ratification, and continued to be so, until the expansion of the principles of nationality called it into question, is, from the evidence afforded by the action of the several states in amending the Constitution, from the language used upon the floor of Congress by senators and representatives, from that used by popular speakers and by the press, and particularly from that of state papers and of the leading expounders of the Constitution in debate and in correspondence, private, official, or professional, equally indisputable.

The retirement of slavery to the country south of Mason and Dixon's line and the Ohio River, and the preponderating development of population and material strength in the country north of this line of delimitation, divided the United States into two sections, and entailed upon them all the evils which sectionalism can inflict. It needs no demonstration that, where different peoples unite in a common form of government, anything inconsistent with the preservation of their unity is dangerous to their welfare, and that sectionalism, or the conflict between interests which are peculiar to sections of territory, is of such a nature. One of the evils, and the main and most virulent one which sectionalism in the United States has developed, has been the sectionalizing as well of social and political principles as of material interests.

This paradoxical effect on principles, which are impulses supposed to be general in their nature, is due to the fact that principles are the sources of rules of action, and inasmuch as the action of political bodies is governed solely by their interests, the motives of action, principles, respond to the interests of a locality and become sectionalized with it. If there be any doubt of this being a vital and active force in politics, this doubt will be dispelled by the most cursory glance at the dealings of the great powers with each other, or, to come nearer home, at the votes in the Congress of the United States affecting the interests of localities; notably those upon the tariff question, which has invariably divided parties. There never has been a time since this question came before Congress, that members of a party which has strenuously maintained that any tariff, except for revenue only, is unconstitutional, have not been found voting for a protective tariff; nor, on the other hand, that members of a party of which "protection" is a cardinal doctrine have not strenuously opposed it. A map of the country, shaded according to the votes for and against a tariff, would, especially in these later days of mineral and commercial development, appear spotted with areas corresponding to the votes in the general legislature, and these areas would consequently indicate the "principles" which had their origin in the interests of these localities.

The bending of "our notions to our dealing" has never been exemplified on a greater scale, or in a clearer manner, than it was in the course run by sectionalism in this country. So long as the chief interest of the North lay in navigation and agriculture, an interest which was not in competition with that of any other section, her principles were general, and the Constitution was a "compact" to which the several states had "acceded" in their capacity of "sovereignties;" there was no tribunal of appeal for the parties to this compact, and the assertions of Virginia and New York in their ratifications of the Constitution, that the powers granted in this instrument, being derived from the people, might be resumed by them, whensoever the same shall be perverted to their injury or oppression, was unquestioned.

Time, however, wrought its changes. The policy of Alexander Hamilton had proved to be favorable to that part of the country where population was concentrated, but it had not been favorable where population was dispersed. It accumulated money in the large cities, making them financial centres; the South had no large cities. It fostered the commercial classes; but, from the constitution of southern society, the commercial class of the South was insignificant, and, to all appearances, would remain such. It undertook to create a manufacturing class, and succeeded in doing so; but the Southerners were not a manufacturing people, for slave labor was not skilled labor, nor could it be made skilled. Moreover, immigration followed northern latitudes in its progress west, and the South thus lacked this augmentation of population, while the balance of representation was inclining against it from day to day. It is not surprising that, as the material importance of the South waned and it began to experience trepidation concerning its political future, the self-importance of the North rose, and that it manifested a disposition to aggrandize wealth and power even at the expense of the South: and this it did by obtaining an adjustment of taxation, the inequality of which was favorable to it, by bounties to navigation and fishing, and above all by protective tariffs. The South was the market of the North: and a tariff for protection transformed New England and Pennsylvania into manufacturing communities whose product was to be taken by the South; for, owing to the lack of a merchant service that should bring foreign productions to her doors, the South would be compelled to buy of the North at the latter's prices.

Such was the view taken by the South of her economical relations to the North. The forecast she made of her fortunes was not a cheering one, nor was it brightened by the reflection that, in ceding the Northwest Territory to the United States, she had increased northern territory, and had provided homes for the immigrants who were rapidly strengthening her rival's ranks. She recalled, too, the debates in the Constitutional Convention which ended, as she conceived, in yielding too much to the North on the questions of representation and taxation; she regretted that she had not made a more determined stand against committing so unreservedly the regulation of commerce to the federal government, and she had South Carolina to remind her of the willingness of New England to allow the claim of right in Spain to control the navigation of the lower Mississippi and to close the mouths of the river, — now that the North had gained possession of the Northwest, it was ready to look on with indifference while the Southwest was rendered valueless to the South. These proofs, as the South chose to consider them, of northern rapacity, and of a settled policy on the part of the North to look to its own interest regardless of the interests of others, confirmed the people of that section in the unfavorable opinion which they had entertained of the northern people for a period long before they had combined with them in resistance to the mother-country. Rightly or wrongly, the South started out in its federal life with a sense of grievance acquired from its political connection with its neighbors, and with the ancient unsocial disposition towards them greatly aggravated: but that it could not lay upon the North the burden of measures which in later days it denounced as unfair and unconstitutional is shown by the facts, that the obnoxious bank was reinstated by the aid of southern votes and the approval of a southern President, and that the tariff of 1816 received southern support and the qualified approbation of John C. Calhoun, the Argus of the South.

The North, it need hardly be said, did not admit that this sense of grievance had any foundation; for, on its part, it had carried away from the Convention the feeling that the South had claimed too much in the settlement of the ratio of representation and taxation, and it retorted that the votes of the South, years after the bank and the protective systems had had a trial, afforded convincive proof that these measures had not been regarded by that section as unfavorable to its interests, and that, consequently, they were to be accepted as conducive to the general welfare; and it pointed to the southern votes on the subject of naturalization as evidence that the incoming tide of immigration was as congenial to the political interest of the South as it was to the material interest of the North. The northern people acknowledged that the South was a market for their manufactures, but they repudiated with abhorrence the notion that they regarded the southern states as Great Britain had regarded all her colonies, as mere factories for her trade, but considered the Union to be a union of all interests, political, social, and economical; that it was a Union of states; and, such was their fidelity to this Union, that they would preserve it at any cost.

How little weight must be given to the professions of loyalty to the Union by either section may be estimated from the fact that, down to the civil war of 1861, there had rarely been a time when the danger of dissolution, at the hands of one side or the other, was not threatening the Union. Recurring to the Spanish claim of right to close the lower Mississippi to our navigation (a contention contemporaneous with the institution of our present government), one of the southern states, South Carolina, made it a reason for hesitation in ratifying the Constitution, and very properly so. It was not in accordance with propriety, on the other hand, that, grievous as the loss of such important navigation might be, southern men should call for the dissolution of a Union which had been just set upon its feet. Nor, as the public utterances and the private correspondence of New England leaders disclose, was there reason or propriety in the threats of dissolution of the general Union, and the formation of a particular one, embracing the New England states only, merely because the rampant federalism of the locality had met with a rebuff. The conduct of New England during the Embargo and the War of 1812 has ever since then received such unsparing condemnation, that merely to mention it is to reopen a mortifying chapter of our history; but the constant threats of dissolution which streamed from southern sources on the slavery question were equally reprehensible with those which had emanated from New England, or with those which the New York Clintonians had been guilty of immediately after the adoption of the Constitution. In fact, if we leave out "the era of good feeling," the sorrowful statement that the continuance of the Union was always a matter of doubt is proved to be true by every page of our history; and it cannot be denied that, from the beginning of our united existence, the danger that threatened it was the irrepressible conflict between the ideas and interests of the North and of the South, or, in a word, "sectionalism."

This sectionalism found expression in the different methods of construing the Constitution. At first, the North, no less than the South, regarded the Constitution as a compact, which had been acceded to by the state-sovereignties as parties, and one which, in the absence of a superior who would enforce conjunction, could be seceded from as it had been acceded to. One cannot read the writings of the days which followed the adoption of the Constitution and fail to see that secession from the Union, or rather the withdrawal and resumption by the states of the delegated powers, was the remedy in contemplation of the generation which made the Constitution; that it was regarded as the logical and natural remedy, and as the only remedy. There is no discussion of a choice of remedies; it was taken for granted that this remedy existed by nature, that it was present to the minds of those who framed the compact, and that, should the time and occasion for applying it occur, it would be resorted to as a matter of course. This general notion precluded the idea of coercion, and, in fact, every suggestion of the kind met with denunciation on all sides. It follows, then, that the "interposition of the states," asserted in the Virginia resolutions to be a "duty," was a mild statement of political obligation, and that nullification became universally repudiated afterwards, not because it was a mere makeshift, but because it was, as the anti-Calhoun party in South Carolina held it to be, illogical. Either the Constitution was a compact, or it was the evidence of a surrender of powers: secession or submission was the only alternative.

Whether the change on the part of the North in its views of the Constitution was due to a sincere disposition to evolve a great and glorious power out of a federation, or whether, according to the taunt of the South, it was due to motives of interest induced by fears of losing its market, the North certainly did exhibit a remarkable change in the way it construed the Constitution. First, it denied that the Constitution was a compact: and this denial carried with it a denial of the right of any state to secede. Second, it denied that the several states or peoples had been parties to the transaction, or that there had been "peoples" at all, but asserted that the Constitution was an ordinance of one whole people of the United States, or nation. Third, that the powers enumerated in this instrument had not been delegated but surrendered, and, moreover, were but outlines to be filled in or to be supplemented by others which should be deemed to be necessary or even convenient by the nation.

With the crystallization of these doctrines into a creed or "platform," the attitude of the North became more and more determined, and she opposed through the Whig party any pretensions made by the South through the Democratic party. She became less and less conciliatory, until at length, throwing aside conciliation, she took a positive stand, and avowed her determination not to permit further territorial extension of slavery. This lent her the appearance of aggression, and the occasion of it was the application of the territory of Missouri to be admitted into the Union.

During its session of 1818, the territorial legislature of Missouri made application for authority to frame a constitution and establish a state government. A bill to effect this purpose was introduced into the House of Representatives at Washington, and reached its consideration in February, 1819, in the course of which Mr. Tallmadge, of New York, offered the following proviso: "That the further introduction of slavery or involuntary servitude shall be prohibited, except for the punishment of crimes, whereof the party shall have been duly convicted; and that all children born within the State after the admission thereof shall be free at the age of twenty-five years." This amendment was to be made a condition precedent to admission to the Union, and it precipitated a debate whose duration and temper disclosed a conflict of principle and sentiment which, now dormant now active, in the course of time became irrepressible, and at last burst forth in a conflict of arms. The reason of this was that, as Rufus King bluntly admitted, it was a struggle for political power, and that this was an effort to extirpate slavery from soil where it existed by law; for this territory was a part of the Louisiana Purchase,[1] in

[1] Louisiana Purchase: 26th October, 1803, an act to enable the President to take possession of the ceded territory passed in the Senate by a vote of 26 to 6 and, on the 28th, in the House by 89 to 23. J. Q. Adams was among the stoutest supporters of the bill, passed in the House on the 29th, for creation of stock to carry the treaty into effect. November 30, the Spanish handed the colony over to the French, and, 20th December, the French transferred it to the United States. 9th March, 1804, St. Louis was handed over by the Spaniards to Captain Stoddard, U. S. Army, who had been commissioned to receive it on behalf

which slavery had always existed, and in which it still existed under the treaty obligations that were conditions of its acquisition. Slave territory it had been under Spanish and French domination, slave territory it had been when acquired by the United States, and slave territory it was when it made its application to enter the Union as a state. There was nothing therefore in its *status* at law to provoke opposition to its admission as a slave state, and such opposition must have had its motive in something else than opposition to unlawful conditions or measures. The most natural motive could be found in the qualities of human nature, and at once it was attributed to the sense of antagonism to slavery and to the spirit of aggrandizement in the North, which sought supremacy of political power at the cost of the South.

There was ground for this alarm in the southern states. In 1819, Alabama had been admitted without the opposition of the free states, although by this admission the South gained a preponderance of votes in the Senate, for the reason, that, when Georgia ceded the territory comprising this state, she made certain stipulations in respect to slavery, that carried this form of labor along with the soil. But so was the soil of which Missouri formed a part, slave territory under conditions just as solemn and effective: for the treaty under which the soil was acquired stipulated, as

of France, and 10th March, 1804, Captain Stoddard transferred it to the United States. The Purchase was at once divided by act of Congress into two parts: all north of 33° north latitude being formed into a district styled the District of Louisiana, and for judicial and administrative purposes being attached to the territory of Indiana. March 3, 1805, an act of Congress erected the District into a Territory of the first or lowest grade, under the name of the Territory of Louisiana. This detached it from Indiana.

conditions to the transfer of possession, that "Louisiana, with all its rights and appurtenances as fully and in the same manner as they had been acquired by the French Republic from Spain,"[1] should be the thing transferred, and Article III, written by Bonaparte himself, further stipulated, that "the inhabitants of the ceded territory shall be incorporated in the Union of the United States, and admitted as soon as possible, according to the principles of the Federal Constitution, to the enjoyment of all the rights, advantages, and immunities of citizens of the United States; and in the mean time they shall be maintained and protected in the free enjoyment of their liberty, property, and the religion which they prefer." If, therefore, the stipulations of Georgia in respect to Alabama had been observed, so should have been the stipulations of France in respect to the Louisiana Purchase, and as no satisfactory reply could be made to this assertion, it is reasonable as well as natural that the restriction insisted upon by the states should have a motive other than the good of all the states. The blunt admission of Mr. King dispelled the last doubt, and that the South was justified in placing an unfavorable interpretation upon this enforced extirpation of slavery from its borders is made clear by the remarks of John Quincy Adams during the debate on the admission of the adjoining territory of Arkansas. Said he, "She is entitled to admission as a slave state . . . by virtue of that article in the treaty for the acquisition of Louisiana which secures to the inhabitants of the ceded territories all the rights, privileges, and immunities of the original citizens of the United States; and stipulates for their admission,

[1] Carr's Missouri, 78.

conformably to that principle, in the Union. Louisiana was purchased as a country wherein slavery was the established law of the land. As Congress have not power in time of peace to abolish slavery in the original states of the Union, they are equally destitute in those parts of the territory ceded by France to the United States under the name of Louisiana, where slavery existed at the time of the acquisition. . . . Arkansas, therefore, comes, and has the right to come, into the Union with her slaves and her slave laws. It is written in the bond, and, however I may lament that it was so written, I must faithfully perform its obligations."[1] This was spoken by a northern man, an ex-President, and carries with it the force not only of the facts, but of an admission. As the circumstances in respect to Arkansas were precisely the same as those of Missouri, it follows that the legal *status* of the two territories was the same, and that Missouri was entitled under the treaty stipulations, and consequently under the laws of the United States, to admission as a slave state, just as Louisiana had been admitted in 1812, and that the attempts on the part of the House of Representatives to force her to put away slavery as a condition precedent to her admission was an unlawful exertion of power, and one not warranted by the Constitution.[2]

But the repugnance of the northeastern part of the Union to the extension of slavery, which had already manifested itself at the time of the acquisition of Louisiana, now assumed an aggressive attitude, and took a

[1] Benton's Abridgment of the Debates, vol. xiii, 33.

[2] Carr's Missouri, 144; Speech of William Pinkney during the debate.

determined stand against the admission of Missouri as a slave state, notwithstanding the perils to the republic that lay in a sectional policy, and a policy that was not inspired by purely political motives, but which found its inspiration in moral sentiment.

To a clear understanding of the scope and effect of this opposition, it must be borne in mind that, at the time of the application of Missouri for admission to the Union, this territory lay on the uttermost western part of the republic. Beyond its limits the Spanish Possessions stretched towards the west: between it and the state of Louisiana on the south was the territory now embraced in the state of Arkansas, then occupied by savages, while to the north of it extended the remainder of the Louisiana Purchase.

The ordinance of 1787 had previously extinguished slavery in the northwest portion, and, as climatic conditions were not favorable to the northward extension of slavery, the only area open to the addition of slave states was the territory now comprised in the states of Arkansas and Missouri. Under the topographical conditions of the United States territory at that time, the physical limitations of slavery may be considered as ascertained, and the further extension of slavery beyond those limits was, to all appearance, an impossibility. It was contemporaneous with the events that led to the Missouri Compromise, that these boundaries were determined in the treaty with Spain by which Florida was acquired. These two events being before the public eye at one and the same time, it seems reasonable that the anti-slavery sentiment should have found a sufficient guaranty against the extension of this institution in the fact that there was no room further for it to expand. There was still another obstacle to slavery extension, and the more formidable that it existed in the indisposition of the South itself to enlarge its area westward. At that time, John Quincy Adams, who, as Secretary of State, was negotiator and ostensible author of the treaty, uttered an expression which was much commented upon, but the more it was discussed the more enigmatical it remained. It was this: "Spain had offered more than we accepted, and she dare not deny it." It is now known [1] that Spain had embraced in her offer to us the country included in the present state of Texas and to the north of it, and that we declined this offer. The reason of our doing so is to be found in a letter from Monroe to Andrew Jackson,[2] and is thus set forth: "Having long known the repugnance with which the eastern portion of our Union, or rather some of those who have enjoyed its confidence (for I do not think that the people themselves have any interest or wish of that kind), have seen its aggrandizement to the West and South, I have been decidedly of opinion that we ought to be content with Florida for the present, and until the public opinion in that quarter shall be reconciled to any further change. I mention these circumstances to show you that our difficulties are not with Spain alone, but are likewise internal, proceeding from various causes, which certain men are prompt to seize and turn to the account of their own ambitious views." In like terms Monroe wrote to Jefferson, who, unlike Jackson, remained unmoved by them, and steadfastly though una-

[1] Benton's Thirty Years in the United States Senate, vol. i, chapter vi.

[2] May 22, 1820.

vailingly opposed the treaty. Thus it appears that unwillingness on the part of southern men to antagonize the North was the real reason that led the United States to reject the offer of territory which, from the nature of the case, would become slave states; and indeed, at that time, throughout the whole South (unless those states now known as "the Cotton states" be excepted), a repugnance to the extension of slavery, if not an abiding one, was as general as it was at the North, and there is no reason to doubt that, but for discordant measures and untoward events, it would have proved to be as lasting.

Having taken its stand upon the Tallmadge amendment, the House passed the bill as amended; whereupon, when it came before the Senate, the amendment was stricken out, and the bill was returned to the House in its original shape. Both bodies, however, refused to yield, and the bill was lost by the adjournment of this Congress *sine die*.

Upon the opening of the Sixteenth Congress in December, 1819, the admission of Missouri again came up, and the action of the House clearly confirmed the truth of Mr. King's assertion that the struggle was for political power. If the interests of the country were henceforth to be governed by sectional considerations, it is evident that any settlement of the question that would annul the preponderance of the South in the Senate and pave the way to the aggrandizement of the northern states would be acceptable to the latter. Accordingly, as an offset to the admission of Alabama, the North presented Maine for admission to the Union. This, the most northeastern possession of the United States, was not the property of the federal

Union, but belonged to Massachusetts, one of the original states. Cut off from the mother-state by the interposition of New Hampshire, this region had experienced the evils of remoteness, and had long indulged in aspirations to sovereignty of its own. Massachusetts was one of the strongholds of the Federalist party, but the sympathies of the inhabitants of Maine were with the Democratic party. The circumstances arising out of the contest over Missouri proved to be Maine's opportunity, and prompt advantage was taken of it. She made her application, and the Senate adroitly took the position that the two measures were to be coupled together, and that if Missouri was to be admitted with restriction of slavery, Maine should not be admitted; but if Missouri came in without such restriction, the admission of Maine should promptly follow. This understanding (for the alternative was not openly admitted) prevailed, and the sooner that many northern Democrats, for the moment swept away from their moorings by the stormy debate on the admission of Missouri, were glad to avail themselves of this opportunity to regain their old footing in their party. As the admission of Maine would secure two democratic senators, and thus offset the disturbance occasioned by the admission of Alabama, while the accession to the democratic side of the Senate of two senators from Missouri would afford still greater democratic preponderance in that body, it is clear that the opportunity to regain their lines was now offered. So far, partisan necessity was satisfied: but the moral element which had intruded itself into the Federal council was not satisfied, and it obstinately demanded compensation for the loss that it would sustain by the admission of Missouri as a slave state. Accordingly, a committee of conference between the Senate and House was appointed, and after a dead-lock to legislation of several weeks, during which the storm raged violently, it reported a series of measures that have been known ever since as the Missouri Compromise. 1. The clause prohibiting slavery was stricken from the bill authorizing the people of the territory to form a constitution. But, 2, it was stipulated that slavery should be excluded from all "the territory ceded by France to the United States, under the name of Louisiana, north of 36° 30′ north latitude." 3. Maine was to be admitted to the Union. The inhabitants of Missouri were left to decide for themselves whether the state should be slave or free, but the admission of Missouri was not guaranteed, however clear was the understanding that she should be admitted.

In this compromise, the advantages were on the part of the North. The South held nothing but its own, but, 1, by the admission of Maine, the North gained supremacy in the Senate. 2. She secured the freedom from slavery of all the vast Northwest, to which already the lines of emigration were trending as the further seat of a dense population: i. e., she extended the advantages she enjoyed under the ordinance of 1787 to the remainder and greater portion of the Northwest, and, 3, she had taken and maintained the position of a power that henceforth was to be consulted and appeased before any expansion of the South could be made.

The first two advantages were political, and, if not above criticism, were at any rate conceded to be legitimate subjects of political action. This cannot be said of the third and last advantage, for it arrayed two sections against each other, and was an unmistakable declaration that the growing power of one of these sections was no longer to be restrained within strictly political limits. The restraints of political character once broken through, what was to regulate or limit the future action of a power that appealed to the vague and unsubstantial inspiration of moral motives?

This compromise was carried into effect, and by a majority of the southern members of each House of Congress; and credit must be given to them for submitting to compromise that which was their undoubted legal right. This action can be explained only by the spirit that animated President Monroe during the negotiation of the Spanish treaty, and by that already noticed as prevailing in the South against the extension of slavery.

The effects of the Missouri Compromise were: 1. The revelation that a balance of power existed between the sections, and that upon its maintenance by compromise depended the preservation of the Union. 2. That henceforth the subject of slavery was not wholly a political one, but that moral considerations had become infused into its consideration, and that the dangerous conjunction of ethics with politics had been established. 3. That sectionalism was recognized by the establishment of a geographical line across which neither party was to step.[1] 4. That North and South acted on the assumption that Congress had absolute power over the territories.

[1] Jefferson to John Holmes, April 22, 1820. Lalor, Compromises, i, 551.

This compromise possessed the weakness inherent to all compromises, namely, that it was founded upon circumstances which were changeable; the history of the United States thenceforth was the history of the endeavors of a divided people to reconcile their compact with constantly changing conditions. If, instead of this imaginary line, there had been a Chinese wall which would have restrained effectually the flood of immigration within the territory north of 36° 30′, and had the territory south of this degree of latitude not been extended by conquest, purchase, or treaty, the Missouri Compromise might have existed forever: but it was founded upon conditions which changed with every movement of the rapidly moving West, and it had to be readapted to the acquisition of Texas, to the acquisition of California, to the admission of Nebraska and Kansas, — in a word, it had to conform to the expansion of the South in territory and to the expansion of the North in population. No hard-and-fast bargain was equal to this task. It came to an end, or rather, the compromise of 1850, which, virtually, was the Missouri Compromise over again, came to an end, amid scenes of discord and bloodshed.

But the great importance of the Missouri Compromise and its successors lies in the fact that the compromise that was so thoroughly an ingredient of the Constitution of the United States was recognized *dehors* the Constitution as the one only force which could bind together two differing peoples and two incongruous forms of anglican civilization. A mere Constitution had proved to be insufficient for this end as early as 1820: from this year to 1861, the bond of union was the principle of compromise which was made a prerequisite to the admission of Missouri into the Union; and so clearly was this recognized as essential to the stability of the Union that, as late as 1860, when it was perceived that the states could no longer hold together on the old basis, the sole attempt to preserve the Union was the endeavor to fan the embers of the Missouri Compromise into new flame by the futile Crittenden Compromise. The only hope of "saving the Union" was by a recurrence to compromise, and with its failure expired the last appearance in our history of compromise as a groundwork of Union.

From 1820 to 1861, the Union rested not upon the compromises of the Constitution, but upon those of legislation, and these legislative compromises were mere bargains between the two great sections of the United States.

CHAPTER XI.

COERCION, OR NON-COERCION?

Condition of affairs at the inauguration of Abraham Lincoln — Coercion, or non-coercion? — Inaugural Address and answer to the Virginia Commissioners — Coercion — The President's Message of July, 1861 — "No state, upon its own mere motion, can lawfully get out of the Union."

WHEN Abraham Lincoln took the presidential oath of office, the whole country was in the direst agitation. The secession of South Carolina had been followed by that of six other states, and the national flag was flying over four forts only on the coast that stretched from Cape Henlopen to the Rio Grande. The eyes of the world were at that moment concentrated upon one of these forts, Sumter, for it had been regularly invested by secession forces, and with each recurring day might come the news that its flag had been lowered in subjection. Allegiance to the United States had been cast off, and the federal government was powerless to execute a single one of its orders [1] throughout the vast region known as the Cotton or Gulf States; Virginia, North Carolina, Tennessee, and Arkansas were arming, ostensibly against all comers, but it was feared that they had the intention of joining the seceded states. In the border states

[1] The United States' postal service was maintained in the seceded states until June 1, 1861; but this was suffered by the Confederate government for motives of convenience and self-interest only.

of Maryland, Kentucky, and Missouri, the population was divided against itself, and the most that the government could hope for was to hold its own within these disputed limits. The Congress that had just terminated [1] had done nothing to effect harmony, so torn and rent had it been by the conflicting parties and factions; it had been inefficacious for conciliation or cure, and the great Peace Convention, called at the instance of Virginia, had proved to be of so little avail that its disheartened members had separated, leaving their beneficent object farther from attainment than ever. Among the last things which the Convention had done was this significant act — it had permitted a resolution to be placed upon its journal expressing the "conviction that the Union, being formed by the assent of the people of the respective states, and being compatible only with freedom and the republican institutions guaranteed to each, cannot and ought not to be maintained by force." The Convention, therefore, deprecated "any effort by the federal government to coerce in any form the said states to reunion or submission, as tending to irreparable breach, and leading to incalculable ills," and it earnestly invoked "the abstinence from all counsels or measures of compulsion towards them." [2]

[1] The 36th Congress.

[2] Ann. Cycl., 1861, 568. The power to coerce a state is not among the powers granted in the Constitution. On the 31st of May, 1787, a clause "authorizing an exertion of the force of the whole against a delinquent state" was considered. Madison vigorously opposed it, and made use of this language: "The use of force against a state would look more like a declaration of war than an infliction of punishment; and would probably be considered by the party attacked as a dissolution of all previous compacts by which it might be bound." Whereupon the Convention dropped the subject and never recurred to

This deprecation of coercion was in accordance with the doctrine of "strict construction of the Constitution," and also with an elaborate opinion by Jeremiah S. Black, late Attorney-General, submitted to President Buchanan, to the effect that there was no constitutional power in the federal government to coerce a refractory state. This opinion of the Attorney-General, and the consequent line of conduct pursued by President Buchanan, had brought down upon these officials unmeasured obloquy at the hands of the dominant party in the North: but the opinion was a logical conclusion of the principle of construction maintained by the Democratic party by whom the President had been chosen. In fact, this legal opinion laid bare to the people the real, underlying cause of the existing trouble — the different and conflicting principles of constitutional construction upheld by the North and by the South, and the obloquy heaped upon the unlucky officials was merely heated denunciation of the doctrine adhered to by the administration.

Nevertheless, the incoming President, Lincoln, was confronted at the outset by the fact that this doctrine had been acted upon by the executive branch of the government down to the very moment in which he had taken the oath of office; that the legislative branch had not denied the principle in word or deed; that the judicial branch had not yet met the question of coercion decisively, and that, scarcely three weeks before, a national convention, composed in greater part of north-

it. Madison afterward said of it: "Any government for the United States formed on the supposed practicability of using force against the unconstitutional proceedings of the states, would prove as visionary and fallacious as the government of Congress," referring to the Congress of the Confederation of 1781.

ern states, had declared that the Union ought not to be maintained by force, and had deprecated any effort by the federal government to coerce the states to reunion or submission. Adherence to the doctrine of strict construction would leave the seceded states undisturbed; would permit the unobstructed secession of states that might desire to secede thereafter, and would relegate reunion to an uncertain but peaceful future: but a construction of the Constitution which would evolve power in the federal government to compel and maintain union by force would unquestionably precipitate civil war. It is not surprising that, with such a choice before it, the whole country was plunged into the direst perplexity: peace or war, Union or Disunion, were the issues of a game upon which its fortune was staked.

If the President were to reflect the doctrines of those who had chosen him, there could be little doubt of his future course; for the victorious Republicans comprised those who were even then shouting for "a strong government," those who doubted that the Constitution which had been suitable enough for a few millions of people and for times of peace would be so for a great population and for times of civil conflict, and those who, like the Abolitionists, looked upon the Constitution as a compact with hell, and welcomed the secession of the states with the joyful exclamation of "All hail, disunion!"[1] This new party embraced the mass of liberal constructionists in the Union, and such had become the antipathy between the northern and southern sections that the triumphant Republicans had taken no greater pains to con-

[1] Wendell Phillips, Boston, January 20, 1861.

ceal their own sectional feeling than had the Southerners theirs, but had openly rejoiced in the fact that "a Northern President," "a President that really represented the North," would take the helm on the ensuing fourth of March. It was to be anticipated, then, that, reflecting the notions of constitutional construction entertained by his party, the incoming President would rely upon "the war powers," and exert the coercive force of one body of the states against the other.

This anticipation was encouraged by the personal antecedents of Abraham Lincoln. He had never taken any other view of the federal Constitution, than that its supremacy was not restricted to the limitations set upon it by itself, but that it was "the supreme law of the land" to the exclusion of everything that it did not grant, and that all that was necessary to establish its "implied powers" was to enunciate them in laws of the United States made "in pursuance thereof."[1]

Only three weeks before, the very day indeed upon which he had left his home and had begun his journey to Washington,[2] he had used this language in reply to an address of welcome at Indianapolis: "By the way, in what consists the special sacredness of a state? I speak not of the position assigned to a state in the Union by the Constitution; for that is the bond we all recognize. That position, however, a state cannot carry out of the Union with it. I speak of that assumed primary right of a state to rule all which is less than itself, and to ruin all which is larger than itself. If a state and a county, in a given case,

[1] Constitution of the United States, Article VI.

[2] February 11, 1861.

should be equal in extent of territory and equal in number of inhabitants, in what, as a matter of principle, is the state better than the county?"[1] Every word which dropped from the lips of the President-elect fell upon anxious ears, and there were not wanting conservative men in his own party to note that, in his consideration of a sovereign state, he had done that which Davis and Toombs and Wigfall were then doing, — not regarding it "in the position assigned to it in the Union by the Constitution," but in a position outside of the Union and of the Constitution; and that the first notice which he had taken of the states was to make light of them. The expression, "By the way, in what consists the special sacredness of a state?" grated on the feelings of these men, and struck despair into the hearts of those in whom reverence for the Constitution was ingrained, and who regarded the states as the sources of the federal system, and as the sole defence against the encroachments or assaults of the general government. The strict-constructionists forthwith charged the President-elect with ignorance or wilfulness in putting a state and a county (a sovereign and a non-sovereign) upon an equality, and also with indulging in a flippant and mocking tone, irreconcilable with reverence for the Constitution or with the gravity of the situation, and which boded ill to the integrity of the sovereignties which composed our federal system. Thus, in wending his way to Washington to become President of the United States, Abraham Lincoln left behind him the appre-

[1] That hostile criticism was not blind to the defectiveness of constitutional principles betrayed by this inquiry is shown by the fact that Jefferson Davis, in his Message of April 29, 1861, refers to this passage as exhibiting "a lamentable and fundamental error."

hension that, in a conflict between states, he, the head of the federal government, would have little knowledge of the nature of the sovereignties with which he would have to deal, and that the states themselves, North as well as South, would meet with no more regard for him than if they were counties.

There were, however, great obstacles to the immediate adoption of coercion. Men and money would have to be raised. Men, it is true, were in plenty, but the question of money was a difficult one in face of the low credit of the government and of the menacing aspect of affairs.[1] The navy was scattered over the face of the globe;[2] the army had been weakened by the resignation of southern officers, and even by the capture of southern garrisons, and the loss of the southern posts would force the government to take its initiative from points exterior to the territory of intended operations. The northern arsenals had been partially depleted, and the southern magazines with their contents were in the hands of secessionists,[3] while the capital itself, situated in the midst of a disaffected population and on the verge of the theatre of war, was manifestly insecure.[4] The great European powers were certain to withhold their sympathy from the North, and were as certain to extend it to the South; already their public prints were predicting

[1] No responsible bidder had offered to take any considerable amount of the Treasury notes authorized by the act of December 17, 1860, at par, at a lower rate of interest than 12 per cent. Message of President Buchanan, January 8, 1861.

[2] Dawes' Report, February 21, 1861: but see Branch's Minority Report.

[3] Report of the Secretary of War, January 15, 1861; also that of February 18, 1861.

[4] Report of the Secretary of War, February 18, 1861.

the downfall of the federal government, and were exultantly pointing to the seceded states as proof of an accomplished dissolution of the Union. Moreover, while the northern wing of the Democratic party was openly opposed to aggression, and while a people who knew nothing but peace and who were averse to war were still deluding themselves with hopes of compromise and harmony, it was extremely doubtful whether a policy of coercion would be sustained. Could the country be depended upon for a long, a costly, and a bloody conflict? The rupture of the Union was having its effect even now in the direction of submission, and as cries of discord and hatred rose in every quarter, and pillar after pillar of the state was falling, men who a week ago had been calling for coercion were faltering or were dumb. The influences that were leading many worthy but timorous men to ask whether the Union were worth the fearful cost, now foreseen, to preserve it, and to doubt if it was longer within the power of man to save it, might affect the President in the same way, and, should he take counsel of his fears, he would find ample support in a resolution adopted by the national Convention which had nominated him to the Presidency, and which denounced "the lawless invasion by armed force on the soil of any state or territory, no matter under what pretext, as among the gravest of crimes." Congress would not be in session at his inauguration; yet, without its authority, any invasion of a state, however trivial, would be lawless, and thus he would begin his term of office by acts without constitutional warrant, and in the teeth of his party's denunciation.

The dreadful scene of the dissolution of the Union,

pictured by Webster, was then before Mr. Lincoln's eyes, as it was before those of his halting countrymen, and to take up coercion would be to augment the existing horror; the Border States were already at his elbow, and, overcome by present evil and shrinking from an unknown future, he might lend an ear to the whisperings, and, content with that which was left, relegate to time and circumstances the reunion of all the states. It was not without reason, therefore, that those who favored armed compulsion should be as anxious as the conservative elements of the North were, and like them await the Inaugural Address with apprehension.

The Inaugural Address was duly delivered, but the country was little wiser than before. North and South interpreted it according to their will; this section declared that it breathed forth threatenings and slaughter; that asserted that it held out the olive branch. A month later, in answer to the Virginia Commissioners, who had been appointed by the state Convention to "respectfully ask him to communicate to this Convention what course he intended to pursue," the President became his own expounder. He repeated, that he would continue to hold "the property and places belonging to the government, and to collect the duties and imposts; but beyond what was necessary for these objects there would be no invasion, no using of force against or among the people anywhere;" but if an unprovoked assault had been made upon Fort Sumter, he should hold himself at liberty to repossess it, and that, in any event, he should repel force by force.[1] He should not attempt to collect the du-

[1] **The position here adopted by President Lincoln is no more nor**

ties and imposts by any armed invasion of any part of the country; not meaning by this, however, that he might not land a force deemed necessary to relieve a fort upon the border of the country.[1] This answer was given to the Commissioners on the fifteenth of April, simultaneous with the President's call for militia to suppress combinations and to cause the laws to be duly executed; to which call Letcher, the Governor of Virginia, replied in these terms: "I have only to say, that the militia of Virginia will not be furnished to the powers at Washington for any such use or purpose as they have in view. Your object is to subjugate the southern states, and a requisition made upon me for such an object, in my judgment not within the purview of the Constitution or the act of 1795, will not be complied with. You have chosen to inaugurate civil war, and having done so, we will meet it in a spirit as determined as the administration has exhibited towards the South."

Fort Sumter had surrendered on the thirteenth, it was evacuated on the fourteenth, and that night the President sent to the Secretary of State a proclamation convening Congress on the fourth of July and calling for troops, which was proclaimed the next day. On the nineteenth, another proclamation declared the ports of the Gulf States and South Carolina to be blockaded. On the twentieth, the federal government seized the telegraphic despatches of the past year in the northern states; on the twenty-seventh, the President extended the blockade to the ports of North Car-

less than that taken by his predecessor, President Buchanan. See Message at the opening of the Second session of the 36th Congress, December, 1860, and also that of January 8, 1861.

[1] See also Message of July 4, 1861.

olina and Virginia, and the government at once set to work to render the blockade effectual. On the third of May, the President issued another proclamation calling into service forty-two thousand men for *three* years, a term, the duration of which, in contrast with the first call, indicates how rapid the expansion of ideas in reference to the magnitude of the work in hand had been since the fourteenth day of April. In this proclamation, too, the President had, of his own motion, increased the regular army by ten regiments, or more than twenty-two thousand men, and had increased the navy by eighteen thousand seamen. On the sixteenth of May, he issued a further proclamation suspending the writ of *habeas corpus* in the localities still occupied by federal troops in Florida, in case the commander of the forces found it necessary, and authorizing him to remove all dangerous or suspected persons from the vicinity of the United States forts. On the twenty-fifth, an armed force aroused John Merryman, a citizen of Maryland, from his bed about two o'clock in the morning and placed him in custody in Fort McHenry. Merryman, the same day, presented his petition to the Chief Justice of the United States for a writ of *habeas corpus*, which, on the twenty-sixth, was served upon General George Cadwalader, whose answer to the writ contained, among other things, this astonishing information; " He has further to inform you, that he is duly authorized by the President of the United States in such cases to suspend the writ of *habeas corpus* for the public safety." The General declined to produce Merryman until instructions had been received from the President, whereupon the Chief Justice ordered an attachment to be issued against Cadwalader, which the official in charge was unable to serve because he "was not permitted to enter the gate." Other instances of the kind occurred in different parts of the country, and by October nineteenth, one hundred and seventy-five prisoners of state had been confined in Fort La Fayette. All of these arrests had been arbitrary. On the fifteenth day of April, the President had called Congress to meet in extra session, on the fourth of July.[1] Long before that time all men throughout the land knew that civil war was upon them.

In every one of these proclamations and in the procedure under them, except that of convening Congress in extra session, the President acted without constitutional power. He raised armies and provided for calling forth the militia to execute the laws of the Union, suppress insurrection, and repel invasion,— powers which by the Constitution belong solely to Congress.[2] He increased the navy of his own motion, and set on foot and extended a blockade, which was an act of war unauthorized by Congress; and with nothing to establish his right to proclaim martial law and to suspend the privilege of the writ of *habeas corpus*, except an opinion of his Attorney-General, he authorized his officers to do so, and arbitrary arrests followed in states not in rebellion. This assumption of powers not conferred upon the President brought upon him much animadversion, the severity of which was by no means mitigated by the apology of "necessity" everywhere advanced by those who sustained him. His course was compared unfavorably with

[1] The first session of the 37th Congress.

[2] Article I., sect. 8.

that of the President of the Confederate States, who took care to act strictly within his Constitution, and whereas Jefferson Davis called the Confederate Congress together within a fortnight, President Lincoln allowed an interim of eleven weeks to elapse before Congress assembled on the fourth of July. This seeming lack of energy might have been a sagacious mode of acquiring the advantage which a knowledge of the action of the Confederate Congress would by that time give our own: but his censors insinuated that the delay was occasioned rather by the opportunity it would afford the President to make precedents for the exercise of "the latent powers," and to usurp the powers of the absent Congress. That President Lincoln was fully aware of the unconstitutionality of his proceedings, and that he desired his party to share the responsibility incurred by him, is clear from the act of August sixth, which was the first in the series of condonation acts. The condonation by one branch of government of the faults of another branch was without validity, and, indeed, was itself merely another unconstitutional act, committed, in this instance, by two branches of the government instead of by one alone: nor is it to be supposed that President or Congressmen regarded this innovation as valid, or as anything else than what it was, — a compliance with the demand of the President that his party should place itself where it could not repudiate his unconstitutional acts.

When Congress met together, the President's Message was received with eagerness, but, like the Inaugural Address, it was not altogether satisfactory. After entering into the details of the reduction of

Fort Sumter, and after placing upon the Confederates the burden of beginning hostilities to which the United States were compelled to respond, he exposed the fallaciousness of the "armed neutrality" of the Border States, in a few pithy sentences. He likewise exhibited with great clearness the sophism upon which the South had seceded from the Union. "The sophism itself," he said, "is, that any state of the Union may, consistently with the national Constitution, and therefore lawfully and peacefully, withdraw from the Union *without the consent of the Union or of any other state.*" Had he contented himself with this statement, which contains the condition of withdrawal from the Union, then admitted to be essential even by rigid constructionists, the consent of all or at least of a majority of the states, — the President would have done well. He went on to say, however, that "this sophism derived much of its currency from the assumption that there is some omnipotent and sacred supremacy pertaining to a state, — to each state of our Federal Union," and to assert, by a historical perversion, that no one of the states had ever been a state "out of the Union." The remarks that followed were an elaboration of the text which he had set forth in his address at Indianapolis, and their tone was adverse in the extreme to the integrity of states. He scouted the notion that a state had ever existed outside of the Union, declaring that the states have their *status* in the Union, and that they have no other legal *status*, and that no one, except Texas, ever had been a sovereignty, assertions susceptible of ominous interpretation to a state which had "gone out," in case the fortune of war should bring it to the day when it was to be brought back. This argumentation has proved unfortunate in lending the name of Abraham Lincoln to a sophism quite as mischievous as the one he had been denouncing. Its importance, at the time of writing, was diminished by the assumption that the President felt called upon to make a rejoinder to the strictures of Jefferson Davis upon his Inaugural Address and Indianapolis speech, and that, in doing so, he had unconsciously overstepped the limits prescribed by historical facts and right reason. Equally weak was the argumentative exculpation of himself for authorizing the suspension of the privilege of the writ of *habeas corpus*, "by the commanding General in proper cases;" an exculpation which terminated in the intimation that he was aware that the Constitution did not specify who was to exercise the power of suspension, and that it was not to "be believed that the framers of this instrument intended that in every case the danger should run its course until Congress could be called together." In relation to other unconstitutional proceedings, the President admitted that "these measures, whether strictly legal or not, were ventured upon *under what appeared to be a popular demand* and *a public necessity;* trusting then, as now, that Congress would readily ratify them," — a trust which seems confidently placed, but which it took Congress thirty-three days before it could bring itself to sustain.

The following paragraph in reference to reconstruction occurs in this message: "Lest there be some uneasiness in the minds of candid men as to what is to be the course of the government towards the Southern States after the rebellion shall have been suppressed, the Executive deems it proper to say, it will be his purpose then, as ever, to be guided by the Constitution and the laws; and that he probably will have no different understanding of the powers and duties of the federal government relatively to the rights of the states and the people, under the Constitution, than that expressed in his Inaugural Address."

But the only expression in the Inaugural Address bearing upon the subject is this: "It follows from these views that no state, upon its own mere motion, can lawfully get out of the Union; that resolves and ordinances to that effect are legally void; and that acts of violence, within any state or states, against the authority of the United States are insurrectionary or revolutionary, according to circumstances. I therefore consider that, in view of the Constitution and the laws, the Union is unbroken."

This makes manifest the President's notion of what the *status* of a seceded state was — it was still in the Union; but what the course of the government towards this state would be after the rebellion should be repressed, is not disclosed. The Inaugural Address has nothing to say about it, and the only notable thing in this clause from the message is the assumption that the rebellion would be suppressed. When we recall what the condition of the country was when this line was penned, we cannot but admire the steadfast trust that the day would surely come when the Union would be restored.

It may be well to anticipate events by saying that the President maintained to the close of his life the doctrine he announced on the day of his inauguration, and which he reiterated in this message, — the doctrine that "no state, upon its own mere motion, can lawfully get out of the Union." It was upon this principle that he came at last into positive opposition with the groups of extremists which were led by Wade and Sumner in the Senate and by Stevens and Henry Winter Davis in the House; a principle which may be said to have expired with him, for it was overcome and thrust aside when "the Congressional policy" overcame and thrust aside his successor.

CHAPTER XII.

DEVELOPMENT OF PRINCIPLES OF CONGRESSIONAL ACTION TOWARDS THE SOUTH.

The Crittenden Resolution of July 22, 1861 — Debate in the Senate upon the Resolution — Sumner's Resolutions — Stevens' *vae victis* policy — Hale on arbitrary arrests — Claim of Congress to absolute power in reconstruction.

In the mean time a notion of reconstruction developed in Congress which was destined to become antagonistic to that of the President and in the end to effect its subversion. It was known as the Congressional Plan of Reconstruction, and was as radical and revolutionary in its nature as was the Presidential Plan. Nevertheless it will be seen, from the vote upon a resolution of Congress now to be considered, that at the outset the notion prevailing in Congress upon the subject was precisely that which had been entertained by the President, and, it may be added, by the country at large, at the time of the President's inauguration.

On the day after the battle of Bull Run,[1] Crittenden, of Kentucky, offered in the House of Representatives the following resolution: —

"That the present deplorable civil war has been forced upon the country by the disunionists of the Southern States, now in arms against the constitutional government, and in arms around the capital;

[1] The 22d of July, 1861: Cong. Globe, 222.

that in this national emergency, Congress, banishing all feelings of mere passion or resentment, will recollect only its duty to the whole country; that this war is not waged on their part in any spirit of oppression, or for any purpose of conquest or subjugation, or purpose of overthrowing or interfering with the rights or established institutions of those States, but to defend and maintain the supremacy of the Constitution, and to preserve the Union with all the dignity, equality, and rights of the several States unimpaired; and that as soon as these objects are accomplished the war ought to cease."

This resolution was adopted by a majority so great that only two members recorded dissenting votes.

Four days afterward, the same resolution, with a few unimportant verbal changes, but otherwise in precisely the same language, was introduced in the Senate by Andrew Johnson, of Tennessee, and was there adopted also by a great majority, only five Senators dissenting, among whom were Southerners who had not yet followed their colleagues to the South, but who were on the point of doing so. The vote in the Senate, therefore, is as significant of northern opinion concerning the object of the war and of the *status* of the rebellious states, as was that of the House, and it may be well to review the remarks of different Senators at the time, inasmuch as they reflect exactly the notions of the North, and also afford a point wherefrom to observe how rapidly and widely these same men changed their opinions. While the resolution was directed to all the southern people, it was intended to affect the Border States immediately and directly.

There can be no question that the political leaders of this locality entertained the hope that their states might perform the part of what nowadays are called "Buffer States." Their hope proved futile, but they thought that by judicious neutrality the broad belt of states separating the combatants might succeed in preventing the continuance of war and might even restore the Union without much bloodshed; a part which would be humane and patriotic in the highest degree, and which would eventuate in confiding the future maintenance of the bond of Union to their keeping; certainly it would have resulted in placing the balance of power in their hands. But to the attainment of this object it was essential that no war of subjugation should be tolerated for a moment, that the right of one state to coerce another should be denied, and that this odious doctrine be repudiated by the belligerents in a manner so positive that the minds of the people of the Border States should be at rest as far as this point was concerned. However feasible this plan might have seemed in times of altercation but before blows had been struck, it is evident that it was nothing short of utopian after blood had been shed. It was asking the North and the South, both, to submit their differences to a third and interested power.[1] The South could do this without risk, for the Border States were slave states, and therefore their interests were on the side of slavery; but for this very reason the North could not subject itself to the tutelage of these states — it would be to submit their cause indirectly

[1] See President Lincoln's message, July 1, 1861. "I see no reason why I should give up my opinions to those of any gentlemen from the Border States." HENRY WILSON.

to the arbitrament of their foes. This plan, therefore, was out of the question, and the uppermost thought of the Border States, now that a pitched battle had been fought, was to stave off the horrors of war from their soil. Nevertheless, whatever the humane or the ambitious designs of the border chiefs, a great part of the border population sympathized with the seceding states, and were at that moment enrolling troops, ostensibly for the defence of their territories, but really with the intention of joining the secessionists. On the other hand, the same dubious plays were being acted on the same stage in the interest of the North. These states were already divided households; the northern and southern sentiment prevailed in contiguous counties. The belt comprising Maryland, Western Virginia, Kentucky, and Northern Missouri was virtually in the military possession of the North, and every consideration urged this government to maintain therein its footing. Accordingly, Congress delayed not a moment to adopt a resolution which was to carry with it an authoritative enunciation of its principles and policy, and one well calculated to allay the apprehension of the border population and to attach the wavering to their side. Such a resolution admitted but little debate, and it is fair to presume that the different Senators meant to convey to the world, as well as to the Border States, the sentiment and doctrine of their own sections of the country, as plainly and directly as was possible.

That the Border States were bitterly opposed to any war that savored of subjugation, and especially of one that threatened the integrity of the states, no matter what the conduct of their citizens, is clearly revealed by the remarks of Senator Willey, of Western Virginia, who said:[1] "There is a fear among many, there is a prejudice wide extended in the public sentiment of Virginia, that the design of this war is subjugation; that the design of this war, literally, in the language of the honorable Senator from Vermont, is to pass our people under the yoke.

"I do not understand such to be the purpose of this war. The Legislature of the state which I represent does not understand such to be the purpose of this war. My constituency are for the preservation of the Union, the vindication of the Constitution, and the execution of the laws. . . . But candor constrains me to say that if any different purpose shall be avowed, if it shall ever be intimated or declared that this is to be a war upon the domestic institution of the South, and upon the rights of private property, every loyal arm on the soil of the Old Dominion will be instantly paralyzed."

Andrew Johnson, who had introduced the resolution,[2] said in explanation of it that "The resolution simply states that we are not waging a war for the subjugation of states. If the Constitution is maintained and the laws carried out, the states take their places and all rebel citizens must submit. That is the whole of it."

Mr. Doolittle, of Wisconsin, admitted very pointedly that the resolution was an act not altogether legislative in its character, but a declaration of a purpose of the government. It was a deed in that sense, which was to have its effect upon the American people.

[1] July 25, 1861: Cong. Globe, 259.
[2] July 24, 1861: Cong. Globe, 243.

Senator Trumbull, of Illinois, drew a clear distinction between a state and the rebellious citizens of a state: he would subjugate the rebels, but in respect to the states, he said very emphatically: "I know that persons in the southern states have sought to make this a controversy between states and the federal Government, and have talked about coercing states and subjugating states; but it has never been proposed, so far as I know, on the part of the Union people of the United States, to subjugate states or coerce states. It is proposed, however, to subjugate citizens who are standing out in defiance of the laws of the Union, and to coerce them into obedience to the laws of the Union."

Senator Fessenden, of Maine, said: "I do not want to carry on this war for the purpose of subjugating the people of any state, in any shape or form; and it is a false idea gotten up by bad men for bad purposes, that it ever has been the purpose of any portion of the people of this country. I am willing, therefore, to meet them face to face, and say I never had that purpose, and have it not now. But we say, notwithstanding we have not that purpose, and distinctly avow it, we have a purpose, and that is to defend the Constitution and the laws of the country, and to put down this revolt at whatever hazard; and it is for them to say whether it is necessary for us, in the course of accomplishing a legitimate and proper object, to subjugate them in order to do it. I hope not; and if it is necessary and we could do it, I should want to keep them subjugated no longer than was necessary to secure that purpose. Thus far it must go, and no further. To that it must go at all events and hazards."

Senator Hale, of New Hampshire, called to the recollection of the Senate his oft-repeated declarations that the Government had no more right, no more legal or constitutional authority, to interfere with slavery in the states than it had to interfere with the condition of the serfs in Russia, or with the rights and wrongs of the laboring classes in England.

The debate, if it may be called one, had turned upon the meaning and force of the word "subjugation," and it had not escaped the notice of John C. Breckinridge, the Senator from Kentucky, who still lingered in the United States Senate, that these exponents of northern sentiment were dwelling upon, and were maintaining, the notion of subjugation, and that the most they had succeeded in doing was to make a distinction between the states and the people of a state. Accordingly, he rose and avowed his belief that the war was being prosecuted, according to the purposes of a majority of those then managing the legislation, for objects of subjugation. He declared his belief that, unless these states which had seceded from the federal Union laid down their arms and surrendered at discretion, the majority in Congress would listen to no terms of settlement, and that those who attempted to mediate would speak to the winds. He believed, therefore, that the war, in the sense and spirit entertained by these Senators, was a war of subjugation, and in saying this, he drew no distinction between a state and its people, but left his language to be construed in the most general and comprehensive sense of which it was capable.

He supported this statement by recalling an assertion of Senator Sherman, made but a few days before, to the effect that, unless the people of certain states in the South yielded willing obedience, he would depopulate those states and people them over again, and this the Kentuckian characterized justly, as not only a war of subjugation but a war of extermination. Breckinridge also recalled an amendment offered by Trumbull to a general bill, but two days before, which had received the vote of a great majority of the Senate, wherein it was provided that any person held to service or labor, who should be employed to aid the rebellion in any form, should be discharged from service and labor. This could apply to slaves only, and was equivalent to a general act of emancipation; a proceeding in flat contradiction to Hale, and also to those who had asserted their respect for the integrity of the states.

These *argumenta ad hominem* of Breckinridge called forth tart and acrimonious replies from the Senators who had been named, and the debate, which had started under such favorable auspices and with such good intentions, speedily degenerated into accusation and recrimination. The result was unsatisfactory: nevertheless, by a vote of thirty to five, the Senate of the United States, and by an almost unanimous vote the House of Representatives, proclaimed to the world that the war on the part of the North was "not prosecuted in any spirit of oppression, nor for any purpose of conquest or subjugation, nor for the purpose of overthrowing or interfering with the rights or established institutions of those states, but to defend and maintain the supremacy of the Constitution and all laws made in pursuance thereof, and to preserve the Union, *with all the dignity, equality, and rights of the several states unimpaired.*" The votes of Congress upon the resolution reflected northern sentiment, though the speeches of the members did not do so.[1]

It is noteworthy that of the northern speakers on the resolution, two of the most prominent and most emphatic, Senators Trumbull and Doolittle, were afterwards to become conspicuous defenders of the Presidential Plan of Reconstruction, and to be the targets of bitterness and obloquy, so great that it may almost be said that they went to their political graves martyrs for the doctrine that a state could not be subjugated nor destroyed, but that once a state, always a state.

Less than five months afterward, on the fourth of December, when Congress was met in regular session, Holman, of Indiana, again offered in the House of Representatives the resolution, word for word, with the following addition: "And whereas, since that time (July 22), no event has occurred to change the policy of the Government: therefore, resolved, That the principles above expressed are solemnly reaffirmed by this House." Whereupon the resolution as offered was laid on the table by a House that was nearly equally divided: for the ayes were but seventy-one, and the nays instead of two were sixty-five — and this after the last southern member had left the House and had gone South. It was a purely federal vote.[2] Inasmuch as this vote was not upon the original resolution, it cannot be accepted as the vote with which the resolution would have been met had it then been offered for the first time; yet we cannot shut

[1] Cong. Globe, 1st sess. 37th Congress, 257–265.

[2] Cong. Globe, 15.

our eyes to this indication of the changed temper of the House. Congress was now fast falling into a mood foreshadowed by Thaddeus Stevens when he exclaimed: "Mr. Speaker, I thought the time had come when the laws of war were to govern our action; when constitutions, if they stood in the way of the laws of war in dealing with the enemy, had no right to intervene."[1]

Of still greater significance than this vote in the House was the offer in the Senate by Charles Sumner of nine resolutions,[2] of which the first one was as follows: "Resolved, that any vote of secession or other act by which any state may undertake to put an end to the supremacy of the Constitution within its territory, is inoperative and void against the Constitution, and when maintained by force it becomes a practical abdication by the state of all rights under the Constitution, while the treason which it involves still further works an instant forfeiture of all those functions and powers essential to the continued existence of the state as a body politic, so that from that time forward the territory falls under the exclusive jurisdiction of Congress, as other territory, and the state being, according to the language of the law, *felo-da-se*, ceases to exist."

This was the first attempt to commit Congress to the *vae victis* policy which was afterwards carried out by that body with the sword. The people, however, yet entertained no notion of the kind, and would have regarded it with alarm and consternation had it appeared on the statute-book. Prudence ruled the day, and Sumner's resolutions were received almost in

[1] August 2, 1861: Cong. Globe, 414.

[2] February 11, 1862: Cong. Globe, 736, 737.

silence: no action was taken upon them nor upon the resolutions which Davis, of Kentucky, offered for the purpose of counteracting them.

It would be impossible to give a full account of the development of the spirit which rapidly led Congress to the point of ignoring the doctrine of the indestructibility of the states, and of ignoring, too, the limitations set upon its action by the Constitution of the United States. Scarcely a day passed without this body being called upon to consider its constitutional limitations. Appropriation bills, confiscation bills, emancipation bills, conquered territory rehabilitation, border state conditions, — a thousand questions were constantly arising upon which the temper and the sentiment of Congress found expression. The change in Congress can be followed easily from the doctrine that a state is indestructible, that it cannot commit treason, that upon its mere motion "it cannot lawfully get out of the Union," to the arbitrary conclusion that its maintenance of secession by force works an "abdication" of all its rights under the Constitution of the United States. Nevertheless, the necessity of a clear comprehension of this departure from ancient and constitutional principles is imperative, and this may be obtained by considering the action and utterance of this body on a few of the most prominent subjects of the day. It will be seen that this action and these utterances became more and more revolutionary as time wore on. The influence and measures of the radicals at last prevailed in Congress, as they have done in the parliamentary bodies of all revolutionary times. Conservatism became a word of scorn; constitutionality was scouted; every infraction of ancient law and of ancient principle was justified by the plea of "necessity," and men like Dixon, of Connecticut, and Wilson, of Massachusetts, actually thanked God on the floor of a body which owed every breath of its existence to law, that a servant of the government, then unknown to the Constitution, the Secretary of State, had had the hardihood to defy the law and to imprison men upon mere suspicion. Sumner's or Stevens' cry of *vae victis* is to-day heard in silence that is disturbed only by a general shudder; to-morrow the mob of legislators are treading upon each other's heels in the effort to run ahead of them.

"I desire to say," was the vaunt of Thaddeus Stevens,[1] "that I know perfectly well, as I said before, I do not speak the sentiments of this side of the House as a party. I know more than that: that for the last fifteen years I have always been a step ahead of the party I have acted with in these matters; but I have never been so far ahead, with the exception of the principles I now enunciate, but that the members of the party have overtaken me and gone ahead; and they will again overtake me, and go with me, before this infamous and bloody rebellion is ended. They will find that they cannot execute the Constitution in the seceding states; that it is a total nullity there, and that this war must be carried on upon principles wholly independent of it. They will come to the conclusion that the adoption of the measures I advocated at the outset of the war, the arming of the negroes, the slaves of the rebels, is the only way left on earth in which these rebels can be exterminated. They will find that they must treat those states now outside of the Union

[1] January 8, 1863: Cong. Globe, 243.

as conquered provinces and settle them with new men, and drive the present rebels as exiles from this country; for I tell you they have the pluck and endurance for which I gave them credit a year and a half ago, in a speech which I made, but which was not relished on this side of the House, nor by the people in the free states. They have such determination, energy, and endurance, that nothing but actual extermination or exile or starvation will ever induce them to surrender to this Government. I do not now ask gentlemen to endorse my views, nor do I speak for anybody but myself; but in order that I may have some credit for sagacity, I ask that gentlemen will write this down in their memories. It will not be two years before they call it up, or before they will adopt my views, or adopt the other alternative of a disgraceful submission by this side of the country." These words had hardly dropped from Stevens' lips, when Owen Lovejoy rose to find fault with them because Stevens had found no warrant for them in the Constitution, but had founded his conceptions solely upon military necessity. "My chief object," said he, "is to repudiate for myself and the Republican party, and the administration, the idea advanced by the gentleman from Pennsylvania, that if it should be necessary, as I believe with him it is, to annihilate these rebels, to extirpate them, and repeople those states with a loyal population, that that exile and that annihilation by military authority would be unconstitutional. Now I claim that this is precisely, if necessary, just what the Constitution imperatively requires of us; that it imposes it upon us as a sacred duty to destroy these rebels, and, to the extent that may be necessary, to exterminate them in order to restore, as a matter of fact, what still exists as a matter of right, the constitutional authority of the government of the United States." [1]

Stevens was too good a lawyer to place the *vae victis* policy on constitutional grounds: he placed it upon the only ground where it could rest, upon necessity, and he hesitated not to brush away the Constitution and all its belongings with an impatient hand; and this he did by denying that the Constitution embraced a state in arms against the government. "I hold and maintain," said he, "that with regard to all the southern states in rebellion, the Constitution has no binding influence and no application." "Are not those seceded states," asked Dunlap, "still members of this Union, and under the laws of the government?" "In my opinion they are not," was the answer. "Then," continued Dunlap, "I would ask the further question, did the ordinances of secession take them out of the Union?" "The ordinances of secession, backed by the armed power which made them a belligerent nation, did take them, so far as present operations are concerned, from under the laws of the nation." "Are they, then, members of the Union?" persisted Dunlap. "They are not, in my judgment," was Stevens' answer.[2]

The vaunt of Stevens, that he was always just ahead of his party, and that, in due course of time, it was sure to catch up with him and even to run ahead, was not an idle one.[3] How readily the constitutionists of

[1] Cong. Globe, 243, 244.

[2] Cong. Globe, 239.

[3] "I believe that not only a majority, but perhaps a very considerable majority of my friends on this floor do not go to the extent to which I go in the doctrines which I have enunciated. They are com-

the Republican party were swept from their moorings is shown by the conduct of no less a man than John P. Hale, Senator of New Hampshire. Hale had been one of the original abolitionists, and had been in sympathy with the group of New England abolitionists, whose agitation had stirred the land from the day of the Missouri Compromise. In one respect he had differed from them: he revered the Constitution, and held in sanctity the personal and political rights of the citizen. To him nothing was a gain which had been acquired at the cost of another's right, and even the triumph of the North, if achieved at the cost of personal liberty, was the worst of defeats. Accordingly, when Senator Trumbull offered a resolution [1] directing the Secretary of State, Seward, to inform the Senate whether, in the loyal states of the Union, any persons had been arrested and imprisoned by the Secretary's orders, and under what law this was done, and Trumbull had been severely reproached for his act on the floor of the Senate by every Republican leader that could find breath to utter his astonishment, Hale had risen in his place, and had uttered these noble sentiments: —

"Instead of feeling grief and mortification and regret at the introduction of this resolution, I thank my friend from Illinois for introducing it. I think it eminently proper, eminently appropriate; and I shall feel mortified if the day has come when any act of your Executive may not be inquired into by his sworn

ing along behind, and will be up shortly, but they are not up yet. Still I do not propose to take one step backward. I hold the doctrines which I have enunciated to be true, and I abide by them." Cong. Globe, 244.

[1] December 1, 1861.

constitutional advisers, the Senate of the United States. If, in answering that resolution, if it passes, the Secretary of State or the President shall deem it proper to send it to us under the seal of executive secrecy, I shall find no fault with that; but the right, the power, the propriety, and the necessity of making this inquiry, to my mind, eminently exists. What is the purpose of this inquiry? Have not arrests been made in violation of the great principles of our Constitution? If they have, let us know it, and let us know the necessity which impelled them. If the fact be that such arrests have been made, and if the necessity exists upon which they were made, then I trust there is magnanimity, there is justice, there is patriotism, there is forbearance enough in this Senate and in this Congress, to throw the mantle over every act that has been prompted by a patriotic impulse to serve the nation and preserve its liberties. You may gain your victories on the sea, you may sweep the enemy from the broad ocean and from all its arms and from all its rivers, until you may hoist, as the Dutch admiral once hoisted at the head of his flag-staff, a broom, indicative that you have swept the ocean of your foes, and you may crush every rebel that is arrayed against you and utterly break their power; and when you have done all that, when you have established a military power such as the earth never saw, and a naval power such as England never aspired to be, and constitutional liberty shall be buried amid the ashes of that conflagration in which you have overcome and destroyed your foes; then, sir, you will have got a barren victory, and with all your glory you will have but achieved your everlasting shame."

These were noble words, and assuredly the sentiments were just, constitutional, and patriotic, but the resolution was buried in committee nevertheless, and the Secretary, now exempt from interference, redoubled his efforts, and the arrests went on merrily for another year, when Senator Saulsbury, of Delaware, offered a similar resolution in which the inquiry was addressed to the Secretary of War, who had been emulating the example of the Secretary of State. Wilson, who was shocked at this arraignment of the administration of the government, thought that instead of the few hundred arrests which had been made, there ought to have been several thousands, and that not one man in ten who should have been arrested had been arrested. Fessenden and Collamer addressed themselves to the hopeless task of defending the *lettres des cachet;* one alone, who could not defend the government, found voice to condemn himself, and this was the way John P. Hale ate his brave words of one short year before: —

"I have regretted the exercise of this power from first to last; but will say that, where the emergencies of the country are such, and the condition of things is such, as to justify a resort to extraordinary proceedings for the safety of the Government, I am willing that the Executive should act upon that old maxim, which, translated into plain English, is, 'The safety of the republic is the supreme law.' I confess, for myself, that nothing in the whole history of the war has so embarrassed me, has left me in such doubt what course to take and pursue, as questions of this character. I have as earnest a desire for the preservation of the Constitution in all its integrity as anybody else; and it matters not to me whether victory or defeat attends our arms, if, when the war is over, it does not leave us a constitutional government. We are at war for that; and I hope we shall make every sacrifice that is necessary to sustain it. That being our object, our end, and our aim, I would not now, while the enemy is in the field, and while the contingencies of battle are pending, and the issues of life or death are suspended upon the result, impede or hinder those who are charged with the execution of the laws by inquiries which are not vital to the government. I do not look upon this as so, because I believe it is one that belongs to the judiciary to examine and settle; and if anybody has made an attempt to apply that remedy and has failed, it will be time enough then to look to some ulterior course."[1]

Thus did a member of an independent branch of the government surrender his will to the keeping of another branch. But if a man like Hale was so easily torn from his antecedents and his principles, and hurried along with the crowd, what could be expected of the less resolute and less principled, those self-seekers who make up the mass of politicians? One can easily see how a man of strong will, like Stevens, could bide his time and wait until the rest of the irresolute crowd had caught up with him, and then smile at their efforts to outdo him.

In 1861, Stevens, superior to the gloom and consternation with which the disaster of Bull Run had enveloped the Capitol, had retorted to Diven with a sneer: "I thought the time had come when the laws of war were to govern our action; when constitutions,

[1] December 8, 1862: Cong. Globe, 28.

if they stood in the way of the laws of war in dealing with the enemy, had no right to intervene. Who says the Constitution must come in, in bar of our action?"[1] This born leader of revolution had not to look long nor far for support in his radicalism. During the debate in the Senate, on the Confiscation bill,[2] Mr. Morrill, of Maine, gravely pronounced an opinion which cannot be passed by unnoticed, and which was designed to have the effect of a judicial opinion upon the powers of Congress. After noting that the nation was in a state of general internal hostility, and that it possessed the power of self-defence, he proceeded to inquire in what department of the government this power was lodged. Sustained by the Constitution,[3] and by the interpretation put upon it by the Supreme Court, in Brown *v.* The United States,[4] he had no difficulty in asserting that it lay in Congress and nowhere else: the Executive was merely "Commander-in-Chief of the Army and Navy." He went on to say: "In the contingency of actual hostilities the nation assumes a new and extraordinary character, involving new relations and conferring new rights, imposing extraordinary obligations on the citizens, and subjecting them to extraordinary penalties. There is, then, no limit on the power of Congress; but it is invested with the absolute powers of war, — the civil functions of the Government are, for the time being, in abeyance when in conflict, and all state and national authority subordinated to the extreme authority of Congress, as the supreme power, in the peril

[1] August 2, 1861: Cong. Globe, 414.
[2] February 25, 1862: Cong. Globe, 942, *et seq.*
[3] Article I. sect. 8.
[4] 1 Cranch.

of external or internal hostilities. The ordinary provisions of the Constitution peculiar to a state of peace, and all laws and municipal regulations, must yield to the force of martial law as resolved by Congress."

The significance of this claim of absolute power in Congress cannot be overrated. It must be borne in mind that the object of the bill under discussion was the confiscation of the property of rebels, particularly of slaves, who on the instant would be set free; but, to confine our observation to the object set forth in the bill, it provided for the confiscation of the real and personal property of those in rebellion. When it is considered that there is no clause in the Constitution expressly conferring this power, it follows that such power could not be exercised unless it was implied by the Constitution. This Senator Howard undertook to attribute to one of the objects of the Constitution enumerated in the preamble, to "insure domestic tranquillity," and the attempts to find a justification for the measure were divers and different. Morrill was not of a tentative disposition: he would not accuse himself in excusing himself; he appealed to the clause in the Constitution which imposed upon Congress the duty of declaring and maintaining war, and he claimed everything, all power, absolute power in Congress, as the shortest way of enabling the radicals to attain their end.

The consequences of this doctrine of the centralization of all power, state and federal, in Congress during a period of "general internal hostility," were far reaching. If once Congress could maintain the position that civil war had centred irresponsible power in that body, subordinating the other branches of government, and that the seceded states had committed *felo-da-se* by actual rebellion, it would be omnipotent, could it unite upon one single plan of action. Already the bold utterances of the radical leadership indicated with sufficient certainty by whom this one plan of action would be supplied. At any rate, a vigorous and self-centred policy of the legislature, sitting as a Committee of Safety as well as a Congress, would find little annoyance from the cautious policy of a President who had inaugurated his administration by saying: "In view of the Constitution and the laws, the Union is unbroken, and, to the extent of my ability, I shall take care, as the Constitution itself expressly enjoins upon me, that the laws of the Union be faithfully executed in all of the states." The expanding radicalism of the Republican party chafed at the restrictions which the Constitution had placed around it: but turn where one would, the Constitution still blocked the way. Stevens saw this, and pushed the Constitution aside; but he was too wise to claim centralization of all powers in Congress before the time for doing so had come. Sumner saw it, and ignoring the Constitution, cried, "Opportunity, opportunity, opportunity. . . . Do not fail to seize it!" Morrill saw it, but relying on the investiture of Congress with declaration and maintenance of war, went farther than them all — it was for Congress to centralize in itself all powers, to subordinate "all state and national authority to the extreme authority of Congress, as the supreme power." This was revolutionary, but then any path that lay over a prostrate Constitution was revolutionary, and this path had already been taken.

CHAPTER XIII.

PLANS OF RECONSTRUCTION.

The Emancipation Proclamation — The Amnesty Proclamation and Presidential Plan of Reconstruction — The Congressional Plan of Reconstruction and debate thereon in the House of Representatives.

DURING the year 1862,[1] President Lincoln, who still clung to the notion of compensated emancipation of slaves, had sent a message to Congress, recommending the adoption of a joint resolution giving pecuniary aid to any slave state that might adopt the gradual abolition of slavery. On May ninth, he issued a proclamation countermanding an order of General Hunter by which the slaves in his department had been declared free; and, on July twelfth, he had addressed an appeal to the representatives from the Border States, to sustain him in his efforts towards gradual and compensated emancipation.[2] Whether the disappointing response to this appeal convinced the

[1] March 6, 1862. "I recommend the adoption of a joint resolution, . . . which shall be substantially as follows: *Resolved*, That the United States ought to coöperate with any state which may adopt gradual abolishment of slavery, giving to such state pecuniary aid, to be used by such state in its discretion, to compensate for the inconveniences, public and private, produced by such change of system." This resolution passed the Senate and the House. McPherson's Hist. Rebellion, 209, 210. See also Message of December 1, 1862: id., 221.

Slavery was abolished in the District of Columbia by act of Congress, April 16, 1862. Id., 211, 212.

[2] McPherson's Hist. Rebellion, 213 *et seq*.

President that he could no longer hope for the realization of his wishes, and disposed him to adopt another course, is not certain. During the ensuing summer, he abandoned this position, and adopting the opinion of the radicals that the war was a war against slavery, and that it would never reach a conclusion satisfactory to the North unless it terminated in the abolition of that institution everywhere upon the soil and territory of the United States, he issued, on September twenty-second, a proclamation to the effect that, on January 1, 1863, all persons held as slaves within any rebellious state should be thenceforward and forever free. Heretofore, slavery within the limits of a state had been universally held to be inviolable under the Constitution, and nothing betrays the revolutionary character of the civil war more clearly than does this proclamation. The President would have issued it earlier than he had done, if the federal reverses in the field had not afforded ground for a misconstruction of the act. The first substantial success, the battle of the Antietam, called forth the Emancipation Proclamation.

This proclamation was not satisfactory to the radicals; it was restricted in its operation to the states in rebellion, and it contained a reiteration of the President's purpose to recommend a grant of pecuniary aid to the Border States for the abolishment of slavery within their limits. A reference to what was considered the antiquated doctrine of African colonization, though in a new guise and under conditions in which the freedmen would be set apart and be debarred the benefits of citizenship, was also offensive to them. When Congress met in December, and the President's

Message came to be read, it was found that he had been as good as his word; for it contained a recommendation that an article amendatory of the Constitution be adopted, whereby compensation to the emancipating states should be provided for by the federal government, and even the form of this article was set forth. These persistent efforts of the President in the direction of gradual and compensated emancipation had been exceedingly distasteful to the radicals; Hickman, of Pennsylvania, in the debate on the resolution of March sixth, going so far as to say: "The President of the United States cannot be ignorant of the fact that he has, thus far, failed to meet the just expectation of the party which elected him to the office he holds; and his friends are to be comforted, not so much by the resolution itself as by the body of the Message, while the people of the Border States will not fail to observe that with the comfort to us is mingled an awful warning to them."

Although the promised Emancipation Proclamation was but a few days in the future, the past was still more certain, and the President's indisposition to accede fully to the dictation of the radicals was the rankling thorn of the moment. Accordingly, on the ninth of December, when the bill for the admission of West Virginia was under discussion in the House, Thaddeus Stevens, in the course of his remarks, thus addressed the President over the heads of his hearers: —

"I hold that none of the states now in rebellion are entitled to the protection of the Constitution, and I am grieved when I hear those high in authority sometimes talking of the constitutional difficulties about enforcing measures against this belligerent power, and the next moment disregarding every vestige and semblance of the Constitution by acts which alone are arbitrary. I hope I do not differ with the Executive in the views which I advocate. But I see the Executive one day saying: "You shall not take the property of rebels to pay the debts which the rebels have brought upon the northern states. Why? Because the Constitution is in the way. And the next day I see him appointing a military governor of Tennessee, and some other places. Where does he find anything in the Constitution to warrant that? If he must look there alone for authority, then all these acts are flagrant usurpations, deserving the condemnation of the community. He must agree with me, or else his acts are as absurd as they are unlawful. . . . Sir, I understand that these proceedings all take place, not under any pretence of legal or constitutional right, but in virtue of the laws of war; and by the laws of nations these laws are just what we choose to make them, so that they are not inconsistent with humanity. I say, then, that we may admit West Virginia as a new state, not by virtue of any provision of the Constitution, but under our absolute power, which the laws of war give us in the circumstances in which we are placed. I shall vote for this bill upon that theory, and upon that alone; for I will not stultify myself by supposing that we have any warrant in the Constitution for this proceeding."

The leaven had worked, and the time had come when Stevens could openly call upon the absolute power of Congress; and the President was warned that any policy that claimed the Constitution as its foundation would not receive the approval of an omnipotent Congress, which regarded the rebellious states not as states but as conquered provinces. The President was given to understand that, if he persisted in his course, there would be two plans of reconstruction in the field, — the President's plan and the Congressional plan.

During the debate of the twenty-second of January, 1864, upon a joint resolution explanatory of the confiscation act, Stevens gave his reasons for denying that the Constitution had the least reference to any one of the provisions of the bill in question.[1] He supported his position, as best he could, by quotations from judicial decisions and from recognized authorities upon the laws of nations. In the course of his argument, he was sharply interrogated concerning his views of the *status* of the rebellious states, and of the power of the government to punish a state in its corporate capacity, but he did not hesitate to avow his position. He scouted the Presidential notion of transforming rebel states into loyal ones: "The idea that loyal citizens, though few, are the state, and in state municipalities may override and govern the disloyal millions, I have not been able to comprehend. If ten men fit to save Sodom can elect a governor and other state officers for and against the eleven hundred thousand Sodomites in Virginia, then the democratic doctrine that the majority shall rule is discarded and dangerously ignored. When the doctrine that the quality and not the number of votes is to decide the right to govern, then we have no longer a republic, but the worst form of despotism. . . . It is mere mockery to say that, according to any principle of popular gov-

[1] Cong. Globe, 316 *et seq.*

ernment yet established, a tithe of the resident inhabitants of an organized state can change its form and carry on government because they are more holy or more loyal than the others. . . . If the United States succeed, how may she treat the vanquished belligerent? . . . Every inch of the soil of the guilty portion of this usurping power should be held to reimburse all the costs of the war; to pay all the damages to private property of loyal men; and to create an ample fund to pay pensions to wounded soldiers and to the bereaved friends of the slain. . . . All this done, and yet the half would be undone. . . . It is not only our right but our duty to knock off every shackle from every limb." While asserting his conclusion that all the people and all the territory of the rebel states were "subject to the laws of war and of nations," he added, "both while the war continues and when it shall be ended."

Stevens was answered by Wadsworth, of Kentucky, who expressed his astonishment how any one could refer the House to the laws of nations in support of this act: "Why, sir," said he, "the usages of nations in modern times forbid the very means which the gentleman would employ, and the whole policy which he advocates." Wadsworth agreed with Stevens that the war powers were vested by the Constitution in Congress, but maintained that the sovereignty lay in the people, and that there was no sovereign but the people; that this sovereign had delegated one part of the sovereignty to the states and another part to the federal government; and that this latter part was to be exercised by Congress and not by the President. "Woe worth the day," he cried, "when the American people consent that that portion of the sovereignty which they delegated to the states shall, by the accident of fortune, or the malice of men, be vested in one man, and he the holder of the sword and the purse! . . . These states are in the Union, and there is no power short of successful revolution that can drive them out of it; and it is no longer worth while for men of intellect and courage to deny the fact — rebellion, double damned as it is, has been met on our part and confronted with revolution: a revolution of the federal government against the states, of the rulers against the people, of the sword against privilege, of power against liberty." In the course of his remarks, he had said: "If the gentleman from Pennsylvania is as logical in action as in argument, the Executive of the United States must meet with his determined opposition. I understand him, indeed, in the very speech to which I have directed my attention, to sneer at the pretence that the Executive of the United States is vested with the federal or state sovereignty at all."[1]

Although the resolution passed the House by the small majority of nine, this majority was sufficient to indicate that the party was "catching up" with Stevens; the two years which he had allowed to it to do so were not much more than half gone.

This debate may be said to have had its origin in the Amnesty Proclamation with which President Lincoln had accompanied his Message at the meeting of Congress in the preceding December,[2] and which provided that when a number of persons in any of the

[1] Cong. Globe, 467 *et seq.*

[2] December 8, 1863: McPherson's Hist. Rebellion, 147.

states south of the Border States (that is to say, where the territory, or the greater part of the territory, was in actual possession of the military force of the rebels), not less than one tenth in number of the votes cast at the Presidential election of 1860, should organize a government, under the conditions set forth, such should be recognized as the true government of that state.

The President was the first in the field with his plan of reconstruction; but it was satisfactory to nobody, and none raised their voices in its behalf except the crowd that thronged the offices and those who were expectants of the Administration's favors. Congress gave it the cold shoulder, for it was looked upon as a clear usurpation of powers which belonged to that body alone; and the people did not welcome it, for it came to them "in shapeless gear;" it was a stranger to them, and a stranger with no attractive nor even propitious demeanor. Democrats and Republicans joined in one cry, that it was a creature unknown to the Constitution, and both, as if inspired with the same motive, fell upon it, stripped it of its raiment, and lashed it in mockery naked through the world. The stifled and half-muttered dissatisfaction with the President that had been growing in his party with the expansion of radicalism now burst forth, and his shortcomings were exposed in unmeasured terms. All that the Democrats had ever accused him of: his weakness, his vacillation, his fostering a personal administration and a personal party, his longing for a second term of the Presidency, his broken promises of the Inaugural Address and of the First Message; his desertion of constitutional principles and constitutional methods, his illegal arrests, his reliance on the military in exclusion of the civil power, his despotic tendencies manifested from the very beginning, all were harped upon, until the wonder grew that men should have voted for the expulsion of members from the House, when outside of the walls of the Capitol their own conduct and language towards the President was quite as improper as anything the dishonored members had ever done or said inside. "There has not been a session but that our first act was to validate his infractions of the Constitution and the laws." Thaddeus Stevens a year before[1] had pictured Lincoln "here and there ordering elections for members of Congress wherever he finds a little collection of three or four consecutive plantations in the rebel states, in order that men may be sent in here to control the proceedings of this Congress, just as we sanctioned the election held by a few people at a little watering-place at Fortress Monroe." Everything that the President had done in the way of setting up governments in the seceded states was now brought home to him in bitterness and derision: "It is a government of proclamations, a ukase government, at the South: at the North, it is a 'little bell' government." Congress had in divers ways asserted that it was vested with absolute power in time of war: "I think differently," retorted Lincoln; "I think that the Constitution vests the commander-in-chief with the law of war in time of war." There was antagonism between Congress and the President; he had thrown down the gauntlet, and Congress had snatched it up.

The Republicans in Congress were not slow to counteract the measures of the President, and on

[1] December 9, 1862: Cong. Globe, 50.

February 15th, 1864,[1] Henry Winter Davis, of Maryland, reported a bill to the House from its Committee on rebellious states, to guarantee to certain states a republican form of government. The bill was founded upon an article[2] of the Constitution to which it was intended to give effect. This bill, anxiously looked for by the country, embodied the Congressional plan of Reconstruction, and was the result of much thought and of many efforts to harmonize the rival and ever-conflicting factions of the Republican party, and to consolidate in one plan the different views entertained concerning the *status* of the rebel states and their relations to the federal government. For it must not be supposed, from what has been said, that the mass of the Republican members had been meek and docile followers of the radical leadership, or that they looked only to Stevens and his group for their ideas and their modes of parliamentary conduct. On the contrary, nowhere was there stronger opposition to the leadership of the radicals than in the Republican ranks; nowhere were the reproaches of radicalism and of "Thad Stevens" and his group of agitators more sarcastic and bitter. In fact, the majority of the Republican members took great pains to pose before the country as men who tolerated the "untenable notions of the radicals," but who did not accede to them. They claimed vehemently that they founded their action on the Constitution: but the difficulty with them was that, in point of fact, their devotion to the Constitution was lip-service, and that they lacked the manliness of Stevens and his followers, who openly and truthfully placed themselves out-

[1] Cong. Globe, 668. [2] Article IV. sect. 4.

side of a Constitution which they could not obey and violate at the same time. The consequence was, that the Republicans were more at sea than were the Radicals; their plans had the confusion and abortiveness which always attends the plans of those who say one thing and do another, and floundering from step to step, they had no resource but to adopt at last the plans which were ready at hand, and these were those of the Radicals.[1] Thus Stevens had substantial grounds for the taunt that he was always ahead of his party, but that it was sure to catch up with him. In the mean time, the majority of the Republican members hugged to themselves the delusion that they controlled the party, and pointed to their views of the relations existing between the federal government and the states in rebellion as evidence of a set of principles distinct from those of the radicals. These views were, that the rebels had not ceased to be citizens of the United States, nor their states to be states of the Union, but that by maintaining armed resistance to the government in virtue of their secession, they had rendered themselves incapable of exercising political privileges under the Constitution, and that, under the clause of the Constitution guaranteeing a republican form of government to the states, it was the right and duty of Congress to reorganize them, when reduced to its power by means of the military. Their plan of reorganization was the one now introduced into the House.[2] It had been awaited by the country

[1] See Henry Wilson's remarks on the extent of abolitionism, viz.: "And I say here now there is not a loyal state, etc.:" June 27, 1864: Cong. Globe, 3308.

[2] H. R. 244. The purpose set forth in the title was, "to guaranty to certain states whose governments have been usurped or overthrown,

with great anxiety, and its provisions were as follows: —

The President was authorized to appoint a Provisional Governor in each of the states declared to be in rebellion, and this governor was charged with the civil administration until a state government had been organized by the people recognized by the President after obtaining the assent of Congress. This governor, as soon as military resistance to the United States had been suppressed, and the people had sufficiently returned to their obedience to the federal Constitution and laws, was to direct the Marshal to enrol all the white male citizens resident in the state, in their respective counties; and wherever a majority of them took the oath of allegiance, the loyal people of the state were to elect delegates to a convention to act upon the reëstablishment of a state government. This convention was required to insert into the state constitution these provisions: 1. That no person who had held or exercised any civil or military office (except offices ministerial, and military officers below a colonel), state or confederate, under the usurping power, should vote for, or be a member of, the legislature or governor. 2. Involuntary servitude was forever prohibited, and the freedom of all persons guaranteed in said state. 3. No debt, state or confederate, created by or under the sanction of the usurping power, should be recognized or paid by the state. The Provisional government was to certify the adoption of the Constitution by the convention, and its ratification by the electors, to the President, who, after

a republican form of government." See Cong. Globe, 3448, July 1, 1864, for its provisions.

obtaining the assent of Congress, was to recognize this government as the constitutional government of the state, by proclamation; and from the date of such recognition, and not before, Senators and Representatives and electors for President and Vice-President might be elected in such state. Until this reorganization was completed, the Provisional Governor was to enforce the federal laws and those of the state which were on the statute-book before the act of secession.

Davis, who had reported the bill, said in its advocacy:[1] "It is entitled to the support of all upon this side of the House, whatever their views may be of the nature of the rebellion, and the relation in which it has placed the people and states in rebellion toward the United States; not less of those who think the rebellion has placed the citizens of the rebel states beyond the protection of the Constitution, and that Congress, therefore, has supreme power over them as conquered enemies, than of that other class who think that they have not ceased to be citizens and states of the United States, though incapable of exercising political privileges under the Constitution, but that Congress is charged with a high political power by the Constitution to guarantee republican governments in the states, and that this is the proper time and the proper mode of exercising it. It is also entitled to the favorable consideration of gentlemen upon the other side of the House, who honestly and deliberately express their judgment that slavery is dead. . . . We are now engaged in suppressing a military usurpation of the authority of the state governments. When that shall have been accomplished, there will

[1] Cong. Globe, 1st sess. 38th Congress, Part 4, Appendix, 82.

be no form of state authority in existence which Congress can recognize. Our success will be the overthrow of all semblance of government in the rebel states. The government of the United States is then, in fact, the only government existing in those states, and it is then charged to guarantee them republican governments. . . . The denial of the right of secession means that all the territory of the United States shall remain under the jurisdiction of the Constitution. If there can be no state government which does not recognize the Constitution, and which the authorities of the United States do not recognize, then there are these alternatives, and these only, — the rebel states must be governed by Congress till they submit and form a state government under the Constitution; or Congress must recognize state governments which do not recognize either Congress or the Constitution of the United States; or there must be an entire absence of all government in the rebel states, and that is anarchy. To recognize a government which does not recognize the Constitution is absurd, for a government is not a constitution; and the recognition of a state government means the acknowledgment of men as governors and legislators and judges actually invested with power to make laws to judge of crimes, to convict the citizens of other states, to demand the surrender of fugitives from justice, to arm and command the militia, to require the United States to repress all opposition to its authority, and to protect it from invasion against our own armies; whose Senators and Representatives are entitled to seats in Congress, and whose electoral votes must be counted in the election of the President of a government which they disown and defy. To accept the alternative of anarchy as the constitutional condition of a state is to assert the failure of the Constitution, and the end of republican government. Until, therefore, Congress recognize a state government, organized under its auspices, there is no government in the rebel states except the authority of Congress. In the absence of all state government, the duty is imposed on Congress to provide by law to keep the peace, to administer justice, to watch over the transmission of decedents' estates, to sanction marriages ; in a word, to administer civil government until the people shall, under its guidance, submit to the Constitution of the United States, and, under the laws which it shall impose and on the conditions Congress may require, reorganize a republican government for themselves, and Congress shall recognize that government."

Davis perceived the difficulty of going to the root of the matter, and removing the cause of the war by an amendment to the Constitution prohibiting slavery everywhere within the limits of the United States. For altogether there were thirty-four states, and it would require three fourths of these, or twenty-six, to effect the alteration. But of these thirty-four states, twenty-five only were represented in Congress, so that if the needed assent were forthcoming, it would still lack validity for the want of one vote. Such would be the result, if the action of all the United States were required in order to validate the amendment. But even if another view were taken, that it was never contemplated that the supreme political power should pass away from the government of the United States, and that, consequently, the requisite three fourths of the states meant three fourths of the states actually represented in Congress, which was the view taken by Thaddeus Stevens, even then, apart from the great delay involved in amending the Constitution, it was doubtful that the assent of three fourths of the states could be obtained, so long as states like New Jersey, Delaware, Maryland, and Kentucky were present to refuse their assent. Moreover, although success should crown the proposed amendment and it should be actually adopted, it would still leave the whole field of the civil administration of the states, previous to the recognition of state governments, all laws necessary to the ascertainment of the will of the people, and all restrictions on the return to power of the leaders of the rebellion, wholly unprovided for. It would not be a remedy for the evils which the bill proposed to meet.

This led him to discuss the Presidential Plan of Reconstruction and to expose its shortcomings: "The next plan is that inaugurated by the President of the United States in the proclamation of the eighth of December, 1863, called the Amnesty Proclamation. That proposes no guardianship of the United States over the reorganization of the governments, no law to prescribe who shall vote, no civil functionaries to see that the law is faithfully executed, no supervising authority to control and judge of the election. But if, in any manner, by the toleration of martial law, lately proclaimed the fundamental law, under the dictation of any military authority, or under the prescription of a provost marshal, something in the form of a government shall be presented, represented to rest on the votes of one tenth of the population, the

President will recognize that, provided it does not contravene the proclamation of freedom and the laws of Congress; and to secure that, an oath is exacted. Now, you will observe that there is no guarantee of law to watch over the organization of that government. It may combine all the population of a state; it may combine one tenth only: or ten governments may come competing for recognition at the door of the executive mansion. The executive authority is pledged; Congress is not pledged. It may be recognized by the military power, and may not be recognized by the civil power, so that it would have a doubtful existence, half civil and half military, neither a temporary government by laws of Congress, nor a state government; something as unknown to the Constitution as the rebel government that refuses to recognize it."

He further considered the effect of the Presidential plan upon the matter of slavery, and demonstrated its inefficacy in this respect: as for the oath, it added nothing to the legality of the law, nothing to its force. On the other hand, the bill under consideration, or the Congressional plan, proposed to preclude the judicial question which might be raised of the validity and effect of the President's proclamation or by an irregular constitutional amendment, by the solution of the political question, and this was to be done by the paramount power of Congress to reorganize governments in the insurgent states, to impose such conditions as it thought necessary to secure the permanence of republican government, to refuse to recognize any governments then which did not prohibit slavery forever. A long and excited debate continued in the House.

It must be borne in mind that, so far as Congress

and the President were concerned, the issue was: Which power shall prevail in the reconstruction of the states, the unconstitutional and executive power, or the constitutional and legislative power? Congress profoundly distrusted Mr. Lincoln. He had hardly been warm in his seat when he had begun the arrests, sometimes hundreds of miles away from the seat of war or where any evil influence could seriously embarrass the conduct of military affairs; he had persistently meddled with the operations of troops in the field; he had issued proclamations to which Congress had not previously given its assent, and the legislature had found it necessary to make its first business, on coming together, to validate illegal and unconstitutional acts, which, if the law and the Constitution were to have sway, must be construed as acts of usurpation. The excessive prominence which the war lent the President was distasteful to the legislators, from the fact that it involved his personality, more or less, in every act of administration; while the additional fact that he controlled the movements of a vast army was a cause of apprehension ever present, and which betrayed itself in the assertion that the President under the Constitution was *nominally* commander-in-chief of the Army and Navy. Congress feared the President and his disposition to exert irresponsibly his enormous power; it secretly took to heart the constant assertion of the Democrats and their proofs that the war had engendered a military despotism and that the President was the despot, and it believed the Wadsworths who cried out, "Woe worth the day when the American people consent that that portion of the sovereignty which they delegated to the states shall, by the accident of fortune, or the malice of men, be vested in one man, and he the holder of the sword and the purse!" The contest, therefore, was between two parties, and irresponsible power was the prize. As far as constitutionality was concerned, the President had little to found his claims upon: Congress, on the other hand, had a great deal, but this was nullified and invalidated by the enormity of its claim to absolute power. In fact, the strife was one of absolutism and between absolutists, and the struggle was for power over a prostrate constitution that was trampled upon by the combatants.

The Democrats, who had become restricted in action to a party of mere protest, were not silent, and the view that they took of the relations of the rebellious states with the federal government, of the powers of Congress and of the true nature of the bill, or rather of the Congressional plan then under consideration, was so lucidly set forth by Pendleton, of Ohio,[1] that a comprehensive view of all sides of the question cannot be obtained without taking his remarks into consideration. He opposed the bill, and in the following manner: "The gentleman maintains two propositions, which lie at the very basis of his views on this subject. He maintains that, by reason of this secession, the seceded states and their citizens have not ceased to be citizens and states of the United States, though incapable of exercising political privileges under the Constitution, but that Congress is charged with a high political power by the Constitution to guarantee republican government in the states, and that this is the proper time and the proper mode of

[1] Cong. Globe, 2105.

exercising it. This act of revolution on the part of the states has evoked the most extraordinary theories upon the relation of the states to the federal government. This theory of the gentleman is one of them. The ratification of the Constitution by Virginia established the relation between herself and the. federal government; it created the link between her and all the states; it announced her assumption of the duties, her title to the rights of the confederating states; it proclaimed her interest in, her power over, her obedience to the common agent of all the states. If Virginia had never ordained that ratification, she would have been an independent state; the Constitution would have been as perfect and the union between the ratifying states would have been as complete as they now are. Virginia repeals that ordinance of ratification, annuls that bond of union, breaks that link of confederation. She repeals but a single law, repeals it by the action of a sovereign convention; leaves her constitution, her laws, her political and social polity untouched. And the gentleman from Maryland tells us that the effect of this repeal is not to destroy the vigor of that law, but it is to subvert the state government, and to render the citizens 'incapable of exercising political privileges;' that the Union remains, but that one party to it has thereby lost its corporate existence, and the other has advanced to the control and government of it.

"Sir, this cannot be. Gentlemen must not palter in a double sense. These acts of secession are either valid or they are invalid. If they are valid, they separated the state from the Union. If they are invalid, they are void; they have no effect; the state officers who act upon them are rebels to the federal government; the states are not destroyed; their constitutions are not abrogated; their officers are committing illegal acts, for which they are liable to punishment; the states have never left the Union, but so soon as their officers shall perform their duties, or other officers shall assume their places, will again perform the duties imposed, and enjoy the privileges conferred by the federal compact, and this not by virtue of a new ratification of the Constitution, nor a new admission by the federal government, but by virtue of the original ratification, and the constant uninterrupted maintenance of position in the federal Union since that date.

"Acts of secession are not invalid to destroy the Union, and valid to destroy the state governments, and the political privileges of their citizens. We have heard much of the twofold relation which citizens of the seceded states may hold to the federal government — that they may be at once belligerents and rebellious citizens. I believe there are some judicial decisions to that effect. Sir, it is impossible. The federal government may possibly have the right to elect in which relation it will deal with them: it cannot deal with them at one and the same time in inconsistent relations. . . . The seceded states are either in the Union or out of it. If in the Union, their constitutions are untouched, their state governments are maintained; their citizens are entitled to all political rights, except so far as they may be deprived of them by the criminal law which they have infracted. This seems incomprehensible to the gentleman from Maryland. In his view the whole state government centres in the men who administer it; so that when they administer it unwisely, or put it in antagonism to the federal government, the state government is dissolved, the state constitution is abrogated, and the state is left, in fact and in form, *de jure* and *de facto*, in anarchy, except so far as the federal government may rightfully intervene. This seems to be substantially the view of the gentleman from Massachusetts [Boutwell]. He enforces the same position, but he does not use the same language.

"I submit that these gentlemen do not see with their usual clearness of vision. If by a plague or other visitation of God, every officer of a state government should at the same moment die, so that not a single person clothed with official power should remain, would the state government be destroyed? Not at all: for the moment it would not be administered, but as soon as officers were elected and assumed their respective duties, it would be instantly in full force and vigor.

"If these states are out of the Union, their state governments are still in force unless otherwise changed. And their citizens are to the federal government as foreigners, and it has in relation to them the same rights, and none other, as it had in relation to British subjects in the war of 1812, or to the Mexicans in 1846. Whatever may be the true relation of the seceded states, the federal government derives no power in relation to them or their citizens from the provision of the Constitution now under consideration, but in the one case derives all its power from the duty of enforcing the 'supreme law of the land,' and in the other 'to declare war.'"

Thus Pendleton declared that the seceded states

were still in the Union, — once a state always a state, and that the federal government derived no power to reconstruct them from the clause in the Constitution guaranteeing them a republican form of government,[1] inasmuch as having had that form in the first instance, and that form being unchanged because it was unchangeable by the act of secession, these states presented nothing upon which this clause could operate, and was therefore inoperative. If this were not so, and the states were out of the Union, then the doctrine of Thaddeus Stevens, that these states were subject to the war powers of the federal government, was correct. This led him to discuss the claim of Congress to absolute power, which he did as follows: —

"The second proposition of the gentleman from Maryland is this. I use his language: 'That clause vests in the Congress of the United States a plenary, supreme, unlimited political jurisdiction, paramount over courts, subject only to the judgment of the people of the United States, embracing within its scope every legislative measure necessary and proper to make it effectual; and what is necessary and proper the Constitution refers in the first place to our judgment, subject to no revision but that of the people.'

"The gentleman states his case too strongly. The duty imposed on Congress is doubtless important, but Congress has no right to use a means of performing it forbidden by the Constitution, no matter how necessary or proper it might be thought to be. But, sir, this doctrine is monstrous. It has no foundation in the Constitution. It subjects all the states to the will of Congress; it places their institutions at the feet of

[1] Article IV. sect. 4.

Congress. It creates in Congress an absolute, unqualified despotism. It asserts the power of Congress in changing the state governments to be 'plenary, supreme, unlimited' — 'subject only to revision by the people of the whole United States.' The rights of the people of the state are nothing; their will is nothing. Congress first decides; the people of the whole Union revise. My own state of Ohio is liable at any moment to be called in question for her constitution. She does not permit negroes to vote. If this doctrine be true, Congress may decide this exclusion is anti-republican, and by force of arms abrogate that constitution and set up another, permitting negroes to vote. From that decision of Congress there is no appeal to the people of Ohio, but only to the people of Massachusetts, and New York, and Wisconsin, at the election of Representatives; and if a majority cannot be elected to reverse the decision, the people of Ohio must submit. Woe be to the day when that doctrine shall be established, for from its centralized despotism we will appeal to the sword! . . .

"This bill, the avowed doctrine of its supporters, sweeps all [the rights of the states] instantly away. It substitutes despotism for self-government; despotism the more severe because vested in a numerous Congress."

CHAPTER XIV.

THE CONGRESSIONAL PLAN OF RECONSTRUCTION.

The Congressional Plan of Reconstruction — Debate in the Senate — Madison on the constitutional guarantee of a republican form of government — Carlile's remarks upon this guarantee — The President withholds his assent to the Reconstruction Bill — His proclamation thereon, and the Manifesto of Senator Wade and Representative Henry Winter Davis.

NOT until July first, though it had been reported on the twenty-seventh of May, was this bill called up in the Senate, when Brown, of Missouri, offered an amendment[1] to the effect that the inhabitants of any state which had been proclaimed to be in rebellion should be incapable of casting a vote for presidential electors or of electing Senators or Representatives in Congress, until the insurrection was abandoned. Wade led off in the debate which opened, and in the course of his remarks he said: "What is the relation that these seceded states hold to the general government now? Gentlemen differ widely on that subject. It is a most important question, however, to be ascertained and declared by Congress, for the Executive ought not to be permitted to handle this great question to his own liking. It does not belong, under the Constitution, to the President to prescribe the rule, and it is a base abandonment of our own powers and our own duties to cast this great principle upon the

[1] Cong. Globe, 3449.

decision of the executive branch of the government. It belongs to us; and the House of Representatives, in the performance of their duty, have in my judgment wisely performed this great function. I know very well that the President from the best motives undertook to fix a rule upon which he would admit these states back into the Union. It was not upon any principle of republicanism; it would not have guaranteed to the states a republican form of government, because he prescribed the rule to be that when one tenth of the population would take a certain oath and agree to come back into the Union, they might come in as states. When we consider that in the light of American principle, to say the least of it, it was absurd. The idea that a state shall take upon itself the great privilege of self-government when there is only one tenth of the people that can stand by the principle is most anti-republican, anomalous, and entirely subversive of the great principles that underlie all our state governments and the general goverment. Majorities must rule, and until majorities can be found loyal and trustworthy for state government, they must be governed by a stronger hand. It is a necessity imposed upon the general government by the Constitution itself."

Such was what a Republican Senator thought of the Presidential Plan of Reconstruction. Senator Wade avowed his conviction that "once a state of this Union, always a state; you cannot by wrong or violence displace the rights of anybody or disorganize the state," but he concluded from the constitutional clause of guarantee that "if a portion of the people undertake to overthrow their government and set up another, it is the manifest duty of the general government immediately to interfere, and if necessary, to interpose the strong arm of its power to prevent such a state of things. Precisely that state of things is upon us," he added, "and this bill proceeds upon that idea, and discards absolutely the notion that states may lose their rights and that they may be abrogated and may be reduced to the condition of territories. It denies any such thing as that."

That Senator Wade was right as far as he went, in his views of the relations in which the seceded states then stood to the federal government under the Constitution, cannot be gainsaid, but he was wrong in supposing that the facts were such as to warrant an application of the clause guaranteeing a republican form of government. No portion of the people had undertaken to overthrow their state government and set up another. On the contrary, the secessionists had preserved their state governments in their integrity, and had confined their efforts in government-destroying to the dissolution of the federal Union. So far as the state governments were concerned, those that had seceded were the same as they had been when in the Union; and that is to say, that they were as republican in form as they had ever been. There was then no ground upon which the federal government could interfere, and no warrant for it to set up a state government. This Carlile, of Virginia, in an able answer to Wade, which was characterized by a ready and thorough knowledge of the Constitution, brought out clearly and distinctly in an argument in which his constitutional position was sustained by the forty-third number of the Federalist, written by

Madison, and comprising a commentary on the guarantee clause.

"It may possibly be asked," said Madison, "what need could there be of such a precaution, and whether it may not become a pretext for alterations in the state governments without the concurrence of the states themselves. These questions admit of ready answers. If the interposition of the general government should not be needed, provision for such an event will be a harmless superfluity only in the Constitution. But who can say what experiments may be produced by the caprice of particular states, by the ambition of enterprising leaders, or by the intrigues and influence of foreign powers? To the second question it may be answered that if the general government should interpose by virtue of this constitutional authority, it will be of course bound to pursue the authority. But the authority extends no further than to a *guarantee* of a republican form of government, which supposes a *preëxisting government* of the form which is to be guaranteed."

Thus far the Federalist, which Carlile proceeded to apply to the case in hand, as follows: "I would have the government of the United States do nothing that it has not the power under the Constitution to do, because I believe that the government of the United States is a government of limited powers. I believe it to be its duty under the grant of power in the Constitution to guarantee the existence of a preëxisting republican government. That government existed in South Carolina; the people have not determined — at least before this war they had not determined — to have any other form than a republican form of government. We had recognized that government as a republican form of government by the recognition of the state in all its departments and the admission of all its national representatives. It is made the duty of the government of the United States, not of Congress; and I desire to call the attention of the Senator to that, because it bears upon his assumption for Congress of power which does not belong to the Executive. It is not alone the duty of Congress to guarantee a republican form of government to the people of the several states; the extent of that guarantee is not limited alone to the means which Congress may employ; but the words of the Constitution are 'the United States shall guarantee.' Hence every department of the government is equally bound; and Congress being the legislative branch of course participates to a greater extent in the discharge of that duty. . . .

"You have no authority to appoint a governor or any civil officer in that state, unless you are compelled to resort to military power to carry out your constitutional obligations and to remove the obstacles which are in the way of the exercise of civil authority through the agents of the people themselves, which they have established by virtue of their existing government. No such power is given under any provision of the Constitution; none could have been given without your entirely changing the whole character of this government, which is based upon the fundamental principle that the military power should always be subordinate to the civil. . . .

"But, sir, the Senator from Ohio says the Union is to be preserved. So say I. Upon what principle are these states to come back into the Union? The people, says the Senator from Ohio, will meet you with that inquiry. Sir, when was ever such an inquiry suggested to the brain of any loyal man in this Union? When was such an inquiry ever put? Never until after a policy different from that which characterized the commencement of this struggle was entered upon by the party in power. All said the Union was to be restored; all accepted the struggle as the use of the military power of the government in the restoration of the Union. What Union? The Union of the Constitution. The Union into which new states are to be admitted. It is not into 'a Union' but into 'this Union' that the states are admitted. What Union? The Union of the Constitution, none other; and he who seeks to preserve the Union can only do it by an observance of the Constitution and the use of the constitutional means to restore it, not reconstruct it. . . . In this Union, created by this Constitution, of limited and delegated powers, all prescribed and written in the instrument, you propose to exercise your legislative power by usurping the rights and liberties of the people, a power which all the people you represent could not use or could not exert without the destruction of the Union which the Constitution formed. There is no power in this government, there is no power in the parties to this government, there is no power in all of the states of this Union, to prescribe a constitution for the little state of Rhode Island. If every other state in the Union, the adhering as well as the rebellious states, if every man, woman, and child in them were to meet and prescribe a constitution for the people of Rhode Island, they would have no power or authority to do so under the Union; and tell me where the people's representatives derive the power to do that which all the people in their collective capacity, save the small minority that constitutes that state, cannot do?"

The amendment was adopted by the close majority of one vote, and then the bill was passed on the second of July. The House, however, did not concur in the amendment, and the Senate receded from it, whereupon the bill went to the President for his approval. This took place in the very closing hour of the session, when the President, in order to facilitate the passage of bills, had gone to the Capitol, and in a private room was affixing his signature to such bills as were then presented to him. What would the President do? Would he succumb to Congress, acknowledge himself to be in the wrong, recognize the paramount authority, the absolute power of the representatives of the states and of the people, and sign the bill? He did nothing of the kind, he neither signed nor vetoed it, he pocketed it; and, indifferent to the strictures upon him of Congress, or rather in defiance of this body and of public opinion, he adopted a course which no President had ever taken before, nor has one ever taken since then. The Constitution requires that, if any bill shall not be returned by the President within ten days (Sundays excepted) after it shall have been presented to him, the same shall be a law, in like manner as if he had signed it, unless the Congress by their adjournment prevent its return, in which case it shall not be a law.[1] Congress had adjourned without the bill being signed, and consequently the bill could not

[1] Article I. sect. 7.

become a law. A President who does not approve of a bill, but who has his reasons for not saying so to Congress, has it in his power, when it is presented to him during the closing days of the session, to prevent its becoming a law and at the same time to save himself from officially annulling it, by "pocketing" it, as it is vulgarly styled, until the adjournment *sine die* of Congress intervenes and accomplishes his object for him. Mr. Lincoln was not and has not been the only President who has availed himself of this constitutional limitation upon legislation, but he was the only one who followed up such action by a proclamation upon the subject. This he did with great promptitude. When the hour of adjournment came and the bill had not been returned with the President's signature, great was the wrath of the Republican members of Congress. They had been checkmated, and they dispersed to their homes in the gloom of discomfiture. Moody and silent, their feelings were by no means soothed by the recollection that it was a presidential election year, that their adversary had already been nominated to the presidency, and that it was necessary to maintain a placid front. But they were not permitted to chew the cud of disappointment in silence; for, on the ninth of July,[1] before, in fact, many of the members had reached their distant homes, the President broke the silence with the thunder he was too ready to use in those days, the thunder of a proclamation. He was not disposed to allow his foes to take the stump in their districts where he would not be present to reply, without having the first word with the people. The Congressional party cursed "this government of proc-

[1] The proclamation is dated on the 8th.

lamations" in their hearts, but there was no help for it. The President was beforehand; he had come out best in the game at the Capitol, and now he would make good use of his popularity to forestall Congress with the people.

The proclamation began with a recital of the facts that, at the late session, Congress had passed a bill to guarantee to certain states whose governments had been usurped or overthrown, a republican form of government, and that this bill had been presented to the President for his approval less than one hour before the *sine die* adjournment of the session, and had not been signed by him; and that the bill contained a plan for restoring the states in rebellion to their proper practical relation in the Union, which plan expressed the sense of Congress upon that subject, and which plan it was then thought fit to lay before the people for their consideration. Therefore, the President made known that, as in the preceding December, when by proclamation he had propounded a plan for restoration, he was unprepared by a formal approval of this bill to be inflexibly committed to any single plan of restoration; and while he was also unprepared to declare that the free-state constitutions and governments already adopted and installed in Arkansas and Louisiana should be set aside and held for naught, thereby repelling and discouraging the loyal citizens who had set up the same as to further effort, or to declare a constitutional competency in Congress to abolish slavery in the states, but was at the same time sincerely hoping and expecting that a constitutional amendment abolishing slavery throughout the nation might be adopted: nevertheless, he was fully satisfied with the system for restoration contained in the bill as one very proper for the loyal people of any state choosing to adopt it; and that he was, and at all times should be, prepared to give the executive aid and assistance to any such people, so soon as military resistance to the United States should be suppressed in any such state, and the people thereof should have sufficiently returned to their obedience to the Constitution and the laws of the United States, — in which cases military governors would be appointed, with directions to proceed according to the bill.[1]

It would be impossible to picture the wrath and dismay of the adherents to the Congressional plan. When they recovered from the blow sufficiently to collect their senses, it was resolved that this proclamation of war between the President and Congress should be answered, and accordingly a "protest" or rather a manifesto was issued, signed by Senator Wade, who had reported the bill in the Senate, and by H. Winter Davis, who had reported it in the House.[2]

It was addressed "To the supporters of the Government," and it began by saying that they had read without surprise, but not without indignation, the proclamation of the President, and that it was impossible to pass in silence this proclamation without neglecting their duty; and that, having taken as much responsibility as any others in supporting the Administration, they were not disposed to fail in the other duty of asserting the rights of Congress. That the President had not signed the bill, and therefore it was not a law, it was nothing; that the proclamation,

[1] July 8, 1864: Appendix.

[2] Appendix.

being neither an approval nor a veto, was a document unknown to the Constitution of the United States, but that, so far as it contained an apology for not signing the bill, it was a political manifesto against the friends of the government, and so far as it proposed to execute a bill which was not a law, it was a grave executive usurpation.

It then went on to say that it was fitting that the facts necessary to enable the friends of the Administration to appreciate the apology and the usurpation should be spread before them, and in the course of this disclosure they revealed some facts which had occurred during the time the bill was on its passage through Congress, that shed great light on the methods adopted by the President and his party to defeat the bill, and, with it, their adversaries. The manifesto declared, in contradiction of the facts asserted by the President in his proclamation, that, during the hour preceding the *sine die* adjournment, other bills had been signed, and that adjournment had been three times postponed by the votes of both Houses, and that the least intimation of a desire for more time by the President to consider this bill would have secured a further postponement. Yet the committee sent to ascertain if the President had any further communication for the House of Representatives reported that he had none; and the friends of the bill, who had anxiously waited on him to ascertain its fate, had already been informed that the President had resolved not to sign it. The time of presentation therefore had nothing to do with his failure to approve it.

Ignorance of its contents was out of the question, for the bill had been discussed for more than a month in the House of Representatives, which passed it on the fourth of May: it had been reported to the Senate on the twenty-seventh of May, without material amendment, and had passed the Senate absolutely as it came from the House, on the second of July. Indeed, at the President's request, a draft of a bill substantially the same in material points, and identical in the points objected to by the proclamation, had been laid before him for his consideration in the winter of 1862–1863. There was therefore no reason to suppose that the provisions of the bill took the President by surprise. On the contrary, there was reason to believe them to have been so well known that this method of preventing the bill from becoming a law without the constitutional responsibility of a veto had been resolved on long before the bill had passed the Senate. For the writers had been informed by a gentleman entitled to entire confidence that, before the twenty-second of June, in New Orleans, it was stated by a member of General Banks' staff, in the presence of other gentlemen in official position, that Senator Doolittle had written a letter to the department that the House Reconstruction Bill would be staved off in the Senate to a period too late in the session to require the President to veto it, and that Mr. Lincoln would retain the bill, if necessary, and thereby ensure its defeat. The writer asserted that the experience of Senator Wade, in his various efforts to get the bill considered in the Senate, was quite in accordance with that plan; and that the fate of the bill had been accurately predicted by letters received from New Orleans before it had passed the Senate.

Had the proclamation stopped there, continued

Wade and Davis, it would have been only one other defeat of the will of the people by executive perversion of the Constitution. But it goes further; and the manifesto proceeds, rather hysterically, to pick the proclamation to pieces, to comment upon it, paragraph by paragraph, and to expose its weakness as well as the unconstitutional measures in general of the President and the Administration. In speaking of the governments already set up by the President, it did not mince matters: "The President persists in recognizing those shadows of governments in Arkansas and Louisiana which Congress formally declared should not be recognized, — whose representatives and senators were repelled by formal votes of both Houses of Congress, — which it was declared formally should have no electoral vote for President and Vice-President. They are mere creatures of his will. They are mere oligarchies, imposed on the people by military orders under the form of election, at which generals, provost-marshals, soldiers, and camp-followers were the chief actors, assisted by a handful of resident citizens, and urged on to premature action by private letters from the President. In neither Louisiana nor Arkansas, before Banks' defeat, did the United States control half the territory or half the population. In Louisiana, General Banks' proclamation candidly declared: 'The fundamental law of the state is martial law.' On that foundation of freedom he erected what the President calls 'the free constitution and government of Louisiana.' But of this state, whose fundamental law was martial law, only sixteen parishes out of forty-eight parishes were held by the United States; and in five of the sixteen we held only our camps. . . . At the farce called an election, the officers of General Banks returned that 11,346 ballots were cast; but whether any or by whom, the people of the United States have no legal assurance; but it is probable that 4000 were cast by soldiers or employés of the United States, military or municipal, but none according to any law, state or national, and 7000 ballots represent the state of Louisiana.

"Such is the free constitution and government of Louisiana; and like it is that of Arkansas. Nothing but the failure of a military expedition deprived us of a like one in the swamps of Florida; and before the Presidential election, like ones may be organized in every rebel state where the United States have a camp. The President, by preventing this bill from becoming a law, holds the electoral votes of the rebel states at the dictation of his personal ambition."

The manifesto was a lengthy document, and discussed the claim of Congress to the exclusive right of reconstruction of the seceded states, the subject of emancipation, the "dictatorial usurpation" of the President, and the illegality of the special oath prescribed in the Amnesty Proclamation, and concluded with the following threat: "The President has greatly presumed on the forbearance which the supporters of his Administration have so long practiced, in view of the arduous conflict in which we are engaged, and the reckless ferocity of our political opponents. But he must understand that our support is of a cause and not of a man; that the authority of Congress is paramount and must be respected; that the whole body of the Union men of Congress will not submit to be impeached by him of rash and unconstitutional legislation; and if he wishes our support, he must confine himself to his executive duties — to obey and execute, not make the laws — to suppress by arms armed rebellion, and leave political reorganization to Congress. . . . Let them (the supporters of the government) consider the remedy of these usurpations, and, having found it, fearlessly execute it."

Lincoln received this counterblast with perfect serenity. This kind of talk was not a new thing to him, and he could snap his fingers at the threat which concluded the manifesto. He had seen the irreconcilables in Congress organize into opposition against him, and had watched this opposition develop day by day until it controlled the floor of Congress. He had witnessed the rejection of the state governments which he had set up, and he had heard the leaders, one after another, in the same breath, denounce him and his belongings, and claim paramount authority in themselves to do as they pleased. As for the abuse, he was used to that, which, after all, was nothing more than what the Democrats and Wendell Phillips had been saying of him all along; and as for the unconstitutionality of his course, it did not lie in the mouths of those who recognized the Constitution only when they would use it as a club to find fault with him on the score of irreverence towards that instrument. The contest was a strife for power between parties neither of whom regarded the Constitution as sacred, and the gist of this episode lay in the complaint which escaped Wade and Davis, when they exclaimed; "Congress passed a bill; the President refused to approve it, and then by proclamation puts as much of it in force as he sees fit, and proposes to execute those parts by officers unknown to the laws of the United States, and not subject to the confirmation of the Senate."

In this cry of despair, the truth was told. Lincoln had patiently waited for the passage of the bill which was to lay before the country the long-promised Congressional Plan of Reconstruction. Then he had put it in his pocket, and, flushed with his success, he had proclaimed to the world that he had converted to his own use the property of the legislature, and that so much of it as suited his purposes he would keep, and the rest he would throw away. He was sure of his ground; he had been nominated for the Presidency, and his election was a foregone conclusion. The conditions were such that the malcontents must eat their leek, and support him or be ostracized. It was too true: all that Congress could show, after its struggle for a whole session with the President, was that it had been outwitted.

CHAPTER XV.

THE CONGRESSIONAL PLAN OF RECONSTRUCTION — CONTINUED.

The debate in the House on the Reconstruction Bill — Last speech of Henry Winter Davis — Failure of Ashley's substitute.

WHEN Congress met in December, the President had been reëlected by the votes of all of the twenty-five states but three; the electoral votes of eleven states not having been counted. The signs of downfall on the side of the rebellion were multiplying thick and fast; but the North, far from relaxing her efforts in the field, redoubled them. The eyes of the country were now riveted upon the armies and the President; and what was going on in Congress became of secondary importance. There was no need to follow up the discomfited party that disputed the possession of power with the President, and accordingly the annual message made but a bare allusion to the reconstructed governments of the South, Arkansas and Louisiana, and was absolutely silent respecting any plan of reconstruction. But the opportunity presented by his complete victory over the opponents of the amendment to the Constitution, abolishing slavery throughout the United States, which the President had recommended at the preceding session of Congress, and which had been rejected, was taken advantage of for a recommendation to reconsider and pass that measure. Notwithstanding the Congress was the same as the one which, less than eight months before, had recorded its rejection of the amendment, the House had now become converted to the views of the President so far as to contradict its record, and to pass the joint resolution adopting the amendment by a vote of one hundred and nineteen to fifty-six.

With the waning forces of the Confederacy daily spurring Congress to action, the subject of reconstruction more and more engaged the attention of this body. On December 15, 1864, Ashley reported in the House the bill which had met with such contemptuous treatment at the hands of the President at the close of the preceding session, but, upon one pretext or another, it went over until January 16, 1865, when Ashley offered a substitute, with instructions from the Select Committee on rebellious states to ask that it might be substituted for the original bill, and it was so ordered. This substitute expressly recognized the governments of Louisiana and Arkansas, and provided that no confederate officer above the grade of colonel should vote for or be a member of the legislature, or governor; that involuntary servitude be forever prohibited, and equal rights before the law be guaranteed; that no debt, state or confederate, created during the rebellion should be recognized; and that all acts, judicial or legislative, for the confiscation or forfeiture of debts or property of any loyal citizen of the United States, should be null and void. Several amendments were proposed, and another substitute was offered by Eliot, of Massachusetts.

The next day, further consideration was postponed until February seventh, notwithstanding Davis' doleful assertion that "A vote to postpone is equivalent to a vote to kill the bill." On February seventh, it was again moved to postpone for two weeks further. On February twentieth, the House debated the bill earnestly,[1] and on the next day, Ashley withdrew the motion which he had made to recommit the bill to the committee, and withdrew also Davis' bill, and introduced another.

Kelley led off in one of those long and tedious harangues which no one listens to nor reads, and which are to be found nowhere in such profusion as in the reports of the congressional debates. Dawes followed in opposition to the bill, and so did Eliot, who had an amendment offered, substituting in effect the Presidential plan for the one contained in the bill. Fernando Wood followed, and called attention to the fact that the title of the bill assumed that the states in rebellion had not a republican form of government, and contended that the bill provided for anything but such a form. He was frequently taken to task by Smith, whose position can readily be known from the fact that he asserted that the proper custodian of the rights and interests of the loyal people in the rebellious states was the President; the truth of which assertion was denied by Wood, who maintained that the President was not the custodian of the rights of any portion of the states, but that when he interfered with civil rights, and the rights of the people, acting in their sovereign capacity to make their own constitution and laws subject to the Constitution of the United States, he was guilty of usurpation; that the Constitution imposed certain executive duties on the President which he was to perform merely as an executive

[1] Cong. Globe, 934 *et seq.*

authority. Le Blond also spoke in opposition to the bill. At this stage, Ashley withdrew the substitute and fell back on the original bill with modifications. This bill did not recognize Louisiana or Arkansas. In withdrawing the substitute, Ashley frankly revealed the schism in the Republican party. The substitute, he said, had been a compromise measure, by which he had sought to conciliate those whose sensibilities had been wounded by the action of the President when he pocketed the original bill at the close of the preceding session. In order to secure universal suffrage to the liberated blacks, he had consented to the conditional recognition of Louisiana, Arkansas, and Tennessee. But he had failed to effect a compromise, and therefore he offered again the original bill, with a provision that the governor should execute such laws only of the old states as related to the protection of persons and property, and that all laws inconsistent with this bill, and all laws recognizing the relation of master and slave, should not be enforced. He would not recognize the governments of Louisiana unless he could secure negro suffrage. At the same time, he had little hope of the success of this bill; for it was very clear to his mind that no bill providing for the reorganization of loyal state governments in the rebel states could pass this Congress.

Henry Winter Davis then followed in one of the most characteristic speeches of his life, and the last important address that he made to the House. He, too, had no hope of the bill passing. His words breathed unconquerable detestation and defiance of President Lincoln. It was the defiance of a proud spirit that recognized the fate which awaited him, but of one which would never kiss the rod that smote him.[1] He dwelt upon two alternatives as the result of the bill failing to pass: either sixty-five representatives and twenty-two senators would claim admission from the South when the war was over, and would be entitled to admission; or the servile tools of the Executive would be there to embarrass legislation, humble Congress, degrade the name of republican government for two years, and then the natural majority of the South, rising indignantly against that humiliating insult, would swamp Congress with rebel representatives and be its masters. These were the alternatives, and there would be no middle ground.

For the members who had voted for the bill in the preceding session, but who, he knew, had deserted him, and were waiting for him to cease speaking in order to vote against it, his contempt was unmeasured. That they should have discovered since the vote of the preceding session that the bill violated the principles of republican government and sanctioned the enormities of slavery was quite as remarkable as that these features should have been overlooked before that vote: but they had been neither overlooked before nor discovered since. The vote was before a pending election: it was the will of the President which had been discovered since. The weight of that species of argument he was not able to estimate: it bade defiance to every rule. It was that subtle, pervading epidemic of the time that penetrated the closest argument as spirit penetrated matter; that diffused itself with the atmosphere of authority, relaxing the energy

[1] Cong. Globe, 2d Sess. 38th Cong., 969.

of the strong, bending down the upright, diverting just men from the path of rectitude, and substituting the will and favor of power for the will and interest of the people, as the rule of legislative action. He addressed the House as follows: [1] "The bill which is now the test, to which amendments are pending, is the same bill which received the assent of both Houses of Congress at the last session, with the following modifications, to suit the tender susceptibilities of gentlemen from Massachusetts. . . . There has been one section added to meet the present aspect of public affairs; that section authorizes the President, instead of pursuing the method prescribed in the bill in reference to the states where military resistance shall have been suppressed, in the event of the legislative authority under the rebellion in any rebel state taking the oath to support the Constitution of the United States, annulling their confiscation laws and ratifying the amendment proposed by this Congress to the Constitution of the United States, before military resistance shall be suppressed in such state, to recognize them as constituting the legal authority of the state, and directing him to report those facts to Congress for its assent and ratification. With these modifications, the bill which is now the test for amendment is the bill which was adopted by this House at the last session. . . .

"It is only the House itself that can reverse that judgment and impeach its assertion of its own powers. Nor need I trouble myself to answer the arguments of the gentlemen who at the last session voted for this bill, and who, in the quiet and repose of the interven-

[1] February 21, 1865: Cong. Globe, 969, 970.

ing period, have criticised in detail the language, and, not stopping there, have found in its substance that it essentially violates the principles of republican government and sanctions the enormities of the laws with which the existence of slavery has covered and defiled the statutes of every rebel state. That these discoveries should have been made since the vote of last session is quite as remarkable as that they should have been overlooked before that vote. But they were neither overlooked before nor discovered since. The vote was before a pending election. It is the will of the President which has been discovered since."

This sarcasm was directed particularly towards Dawes and Eliot, of Massachusetts. He then predicted the course events would take: that by the next December, possibly by the fourth of July, the rebellion would be ended, and sixty-five representatives and twenty-two senators from the subjugated states would be claiming admission. This consequence, which the Democrats would have witnessed with equanimity, was fraught with horror to the speaker, who exclaimed: "I am no prophet, but that is the history of next December, if this bill be defeated; and I expect it not to become a law."

Should, however, the President do what Davis averred that there was not the least reason to suppose that he desired to do, namely, treat those who held power in the South as rebels and not as governors or legislators, and then set to work to hunt out the pliant and supple "Union men," so-called, who had cringed before the storm, but who would be willing to govern their fellow-citizens under the protection of United States bayonets; should "representatives like what

Louisiana has sent here, with such a backing of votes as she has given, appear here at the doors of this hall, whose representatives are they? . . . In Louisiana they are the representatives of the bayonets of General Banks and the will of the President, as expressed in his secret letter to General Banks. If you admit such representatives, you must admit, on the same basis and under the same influences, representatives from every state from Texas to Virginia. . . . If the rebel representatives are not here in December next, you will have here servile tools of the Executive who will embarrass your legislation, humble your Congress, degrade the name of republican government for two years, and then the natural majority of the South, rising indignantly against that humiliating insult, will swamp you here with rebel representatives, and be your masters. These are their alternatives, and there is no middle ground. . . .

"Sir, my successor may vote as he pleases. But when I leave this hall, there shall be no vote from the third Congressional District of Maryland that recognizes anything but the body and mass of the people of any state as entitled to govern them, and to govern the people that I represent. And they who may wish to substitute one tenth, or any other fractional minority, for that great power of the people to govern may take, and shall take, the odium. Ay! I shall brand it upon them that in the middle of the nineteenth century, in the only free republic that the world knows, where alone the principles of popular government are the rules of authority, they have gone to the dark ages for their models, reviving the wretched examples of the most odious governments the world has ever seen, and propose to stain the national triumph by creating a wretched, low, vulgar, corrupt, and cowardly oligarchy to govern the freemen of the United States — the national arms to guarantee and enforce their oppressions. Not by my vote, sir; not by my vote!"

Thus bitterly, and not without a touch of pathos, did the author of that which was known far and wide as "the Reconstruction Bill" breathe his forebodings of the future and his defiance of the President. He and Thaddeus Stevens had united in moving the resolution for a special committee, and there is little doubt that, though they did not agree in their views respecting the relations of the seceded states with the federal government, they were united in their distrust of President Lincoln, and that Davis joined forces with Stevens in order to wrest from what he considered Lincoln's usurping hand the power over the states that were being reduced to submission.[1] The Amnesty Proclamation, with its assertion of the right of the executive branch of the government to reconstruct the seceded states, had startled, not the Democrats alone who had made it their business to cry aloud, but it had startled and shocked the constitutionists, who, like Davis, still lingered in the Republican party, and it had roused to wrath the congressional radicals whose domain the President had invaded. Davis could not break with a party in which lay his sole influence, nor could he follow the crowd who had "discovered the will of the President" since

[1] On the final vote to lay the bill and amendments on the table, Stevens voted to do so. Stevens, in his speech in the House, May 2, 1864: Cong. Globe, 2042, bitterly resented Blair's insinuations of his hostility to the President; but he protested too much, and he damned the President with faint praise.

the presidential election. Trumbull and Cowan were fast bringing upon themselves the hatred of the men from whom they were daily getting farther and farther away; Hale had not secured the thrift that follows fawning: Davis could not and would not tempt their fate. Nor could he join the radicals. He had nowhere to go, and he was alone. A lover of the Constitution, albeit an indiscreet one, he was out of place among those who were its enemies: he made the mistake of supposing that good intentions were good principles; he awoke to find that he had read the Constitution wrong, and that his allies had not sought his company for the good that was in it, but for the uses to which they could put him. The alliance between Thaddeus Stevens and Henry Winter Davis was an unnatural alliance, and all men but Davis saw what it really amounted to. The scales fell from his eyes when he beheld Dawes and Eliot in the enemy's camp, and heard them protest that they "had never known the man." This was the last great effort of Henry Winter Davis' life, and it ended in bitter failure; he could hardly be said to have outlived his disappointment, for with the closing year he died.

The bill was laid on the table by a vote of ninety-one to sixty-four. The Democrats, who had nothing but a choice of evils, voted with the radicals, inasmuch as the negro suffrage, admitted in the seventh section, was restricted, and because they could not recognize the President's unconstitutional reorganization of Louisiana and Arkansas. The next day, Ashley endeavored again to get his substitute before the House, but he was unsuccessful, and the bill was laid on the table by a vote of eighty to sixty-five; not voting, thirty-seven. This was on the twenty-second of February, and the session closed on the fourth of March without further attempt to pass the Reconstruction Bill. Throughout the whole matter, Ashley, as the witty Cox did not fail to point out, was on both sides of the fence at once. He inserted the word "white," yet declared to the House that he would vote to strike it out, and he inserted a clause for the recognition of Louisiana and Arkansas, and yet avowed his disbelief that their reorganization was a valid one. The fact is, that Ashley, who was bent upon negro suffrage, was willing to sacrifice anything in the present, so long as he had reason to hope for success in the future. "I do not expect to pass this bill now," said he. "At the next session, when a new Congress fresh from the people shall have assembled, with the nation and its representatives far in advance of the present Congress, I hope to pass even a better bill. I know that the loyal people of this country will never be guilty of the infamy of inviting the loyal blacks to unite with them in fighting our battles, and after our triumph deny these loyal blacks political rights." [1]

[1] 38th Cong.; Cong. Globe, 1002.

CHAPTER XVI.

ENFORCEMENT OF THE PRESIDENTIAL PLAN OF RECONSTRUCTION.

The reconstruction of Tennessee — North Carolina — Arkansas — Louisiana.

As the reconstruction of the states lately in rebellion originated during the first administration of President Lincoln, and at the time of his death was in process of operation, a brief survey of the progress made under his auspices is necessary to understand the part performed by his successor, and the attitude assumed towards "the Presidential plan" by Congress.

The first one of the rebellious states that was occupied by the United States forces to such an extent as to compel the federal government to consider the subject of actual reconstruction was Tennessee. At the close of February, 1862, the Confederates abandoned Nashville, the capital of the state, and on the twenty-fifth, the federal army occupied this city. In anticipation of this occupation, Gen. U. S. Grant had issued, on the twenty-second, an order declaring that no courts would be allowed to act under state authority, but that all cases coming within reach of the military arm would be adjudicated by the authorities which the United States government had established. Martial law was declared to extend over west Tennessee, but whenever a number of citizens sufficient to maintain law and order over the territory should return to their allegiance, this military restriction would be removed. The President about the same time appointed Andrew Johnson, a former governor of Tennessee, and at this moment holding a seat as a member of the United States Senate from this state, military governor, with the rank of brigadier-general.

Thus the first of the military governors, and the first agent of the President in the work of reconstruction, was the man who was to succeed Mr. Lincoln, and who was to take up this work as it fell from his hands. This nomination was confirmed by the Senate on March fifth, and on the twelfth the new official reached Nashville, and on the next evening made an address, which was afterwards printed and circulated under the style of "An Appeal to the People of Tennessee."

It is to be noted that the regular governor of the state, Harris, being a Confederate, had, with his officials and the state archives, left the capital for military reasons and betaken himself to Memphis, whither he had summoned the legislature. This had left the parts of the state which were in the occupation of the federal forces without administration of state government. In his address or appeal, Johnson set forth these facts, asserting that the state government had disappeared; that the executive had abdicated; that the legislature had dissolved; and that the judiciary was in abeyance, and that the national government was at this moment attempting to discharge its obligations to guarantee to every state a republican form of government. The reason and purpose of his appointment as military governor should be given in his own words, which are as follows: "I have been appointed military governor for the time being, to preserve the public property of the United States, to give the protection of law actively enforced to her citizens, and as speedily as may be, to restore her government to the same condition as before the existing rebellion."

The great prominence attained afterwards by Johnson as "the Reconstruction President," and the fact that he himself was the very first man commissioned to undertake the work of rehabilitation, lends to his words weight that otherwise they might not have. It is the future of reconstruction (now past history) that reflects so great importance upon every word and action of the military governor of Tennessee. The fact, then, that he asserted that he had been appointed on account of "the *absence* of the *regular* and *established state authorities*," and for the purpose of "*restoring* her government to the *same condition as before the existing rebellion*," and that his appointment was a "*military*" one, becomes of the highest importance when uttered by one who, at a later day, when he fell heir to a system of reconstruction of which his own appointment was the inception, appointed *provisional* governors, because the rebellious states "had been deprived of all civil government," and "for the purpose of enabling the *loyal* people of said state to organize a state government." For it shows that at the time of his appointment as governor the *restoration* of the ancient government was still the object of President Lincoln's exertion, and that Johnson's military character was the use of the military power merely as an instrument to attain this end. That his appointment was made with the consent of the Senate first being had, proves conclusively that President Lincoln, as late as the spring of 1862, had not reached the point of appropriating to his sole use the powers involved in the work of reconstruction. Indeed, the natural inference is that no "Presidential Plan" of reconstruction was yet present in the mind of the President, that "restoration" of the old state governments was still the primary object of federal endeavor, and that the part of the executive branch of the government was merely to perform such duties as would enable the restored sections to send senators and representatives to Washington, where the rest of restoration would be effected or denied by Congress, according to its decision upon the admission or rejection of these members to their respective houses.

The vacated offices were filled by his appointment for the reason that "otherwise anarchy would prevail." [1]

[1] It may be well to reproduce here Johnson's views of the relations in which the individual citizens of the state stood towards the federal government: "Those," said he, "who through the dark and weary night of the rebellion have maintained their allegiance to the federal government will be honored. The erring and misguided will be welcomed on their return. And while it may become necessary, in vindicating the violated majesty of the law, and in reasserting its imperial sway, to punish intelligent and conscious treason in high places, no merely retaliatory or vindictive policy will be adopted. To those, especially, who in a private, unofficial capacity have assumed an attitude of hostility to the government, a full and complete amnesty for all past acts and declarations is offered, upon the one condition of their again yielding themselves peaceful citizens to the just supremacy of the laws. This I advise them to do for their own good, and for the peace and welfare of our beloved state."

As the state of Tennessee was then the theatre of conflict between great armies, the territory under the protection of one flag or the other was constantly changing its dimensions. The conditions of active warfare did not permit the inhabitants freedom of action sufficient to warrant the reëstablishment of civil government, at least on the part of the federals, and the military governorship was not productive of the benefits hoped for at Washington. That the states in rebellion were regarded as being still in the Union, and that their ancient governments were objects of restoration, is manifest from a speech made by Governor Johnson as late as September, 1863, in which he said: "Tennessee is not out of the Union, never has been, and never will be out. The bonds of the Constitution and the federal power will always prevent that. This government is perpetual; provision is made for reforming the government and amending the Constitution, and admitting states into the Union; not for letting them out of it. . . . The United States sends an agent or a military governor, whichever you please to call him, to aid you in restoring your government. Whenever you desire, in good faith, to restore civil authority, you can do so, and a proclamation for an election will be issued as speedily as it is practicable to hold one. One by one all the agencies of your state government will be set in motion. A legislature will be elected, judges will be appointed temporarily, until you can elect them at the polls; and so of sheriffs, county-court judges, justices, and other officers, until the way is fairly open for the people, and all the parts of civil government resume their ordinary functions. This is no nice, intricate.

metaphysical question. It is a plain, common sense matter, and there is nothing in the way but obstinacy."

It was not until 1864, after the Amnesty Proclamation of the President had been issued, that the state was sufficiently free from hostilities to warrant general efforts towards restoration, and at first these efforts were altogether fruitless. In the mean time, the military governor never ceased to give assurance of his readiness to appoint officers and establish tribunals whenever the people showed a desire for civil government and were willing to sustain his appointments. At last the State Executive Committee of the Republican party issued a call to the people of Tennessee for a convention to meet in Nashville, January 9, 1865, to nominate a ticket which, it was generally understood, would consist of the names of persons to compose another and later convention. This second body was to revise the state constitution and submit it to the people for adoption or rejection. The convention met on January ninth, but instead of cutting out work for a second convention, took the whole thing upon itself, and submitted to the people amendments abolishing slavery, and prohibiting the legislature from making any law recognizing the right of property in man. A schedule was likewise adopted and submitted to the people, annulling, among other things, the ordinance of secession and all laws and ordinances of the seceded state government, and confirming the appointments of Governor Johnson. If these amendments and alterations should be adopted and ratified by a popular majority on February twenty-second, then an election for governor and members of the legislature was to be held on March fourth, upon the basis prescribed by the old act of 1852, and the legislature was to meet on April third. The convention nominated W. G. Brownlow for governor, and persons for senators and representatives in the legislature, as well as those who were to hold the elections, and then adjourned. On February twenty-second, the proceedings of the convention were ratified by the people, and the military governor made due proclamation of this fact. Brownlow and the members of the legislature nominated by the convention were chosen at the ensuing election without opposition.

On the third of April, the legislature met at Nashville, and on the fifth, ratified the pending amendment to the Constitution of the United States. In the mean time, on the fourth of March, Andrew Johnson had taken the oath of office, and had become Vice-President of the United States.

The federal forces having obtained a footing in North Carolina sufficient, in the view of President Lincoln, to warrant an attempt to set up a government under that of the United States, Edward Stanley was appointed military governor of this state, and instructions issued to him from the Secretary of War,[1] similar to those which had been given to Governor Johnson, of Tennessee. In these instructions it was said, that "the great purpose of your appointment is to reëstablish the authority of the federal government in the state of North Carolina, and to provide the means of maintaining peace and security to the loyal inhabitants of that state until *they* shall be able to establish a civil government. . . . It is not deemed

[1] May 2, 1862.

necessary to give any specific instructions, but rather to confide in your sound discretion to adopt such measures as circumstances may demand. You may rely upon the perfect confidence and full support of this department in the performance of your duties." Although the people flocked into the lines to hear what the governor had to say to them in a public address,[1] they were little persuaded by his appeals to them to resume their allegiance, and the war came to an end without any progress towards the restoration of this state being effected.

In Arkansas, John S. Phelps, of Missouri, was appointed military governor, in 1862, but it was not until January 8, 1864, that, under the encouragement given by the Amnesty Proclamation, a convention met to revise the state constitution. The amended constitution, prohibiting slavery, was ordered by the convention to be submitted to the people on March fourteenth. Isaac Murphy was appointed provisional governor, and with other officials was inducted into office on January twenty-second. On January twentieth, however, President Lincoln, in ignorance of the convention and its proceedings, on the petition of sundry citizens of the state, ordered General Steele, commander of that military district, to hold an election on the twenty-eighth of March, for the election of a governor. In this order it is distinctly declared "that it be assumed at that election, and thenceforward, *that the constitution and laws of the state as before the rebellion are in full force*, except that the constitution is so modified as to declare that there

[1] June 17.

shall be neither slavery nor involuntary servitude, . . . that, in all other respects, said election may be conducted according to said modified constitution and laws."

From this it will appear that even after the Amnesty Proclamation, President Lincoln maintained the same view of the state of Arkansas that he had done of Tennessee in 1862, viz.: that it was the ancient constitution which was to be restored. It is true that it was to be modified, and that a strict-constructionist would admit as little right in him to modify as to create a constitution, and that even to modify would be to destroy. But apart from the constitutionality or unconstitutionality of the President's act, and considering his view of reconstruction only, it is evident that, so far as Arkansas was concerned, his plan recognized the ancient constitution as existing, and that no other was present to his mind.

When President Lincoln was notified of the convention and its work, he left the matter to the commander of the department, who proceeded to hold the election, which returned 12,177 in favor of the amended constitution and 226 against it. A governor and other state and county officers were also elected, and when the legislature assembled, it chose two United States senators.

In 1862, George F. Shepley was constituted military governor of Louisiana, with the rank of brigadier-general, and, by order of the President of the United States, a Provisional Court, "which shall be a court of record for the state of Louisiana," was constituted, and Charles A. Peabody, of New York, was appointed to be the judge to hold this court. The jurisdiction of the Provisional Court was illimitable; it comprehended everything that any court can take cognizance of, and, moreover, the judgments of this judge were to be final and conclusive. His commission was described succinctly in the order itself: "A copy of this order, certified by the Secretary of War, and delivered to such judge, shall be deemed and held to be a sufficient commission." The reason given in this order for its appearance was that the insurrection had temporarily subverted and swept away the institutions of that state, including the judiciary and the judicial authorities of the Union, so that it had become necessary to hold the state in military occupation.

The necessity of holding the state in military occupation can be readily accepted, when it is recalled that, for a long time afterward, the United States could maintain its jurisdiction by force of arms only, upon a very circumscribed territory, which, nine months afterward, had become narrowed to the range of the federal cannon in the works at New Orleans. For nearly two years after the constitution of the commission, the United States, outside of their military lines, could not serve a writ in the whole state of Louisiana.

In the following year, notwithstanding the disputed occupancy of the state by armed forces, movements for the reorganization of Louisiana as a federal state were set on foot. In the early summer of 1863, a "committee appointed by the planters of the state of Louisiana" appeared at Washington, and represented to President Lincoln that they had been delegated to seek of the general government a full recognition of all the rights of the state as they existed previous to the passage of an act of secession, upon the principle of the existence of the state constitution unimpaired, and no legal act having transpired that could in any way deprive them of the advantage conferred by the constitution: that under this constitution Louisiana wished to return to its full allegiance, in the enjoyment of all rights and privileges exercised by the other states under the federal Constitution. With the view of accomplishing this object, they requested the President, as the commander-in-chief of the army, to direct the military governor to order an election on the first Monday of November, in conformity with the constitution and laws of the state, for all state and federal offices.

The President said in response that, since receiving their application, reliable information had reached him that a respectable portion of the Louisiana people desired to amend their state constitution, and that they contemplated holding a convention for that purpose. This he deemed a sufficient reason for not giving the committee the authority they were seeking to use under the existing constitution. As to an election in November, there was abundant time, without any order or proclamation from him just then.

This committee represented a party which took the position that the state was still a state in the Union, but one whose operation, so far as the federal government was concerned, had been suspended: it is also apparent that, whatever the views of the President on this subject, he was not disposed to commit himself to a recognition either of this principle or of its upholders.

In fact, the application of this committee to the

President was in counteraction of a party which had already taken initiatory steps towards reorganization, and which held the contrary notion, that the constitution of the state, the state itself, had been subverted and destroyed by the act of secession and by the war, and that the construction of an entirely new state devolved upon the conqueror of the soil. That this fundamental notion of reconstruction was not confined to the Free State, or radical party, but was entertained also by high officials that had been appointed by the President, is evident from the opinion which the Chief Justice, Peabody, himself filed during the following year, 1864, in the cases of the United States *vs.* Reiter and the United States *vs.* Louis.[1] The words of the judge are worthy of quotation, and it may be said by way of anticipation that, so far as the relations of the states in rebellion to the federal government are concerned, the decision of the Supreme Court of the United States is exactly contrary. His Honor said: "These institutions having been formed, established, and administered by the government existing previous to and at the time of the conquest confessedly hostile to the government of the United States, were the only institutions found there at the time the military authority of the United States was by force of its arms established there. By the conquest of the country, in this case as in others, the previously existing government and the power by which it was administered were subverted and swept away, and those of the conquering power were substituted in their places.

[1] These two cases, which involved the same question of the jurisdiction of the court, were considered together. McPherson's Polit. Hist. Rebellion.

This is the necessary consequence of a conquest of the country, — a transfer of the control, government, and sovereignty of it from one party to another. They may be transferred to and adopted by the new governing power, and may be used and operated by it. However there may be retained in use by the new governing power some of the features or institutions of the government which has been supplanted, it is nevertheless wholly another government, and derives its life and all its vital qualities from a new source, — the new sovereignty installed by the conquest. A conquest necessarily operates the extinguishment of the power of the party conquered in the country which is the subject of conquest, and the establishment there of the power of the conqueror. Without this there is no conquest of a country, and there can he none.

"When the power previously dominant in a country has been extinguished by that of another party, and rendered incapable of governing it further, and a new one has been established in its stead, it is both the right and the duty of the party thus coming into power to see to it that a government wholesome and salutary shall be established and administered; and as in such a case there is only one power, that of the new party succeeding, capable of giving and administering the government, it follows that it is the duty as well as the right of that power to do it.

"So the government of the United States having conquered and expelled from the territory of country theretofore known as the state of Louisiana the power by which the government of it had been theretofore administered, and having established there its own power, was bound by the laws of war, as well as the dictates of humanity, to give to the territory thus bereft a government in the place and stead of the one deposed or overthrown: such an one as should reasonably secure the safety and welcome of the people thus reduced to subjection, in some manner, not inconsistent, to be sure, with the proper interests of the governing power, and the maintenance of it in its supremacy there."

Thus far the Chief Justice of the Provisional Court: a court which, to use its own words, had "not its origin or foundation in any constitutional or legislative enactment, — was not the creature of any regularly organized constitutional or legislative body." As the President had made the judgment of this court final and conclusive, he must have done so in the confidence that not only would it administer immutable justice, but that it would reflect his ideas upon the subject of reconstruction: for otherwise, its judgments would obstruct the progress of his plan, and it is incredible that he should himself raise obstructions to his own work. Nevertheless, in sentiment, as well as in bad English, this judicial opinion smacks of Thaddeus Stevens' speech on the admission of West Virginia, and of others of his harangues. These views are clear and simple: the preëxisting government had been "subverted and swept away," and no matter how much some of its features might be drawn upon in order to constitute the new government, which it was the duty of the conqueror to bestow, this new, "wholesome and salutary government" was "wholly another government."

In Louisiana, most of the territory was in possession of the enemy, and the old and established government of the state was entirely so. The conditions were not favorable to a general expression of the people in behalf of change in the organic law, and even if such an expression could be obtained, it would be impossible for latter-day organizers to take the first step essential to the establishment of a new state, namely, to oust the old government. The citizens were in the confederate army, the confederate armies held the territory, and the confederate officials had possession of the government. Viewed from the federal standpoint, the state of Louisiana presented a very restricted theatre of politics: "The city of New Orleans," said General Banks in the spring of 1864, "is really the state of Louisiana;" and it seems as if Chief Justice Peabody would have exhibited greater deference to the reality of the situation if he had forborne to claim jurisdiction on the ground that *the state* of Louisiana had been conquered, or that the preëxisting government (which was then in operation at Shreveport) had been "subverted and swept away."

There being no constitutional way open to a general expression of the people respecting a change of government, it was necessary for unofficial persons to move in the matter and to adopt extraordinary means. We have seen that one way was a delegation "of planters" to present themselves to the President, and it has been remarked already that this movement was done in order to counteract another then on foot. This primary movement was one undertaken by the "Free State General Committee," which was a committee representing the different Union associations of the city of New Orleans and the adjoining parish of Jefferson. This committee, of which Thomas J. Durant was chairman, submitted its plans to the Military Governor, Shepley, who approved them, and who agreed to order a registration of voters, which, under the laws in force previous to the secession of the state, was exacted in New Orleans only. But this registration was to have no reference to old laws: it was to be upon a new system requiring an oath of allegiance, and it was to extend into the country parishes. The governor kept his word and ordered the registration, which was suspended, however, by a power the Executive had not consulted, the enemy.

The principle at issue between the two parties, the "planters" or conservatives, and the Free State men or radicals, can easily be guessed: It was whether the ancient state government was the true and present government, or no. If it were, then the constitution of 1852 was still in force, because the ordinance of secession and the constitution of 1861, presented by the confederate convention, were void: if it were not, then the constitution of 1852, with its amendments of 1861, had been overthrown by the rebellion of the people of the state, and the subsequent "conquest" had not restored the ancient political institutions. The war "has converted into dust and ashes all the constitutions which Louisiana has ever made," said a radical editor, who expressed the feelings of his party by declaring that the war was nothing but a conflict of the ideas of liberty and slavery, that there would be neither progress nor regress until this conflict was settled, and that a convention should be called as soon as possible, to declare that Louisiana then was and forever would be a free state.

The validity of the steps taken has been greatly disputed, and many of them are clouded with doubt. There was much crimination and recrimination. The

Free State men fell out with the President. They asserted that when General Shepley took their plan to Washington, it had been approved in a cabinet meeting, accepted as the plan upon which the Executive was to act, and that an order had actually issued from the War Department to the General, as Military Governor, to carry the scheme into effect. This they declared had occurred in August, and that not only toward the end of this month the President had written to General Banks approving of the registration and expressing the hope that the work of the convention would be finished in time to hold the elections before the next session of Congress, but that in October he had complained that matters were going too slow, and that, in view of the military situation in Louisiana, he would recognize a state government organized by any part of the population under federal control. Nothing, however, was done; no general election was held, though it was asserted that a few parishes had voted, and persons claiming to have been elected members of Congress actually appeared at Washington: but they were rejected.

The registration had proceeded from time to time, when, to the consternation of the Free State party, the President suddenly took the matter of reconstruction in Louisiana entirely into his own hands. The affiliation of these radicals with the radical faction in Congress, whose alienation from the President had now become a matter of notoriety, would have been reason sufficient for the President's action; there was, however, an all-controlling one in the fact that he had recently issued the Amnesty Proclamation, and by this Proclamation had taken upon himself the work of reconstruction wherever practicable.

CHAPTER XVII.

ENFORCEMENT OF THE PRESIDENTIAL PLAN OF RECONSTRUCTION — CONTINUED.

The reconstruction of Louisiana continued.

On the eighth of January, 1864, General Banks, commander of this department, announced that he should issue a proclamation ordering an election of state officers; and in spite of appeals to him to permit the Free State men to go on with their convention, he did so, on the eleventh of the same month. This proclamation, which has been applauded and excoriated by Congress, was addressed to the people of Louisiana, and set forth that, in pursuance of authority vested in him, the commander of the department, by the President of the United States, and being assured that more than one tenth of the voters had taken the oath of allegiance, he invited the loyal citizens of the state qualified to vote, to assemble on the twenty-second of February and elect a governor and other state officers, who, for the time being, should constitute the civil government of the state, *under the constitution and laws of Louisiana*, except so much as relate to slavery, "which being inconsistent with the present condition of public affairs, and plainly inapplicable to any class of persons now existing within its limits, must be suspended, and they are thereupon and hereby declared to be inoperative and void." The oath of allegiance prescribed by the President's Amnesty Proclamation, with the condition affixed to the election franchise by the constitution of Louisiana (that is to say, that those entitled to this franchise should be white), would constitute the qualifications of voters. The registration, so far as it was not inconsistent with the proclamations or other orders of the President, was confirmed, and an election of delegates to a convention for the revision of the constitution, to be held on the first Monday of April, 1864, was announced, and it was stated that arrangements would be made for the early election of members of Congress for the state. An assertion then followed, which, however true the fact it contained might be, shocked the conservative sentiment of the North, and which, when the radicals in Congress espoused the cause of the Free State men, served as a text for many a radical denunciation. Why this assertion should have stirred the feeling of the people so much can be accounted for only by the well-known quality in human nature, which causes men to be shocked by the expression of a truth, though they have become perfectly reconciled to the truth itself. Everybody, north and south, knew perfectly well that the federal possession of any part of Louisiana was purely a military one; they knew that any attempt to organize a government must be absolutely dependent upon federal bayonets for support. In those days it took the people very little while to become familiar with the fact that when the federal government obtained a footing on southern territory, it kept it at the cost of military vigilance and military law; yet when General Banks abrogated so much of the constitution and laws of a sovereign state as seemed good to him, and followed up this iconoclasm with the blunt assertion that "the fundamental law of the state is martial law," indignation burst out everywhere in the North, except at the White House, and among the adherents of the President. To say, however, that this indignation was general is to say too much. Outside of the Democratic party, Mr. Lincoln had the confidence of the middle and lower classes: there was his strength, and from these classes little or nothing was heard in protestation. The fact is, that these classes hardly knew what was going on in such a far-away place as a gulf state, and if they did, they had no appreciation of an event so significant as the subversion of a state government and the erection of another on its ruins by military force: throughout the Republican party, on the contrary, the avowal that the fundamental law of the state was martial law was accepted without cavil. The radical faction in Congress had no popular following outside of their scattered districts, the Democrats were not hearkened to, and thus the mass of the people comprised those whose knowledge of constitutional procedure was indicated by the expression, "Lincoln will do what is right." But it was quite different in Congress. There the conservative Republican redoubled his efforts to wrest the power of reconstruction from the President's grasp: there the Radical sunk the fact that the acts of the conqueror were in consonance with his own teachings, in the exasperating one that the negro was not made a citizen, and reviled the President: and there the Democrat pointed to this order of Banks as a realization of his oft-told prophecies.

As for the Free State men in Louisiana, they cried aloud in the bitterness of their disappointment, and told some truths about Banks and his order. They protested that, in asserting the supremacy of martial law, this general had declared it to be superior to the Constitution, and that he could amend this instrument when and how he pleased; that the slavery laws which he had rendered inoperative had not been touched by the President, and that his assumptions of power were dangerous to the liberties of the people and to republican government.

When the election was held on February 22, 1864, and Michael Hahn, the government nominee, had been returned Governor by an overwhelming majority, the Free State men declared that the result of the election was merely the registration of a military edict, and was worthy of no respect from the representatives and Executive of the nation; that no state government had been created by this election, nor had one been erected in conformity with the Amnesty Proclamation. They set forth these views at length in a protest, which concluded as follows: "The commanding general says that he will order the election of members of a constitutional convention, and that he will, by a subsequent order, fix the basis of representation, the number of delegates, and the details of the election. This will put the whole matter under military control, and the experience of the last election shows that only such a convention can be had as the overshadowing influence of the military authority will permit. Under an election thus ordered, and a constitution thus established, a republican form of government cannot be formed. It is simply a fraud to call it the reëstablishment of a state government. In these circumstances, the only course left to the truly loyal citizens of Louisiana is to protest against the recognition of this pretended government, and to appeal to the calm judgment of the nation to procure such action from Congress as will forbid military commanders to usurp the powers which belong to Congress alone, or to the loyal people of Louisiana." It will not escape the notice of the reader that this lamentation emanated from the party which in the beginning of its attempts to form a civil government had invoked the help of King Stork.

On February 3, 1864, Banks issued his general regulations concerning plantation labor, and on February twenty-second, the election, as has been seen, was held. The inauguration of Governor Hahn took place on March fourth, and on the fifteenth, the following letter was addressed to him from Washington; it is brief and emphatic: "Until further orders, you are hereby invested with the powers exercised hitherto by the Military Governor of Louisiana. Yours truly, Abraham Lincoln." The President seems to have taken upon himself to make good the assertion of the Free State radicals, that "the result of the election was merely the registration of a military edict."

General Banks having issued an order, on March eleventh, for an election of delegates to a convention to be held "for the revision and amendment of the constitution of Louisiana," Governor Hahn, on the sixteenth, made proclamation to the sheriffs, and the election was had on the twenty-eighth. It assembled on the sixth of April, and after a session of seventy-eight days, adjourned on July twenty-fifth; whereupon the governor at once issued a proclamation, appointing September fifth as the day on which the vote of the people should be taken upon the adoption or rejection of the constitution which had been submitted by the convention. This constitution ordained the emancipation of the slaves, and prohibited property in man forever. It made all men equal before the law, but did not give the negro the elective franchise. This constitution was adopted by a vote of 6836 to 1566. In the city of New Orleans, the vote stood 4664 to 789. The government was organized on the third of October.

At this election five congressmen were chosen,[1] as well as members of the legislature. The members of the legislature were almost all Free State men, and this legislature subsequently chose seven electors of President and Vice-President. How restricted in territory the jurisdiction of these officials and these bodies was, may be inferred from the fact that more than three fourths of the state was in possession of the enemy: and how slow the task of reconstruction, and how slight the deference that was paid to this "civil government," is apparent from an order of General Hurlbut, commander of the district. In this order he makes use of the following language: "Upon the

[1] In 1862, two congressmen, Messrs. Hahn and Flanders, were elected from the New Orleans districts, according to instructions for an election from President Lincoln to the general commanding. These persons were admitted to their seats in the House of Representatives by a vote taken February 9, 1863. They were elected for unexpired terms which expired on the 4th of March ensuing. At the next session of Congress two others appeared, but were not recognized as members after the organization of the House.

official report of the Attorney-General of the state of Louisiana, that the ordinary courts of justice are insufficient to punish the offenders named by him, and in consideration that *the state government and courts of Louisiana owe their present existence to military authority*, it is ordered that . . . those arrested for peculation and other offences be sent for trial before the Military Commission now in session in the city of New Orleans . . . and that the Attorney-General of the state of Louisiana be admitted to appear before said commissioner as public prosecutor." Thus, on December 27, 1864, the date of this order, the assertion of the radicals, that "under an election thus ordered, and a constitution thus established, a republican form of government cannot be formed," was verified to the letter.

The five members of Congress elected on the fifth of September, 1864, duly presented themselves at Washington for admission to the House of Representatives; their credentials were referred to the committee of elections, accompanied by a petition remonstrating against the reception of these men as members.[1] There was also a remonstrance against the representation of Louisiana in the Electoral College, for the choice of President and Vice-President of the United States. The legislature had likewise elected two senators of the United States, who presented themselves at Washington but were not admitted. As for the five congressmen, the committee of elections in the House reported that their election depended upon the effect which the House was disposed to give to the efforts to reorganize a

[1] 2d Sess. 38th Cong.: Cong. Globe, Part I. 2.

state government in Louisiana; that neither a law of the state nor of the nation to meet the case was possible, and it followed that the power to restore a lost state government in Louisiana existed nowhere unless in "the people," the original source of all political power in this country; that the people cannot be required to conform to any particular mode, for that presupposes a power to prescribe outside of themselves, which it has been seen does not exist. Therefore, it followed further that if this work of reorganizing and reëstablishing a state government was the work of the people, it was the legitimate exercise of an inalienable and inherent right, and, if republican in form, was entitled not only to recognition, but also to the "guarantee" of the constitution. The committee then inquired how far this effort to restore constitutional government had been the work of the people of Louisiana, and make this astonishing statement: that "the evidence before the committee, and all the information they could obtain, satisfied them that the movement which resulted in the election of state officers, the calling of a convention to revise and amend the constitution, the ratification of such a revisal and amendment by popular vote, and the subsequent election of representatives in Congress, was not only participated in by a large majority, almost approaching to unanimity, but that the loyal people constituted a majority of all the people of the state." They also added that the election was held under the auspices of a new state organization which had arisen from the ruins of the old, in as much conformity to law as the nature of the case would permit.

The conclusions of the committee did not meet the

adoption which is the good fortune of statements that prove themselves. In fact, where they were not received with indignation, they were held in derision. In Louisiana itself, the acting governor, Wells, who had taken the helm, on Hahn receiving an election to the United States Senate, issued a proclamation on May 3, 1865, which reveals very clearly what he thought of the voters in these elections. He says that according to the official statement of the Register of voters for the city of New Orleans, nearly five thousand persons were at that time registered on the books who did not possess the qualifications required by law to become voters. He thereupon declared the old books for the city of New Orleans to be closed from that date, and the registration of all persons contained therein, as well as all certificates issued by virtue of the records and conferring the right to vote, to be null and void; and he ordered a new set of books to be opened, and a new registration to be made. This brought down upon him the censure of General Banks.

As for the members of Congress themselves, incredulity and derision divided the honors when it was gravely declared that the applicants for admission had been elected by a large majority of the people. That the vote approached unanimity was apparent: but why should it not be so? That it constituted a large majority was a statement, the audacity of which could be surpassed only by the assertion, made in the same breath, that "the loyal people constituted a majority of all the people of the state." When Wells' proclamation was issued, the doubters, or rather the scoffers, received it as proof of the truth of their suspicions. The vote of the whole city of New Orleans on the constitution was 5453, and of these 789 were against and 4664 for adoption. The scoffers declared that the 4664 was the riff-raff fraudulently registered, and that the discrepancy of 336 accounted for the halt, the blind, and those who were sick and in jail.

The House took no further action on the matter than to vote rather surlily a sum of money from the applicants sufficient to pay their expenses while in Washington and on their way home. "If we make such large payments to men coming here in this way, we do not know when they will stop coming," said Washburne. "I ask the gentleman to strike out the words 'claimants for seats,'" cried Thaddeus Stevens. "I do not want to recognize the idea that anybody on earth thinks that these men are entitled to seats."[1]

The "reconstruction" of Louisiana in 1864 was the first instance of the kind under the plan set forth in the Amnesty Proclamation; and the first fruits of this plan were scanned with eager and critical gaze throughout the Union. The conclusion was extremely disappointing. The flagrant use of the military, the character of the "loyal people of Louisiana," too plainly recognized as the scum of New Orleans, a city with the worst of reputations in respect to the vicious element that haunts all cities, the fraudulent registration by which this class was turned into voters, the unblushing way in which the military commander threatened these voters if they were slow to execute his will, the lightness of the vote which showed that the reputable classes had either rejected amnesty or

[1] Cong. Globe, 2d Sess. 38th Congress, 1395.

had refused to go to the polls, the knowledge that what was done in the name of the state was applicable only to the narrow limits of a single city, — all this was more than disappointing, it was shocking. Was it for this that the country had condoned the use by the President of powers which belonged only to the people and to the states in Congress assembled? The organization of camp-followers and of a city's riff-raff, the dubbing them with the title of "the truly loyal people," the giving them the name of "citizens," and the calling their institution of a military despotism the "reconstruction of a sovereign state," was too much. It did not take the keen-witted people of the North long to see this travesty on government in its true light, and in spite of the fear of suppression, the press began to bristle with sarcasm and to jeer at this scarecrow of a state.

It was not the intelligent few, however, who could make their voices heard with effect, nor was it the small minority of fearless journals that could rouse a people always ready to shift from their shoulders the responsibility of being free men. It was in Congress that the truth of the matter was exposed, and this not so much by the denunciation of the opposition, as by the quarrelling and bickering of contending factions. The truth about Louisiana owed more to the quarrels that were going on within the Republican party than it did to anything else.

The reconstruction of Louisiana by the President and General Banks did more to precipitate a conflict upon Congress than any other single thing had yet done. This conflict soon became apparent in many things, but in nothing so much as in the debate in the

House on the bill to guarantee to certain states whose governments had been usurped or overthrown a republican form of government, and in the Senate, in the debate on the joint resolution declaring that the eleven rebellious states were not entitled to representation in the Electoral College,[1] and also in the debate in the Senate on the joint resolution recognizing the government of the state of Louisiana.[2] This strife would have occurred sooner or later, because the causes of strife existed within the Republican party; but it occurred when it did because, when the Amnesty Proclamation laid before the country the Presidential Plan of reconstruction, the congressional party for the first time was made aware of the extent of the President's assumption of the powers of Congress, of the means by which he proposed to secure these powers in his own hands, and of his intentions in these respects for future action. The situation was like that existing when an army has been watching the gradual encroachment of its opponent, but has not yet seen any movement which betrayed the force and intention of the enemy. When, at last, a decisive movement takes place, then it becomes as active in defence or in counteracting as its antagonist is in invasion: both camps are astir. So it was in this instance: the congressional faction had been for a long while eying the President askance; he had been assuming too much power by proclamation in the South, and he had been assuming too much power by direct and personal government in the North. So long as the sympathizers with rebellion, the Democrats, and those not belong-

[1] February 1, 1865: Cong. Globe, 533 *et seq.*

[2] February 23, 1865: Cong. Globe, 1061 *et seq.*

ing to the Republican party, were objects of the presidential suspicion and discipline in the North, the congressional faction had been deaf to the outcries of the victims, and had made it their first business, on meeting at Washington, to pass acts condoning these outrages and exculpating the President. But that which the Democrats on the floor of Congress and on the stump had long and constantly predicted, and had warned the Republicans to heed, at last took place, — the President exceeded his powers with respect to reconstruction, and turned his back upon Congress. This usurpation of the legislative power was first announced emphatically, though indirectly, by the Amnesty Proclamation, and this proclamation became at once the cause of opposition in Congress by members of the President's own political party. When the details of the Louisiana reorganization came to hand, it became evident that speedy opposition was necessary, and that this opposition, to be effective, must not stop short of ignoring what the President had done already, but should set a bar upon any like procedure in the future. This was the first instance of Presidential reconstruction, and it had ended in that state in setting up a military despotism, of which the President was the head. There were ten more states in which he could do the same thing, so that, unless prevented, the end of reconstruction of the rebellious states would find him the virtual dictator of the whole South. This would not be the end of the matter. He had interfered as readily in the affairs of the Border States as he had done in Louisiana, and in the same character, to wit, that of commander-in-chief.[1]

[1] Senator Powell: Cong. Globe, 2d Sess. 38th Congress, 557.

He had sustained interference by force of arms in these states with the same readiness which he had exhibited in Arkansas and Louisiana, and the alarmed imagination of senators and representatives pictured him absolute military dictator of the whole country south of Mason and Dixon's line; while in the North, the closed newspaper offices and the prisons crowded with political prisoners, against numbers of whom there had been no charges, showed what they might expect of one so powerful, and of whose readiness to exert unconstitutional power there now could be no doubt. In the three years and a quarter in which he had been President, his course had been strewn with unconstitutional acts; he had left few precedents lacking for a future usurper; the people not only had ratified these acts and these precedents by an immense majority, as the people in all times and places have done when they have had the opportunity, but they had given him four years more in which to complete his work; and worse than all, he had not only usurped the powers of the people and of the states, but he had shown his contempt of Congress in a manner not to be mistaken. Already, they saw him at the head of his troops before the Speaker's chair, and heard him cry, "Take away that bauble!"

Such were the imaginings of the President's own party members in Congress. The radicals mistrusted him because he had not gone far enough and had not enfranchised, as well as liberated, the Louisiana negro; the conservatives, if such a term can be applied to those of the Republican party who were not radical abolitionists, opposed him because he had taken to himself the exercise of power which properly belonged to them. The third faction, the President's own following in Congress, had been greatly strengthened in spirit and number by the result of the election and the consequent new lease of power, and by the obvious wane of the rebellion: this faction included those who were known as War Democrats. The President, therefore, had no mean support in the Senate and in the House, particularly when it is considered that the radicals were always ready to sustain any of his measures which affected the South and were not repugnant to their views of the slave question.

CHAPTER XVIII.

ENFORCEMENT OF THE PRESIDENTIAL PLAN OF RECONSTRUCTION — CONTINUED.

The reconstruction of Louisiana continued — Debate in the Senate upon the recognition of Louisiana as a state.

On the eighteenth of February, 1865, the Committee on the Judiciary, to whom were referred the credentials of two persons claiming seats as senators from the state of Louisiana, made a report on the subject to the Senate, accompanied by a joint resolution which recognized the new government of that state as the legitimate government,[1] and on the twenty-third of the same month, this resolution was considered as in committee of the whole.[2]

The debate lasted several days, and before it terminated, many of the leading members of the Senate had taken part in a discussion which was not confined to the conditions of the state of Louisiana, but which embraced even the general question, What is a state? In this discussion the line was drawn sharply between the presidential faction, on one side, and the allied congressional and radical factions on the other; the former being led by Trumbull, Henderson, Pomeroy, and Doolittle, and the latter by Sumner, Howard, and Wade.

In answer to a question why Arkansas was excluded

[1] Cong. Globe, 903.

[2] Cong. Globe, 1011.

from the resolution, Trumbull, the chairman of the committee reporting, said that the facts were not precisely the same in the two states, but that the principle upon which the committee acted, if adopted, would be applicable to any other state. Sumner at once moved to strike out all of the resolution after the enacting clause, and to insert a resolution that neither the people nor the legislature of a state proclaimed to be in insurrection should elect representatives or senators to Congress until the President should have proclaimed that armed hostility had ceased in that state, nor until its people had adopted a constitution not repugnant to the Constitution and laws of the United States; nor until, by a law of Congress, such state should have been declared to be entitled to representation in Congress. Trumbull objected to this, because, being prospective, it would not apply to the case in hand, and because it would put it in the power of the President to keep out a state forever by refusing to issue his proclamation. The Senate thought so, too, and rejected Sumner's amendment by an emphatic majority.

On the day following, Powell continued the debate[1] by saying that the object in recognizing Louisiana at that time was to allow the state to vote for the proposed amendment to the Constitution of the United States.[2] The admission of senators and representatives from Louisiana would be an immediate result of the passage of the resolution.

[1] Cong. Globe, 2d Sess. 38th Cong., 1061.

[2] "Article XIII. Sec. I. Neither slavery nor involuntary servitude, except as a punishment for crime whereof the party shall have been duly convicted, shall exist within the United States, or any place subject to their jurisdiction."

Powell, in a forcible address, objected to the recognition on the grounds that the state had never been out of the Union, and therefore it needed no recognition; for whenever the facts were established that the people of the state had ceased resistance to the federal government, and had determined to be loyal, and a majority of them had elected their senators and representatives, Congress should then admit these senators and representatives. But he was going to show that beyond the possibility of a doubt the people of Louisiana who formed this state government had not asked of their own free volition, but that they had been coerced to do what they did, and that the constitution presented as the fundamental law was not a constitution made by the free suffrages of the people of that state.

This he proceeded to do at length by taking up the test oath prescribed by the President and exposing its "degrading" character and its unconstitutionality. Its unconstitutionality spoke for itself; the oath was a condition precedent to becoming a qualified voter, and one feature of it was that a man swore to support all the proclamations of the President already issued on the subject of slavery, and all the proclamations that he might make on that subject in the future. No one who was a free man, and who understood his civil and political rights, would so prostitute himself as to take that oath; there was a large class of loyal men in Louisiana who refused to take it; all such were excluded from voting. No senator ever had defended that odious feature. He then discussed the one tenth minimum of loyalty which the President had laid down as a fundamental principle of reconstruction, and observed that one tenth of the voters in 1860, was much less than one tenth of those qualified to vote in the state, because there never had been an election in which all the voters of a state had gone to the polls and cast their votes. At the very threshold, then, the principle that majorities should rule was repudiated, for it was not the majority, but less than one tenth of the voters, that was to rule. When the President prescribed the qualifications of voters, he had amended the constitution of the state of Louisiana as it existed before the rebellion, and to which his orders had referred; for the qualifications of voters were prescribed in that instrument.

Powell then turned his attention to the part performed by General Banks. There is no need of recapitulating the account of Banks' misdeeds, but Powell cast a ray of light upon one feature of the General's procedure which should not be overlooked. He said that when Banks made his statement before the Judiciary Committee, which he did with a great flourish of trumpets, and seeming to be animated with that kind of zeal which would entitle him to be called, in the language of lawyers, "a swift witness," he was requested to lay before the committee all his proclamations and orders. Among these should have been a second proclamation which the General had issued; but it was not forthcoming. Then Powell had a resolution passed by the Senate, calling upon the President to send it to that body; but by this time Lincoln complied with the requests of Congress when he felt like doing so, and when he did not feel in the humor, he paid no attention to them. In this instance the request of the Senate fell on a deaf ear; the President gave no heed to that body. Now Powell remembered having read the order soon after it was issued, and in a report, made by a committee in the House of Representatives in a Louisiana election case, he found an extract from Banks' order which was issued a little before the election. Bearing in mind that Banks had said before the Committee that he desired to state, in the most unqualified terms, that "no effort whatever was made on the part of the military authorities to influence the citizens of the state either in the selection of candidates or in the election of officers, and that the direct influence of the government of the United States was less in Louisiana than in the election probably of any other state of the Union," the following extract from the order in question certainly justifies Powell in asserting that Banks was "wholly unworthy of confidence when he testified concerning this matter." The extract from the order is as follows: "Those who have exercised, or are entitled to the rights of citizens of the United States, *will be required to participate* in the measures necessary for the reëstablishment of civil government. . . . *Indifference will be treated as a crime and faction as treason.*"[1] "No wonder," exclaimed Powell, "that Banks never brought to our view that odious order in which he threatens these people with punishment if they do not come and vote; for that is the plain English of it."

Powell was not quite correct in giving the source of this astonishing extract. It is to be found, not in a second proclamation, but in the order relative to the regulation of labor[2] which is prescribed or suggested

[1] The italics are not Banks'.

[2] General Orders No. 23.

in the Amnesty Proclamation, and which in this case was issued by General Banks.[1] Except those clauses which relate directly to the military, the order is really addressed to master and man, and it adds force to Powell's interpretation, that those whom it was designed to affect were, in great majority, the semi-barbarous slaves lately emancipated by military service and special order. It consists of twenty-five paragraphs, of which the concluding seven bristle with generalities, and, as may be readily imagined of Banks, are sophomoric in style, and are hardly worth the trouble of picking to pieces. In the midst of this nebulous formation appears the nucleus contained in the foregoing extract. It certainly is direful, but it must not be forgotten that when Banks prodded with the bayonet, he never failed to accompany the infliction by telling the victims that civil government must and would prevail some day or other. This very paragraph closed with an instance in point: "War can never cease except as civil governments crush out contest, and secure the supremacy of moral over physical power. The yellow harvest must wave over the crimson field of blood, and the representatives of the people displace the agents of purely military power." It is surprising that, when the Powells in Congress exposed Banks' subordination of the civil to the military authority, the Doolittles and Howes did not point to the moral suasion with which he accompanied the thrusts of his bayonets.

Henderson followed. It will be remembered that he had strenuously maintained that the rebellious states had never been out of the Union, and during the

[1] February 3, 1864; An. Cycl. 1863, 596.

course of his remarks there ensued a colloquy between him and Sumner, in which the senator from Massachusetts denied that he had ever stated that any act of secession took a state out, and that he had always said just the contrary, — the government of the state had been subverted by secession. "No act of secession can take a state out of this Union, but the state continues under the Constitution of the United States, subject to all its requirements and behests. The government of the state is subverted by secession."[1] This admission in direct contradiction of his own resolution was extracted from the senator, and not without persistent effort, by Henderson, of Missouri, to whom Sumner further asserted that, under the constitutional provision for a guarantee of a republican form of government, "it is the bounden duty of the United States, by act of Congress, to guarantee complete freedom to every citizen, and immunity from all oppression, and absolute equality before the law. No government that does not guarantee these things can be recognized as republican in form according to the theory of the Constitution of the United States, if the United States are called to enforce the constitutional guarantee."[2] Thus Sumner, a radical of the radicals, abandoned the position he had formerly occupied along with Stevens, respecting the *status* of the insurrectionary states. He was compelled to acknowledge that they were still in the Union; nevertheless, he continued to claim for Congress the power of settling the question, and, most significant of all, he proclaimed to the world that henceforth a republican form of government was incompatible with the existence of slavery, and where

[1] Cong. Globe, 1067. [2] Id.: id.

that institution was a feature of the state, this state should not be recognized: thus he saved his radicalism.

Henderson kept pressing Sumner, and at length asked him if Congress could interfere with the right of suffrage in one of the states of the Union. Sumner evaded the question by saying that, *at the present time*, under the guarantee clause, it was the bounden duty of the United States by act of Congress to guarantee complete freedom to every citizen and absolute equality before the law. No government that does not guarantee these things could be recognized as republican. "If the loyal men, white and black, recognize it, then it will be republican in form." Whereupon Henderson quoted Madison's limitation of this guarantee to a preëxisting government, and also the following passage from the Federalist[1] by the same authority: "As long, therefore, as the existing republican forms are continued by the states, they are guaranteed by the federal constitution. Whenever the states may choose to substitute other republican forms, they have a right to do so, and to claim the federal guarantee for the latter." Henderson, nevertheless, sustained the presidential reorganization of Louisiana. He thought that when a majority of the people of a state pass an ordinance of secession, one of three things must be true: either this ordinance is valid; or the loyal minority have a right to institute government for their protection; or, lastly, Congress may proceed to govern the state for all time to come, with the hard and oppressive hand of military rule. He believed in the loyal minority instituting a government for its

[1] Number 43.

protection, and, in the case of Louisiana, thought that the mere fact that General Banks had provided a way for the loyal men to express their sentiments did not invalidate their action. He admitted that Banks had no legal authority to do a great many things that he had done, but he declared the question to be, Was this constitution the will of the loyal men of that state? He then took Howard to task for having said that he would keep the rebellious people in tutelage for five, ten, or twenty years. Howard at once interposed, saying that he had added, "if that length of time should be necessary to reproduce loyalty in a seceded state, and thus to restore them to the Union as a loyal people." But Henderson quoted Howard's exact words, and referred him to the page of the Congressional Globe[1] on which appeared a remark, which, as evidence of the feeling of some of the northern leaders towards the southern people, should be repeated. It is thus given: "I never will consent to admit into this Union a state, a majority of whose people are hostile and unfriendly to the government of my country. I prefer to hold them in tutelage (for that is really the word) one year, five years, ten years, even twenty years, rather than run the risk of a repetition of this rebellion, which has cost us so much blood and treasure."

Howard might have saved himself the mortification of a contradiction by sticking to his text; for, one year afterwards, this assumption and this policy had become the groundwork of the congressional action in southern reconstruction.

In this debate Henderson laid down the principles

[1] 2d. Sess. 38th Cong. p. 554.

of the Presidential Plan so clearly and succinctly that his analysis and summary is worthy of reproduction. It is as follows: —

"1. That the seceded states are still in the Union, and cannot get out of it except through an amendment of the Constitution permitting it.

"2. The seceded states being still in the Union are entitled to claim all the rights accorded to other states.

"3. That each state now in the Union has the right to stand upon the form of its constitution as it existed at the time of its admission. The people of such state may change its constitution, provided they retain a republican form of government; but neither the President nor Congress can reform, alter, or amend such constitution, nor prescribe any alteration or amendment as a condition of association with the other states of the Union. The General Government may properly lend its aid to enable the people to express their will; but any attempt to exercise power constitutionally reserved to the state, beyond what may be demanded by the immediate exigencies of war, will not tend to restore the Union, but rather to destroy our whole system of government.

"4. When citizens of a state rebel and take up arms against the General Government, they lose their rights as citizens of the United States, and they necessarily forfeit those rights and franchises in their respective states which depend on United States citizenship.

"5. If a seceded state be still in the Union, entitled to recognition as a state, and a majority of the people have voluntarily withdrawn their allegiance, the loyal minority constitute the state and should govern it.

"6. Congress should not reject the governments presented, because of mere irregularity in the proceedings leading to their reorganization.

"7. If Congress has no right to make and impose a constitution upon the people of any state; if its power extends no further than to guarantee preëxisting republican forms of government; if the state still exists, and the loyal men are entitled to exercise the functions of its government, it follows that the only questions to be examined here are, first, Is the constitution the will of the loyal men qualified to act? and, second, Is it republican in form?

"8. The constitutions of Louisiana and Arkansas are thought to be republican in form, and it is admitted that the loyal men of those states respectively acquiesce in them. Hence the duty of Congress to recognize them, and the duty of each House to admit their representatives."

The first three of these clauses embody principles which were acceptable not only to the supporters of the Presidential Plan, but also to the Democrats or strict-constructionists themselves, who might have accepted even the fourth clause were not the language susceptible to interpretation so broad that the principle contained in the third clause would be endangered or even sacrificed. But the remaining clauses would certainly be rejected by the Democrats. For, so long as the conditions of the fifth clause existed, a Democrat would not recognize them at all as conditions for "reconstruction:" until a majority of the people should resume their "allegiance" in good faith, he would regard the recognition of the state as out of the question. When such majority existed, and manifested its obedience to the Constitution and the laws, no "reconstruction" would be necessary: for all that would be necessary for "restoration" of the Union would be election of state officers who acknowledged the federal government, and the reception of its senators and representatives by the two houses of Congress. Such being his view of the case, he would dismiss the sixth, seventh, and eighth clauses without further consideration; for, if he would never assent to the proposition that a minority, however loyal, constituted the state, neither would he recognize any proceedings by a power other than that of the people of the state for the "reorganization," however clear of irregularity, nor even admit that the constitution of a state should express the will of anybody but the whole people. He would say with Powell: "Senators, before they can vote for this resolution, must maintain the doctrine contained in the President's proclamation of the eighth of December, 1863, when he proposed that one tenth of the loyal voters of a state, who would comply with the conditions set forth in his proclamation, should form a state government. They must further maintain that the President of the United States, of his own volition, has power by decretal order to alter the constitution of a state. They must maintain further that the President of the United States has the power to prescribe the qualifications of voters and the qualifications of candidates for office in the state. They must further believe, not only that the President possesses these powers, but that Major-General Banks possessed these powers in the state of Louisiana by virtue of a major-general of the army commanding in that district." Assuredly, he could never countenance the conclusion that Louisiana and Arkansas should be restored to the Union merely for the reasons given by the President and his adherents, including Henderson. He could almost say with Sumner:[1] "The pretended state government in Louisiana is utterly indefensible, whether you look at its origin or its character."

If the leading clauses contain the principles and the conditions from which the reconstruction of Louisiana and its restoration to the Union are to follow, it is indeed difficult to comprehend the logical sequence which the whole series of Henderson must have presented to the mind of a Democrat. In fact, this manifesto of principles did not harmonize with the actual proceedings of the President in the reconstruction of Louisiana and Arkansas.

At this stage of the debate, Sumner offered a substitute for the resolution of recognition, which embodied the grounds of opposition entertained by the radicals to the Presidential Plan, and their demand for negro suffrage. It set forth that it was the duty of the United States, at the earliest practicable moment, to reëstablish by act of Congress republican governments in those states where loyal governments had been vacated by the existing rebellion; that this important duty was imposed by the Constitution in express terms on "the United States," and not on individuals or classes of individuals, or on any military commander or executive officer, but it must be performed by the United States, represented by the President and both Houses of Congress; that in de-

[1] Cong. Globe, February 24, 1129.

termining the extent of this duty, and in the absence of any precise definition of the term "republican form of government," no error would be committed if the consent of the governed should be insisted upon as the only just foundation of government, and that all men should be equal before the law; that it was plain that, in the performance of the constitutional guarantee, there could be no power under the Constitution to disfranchise loyal people, or to recognize any such disfranchisement, especially when it might hand over the loyal majority to the control of the disloyal minority; nor could there be any such power to discriminate in favor of the rebellion by admitting to the electoral franchise rebels who had forfeited all rights, and by excluding loyal persons who had never forfeited any right; that the reëstablishment of no state should be allowed without proper safeguards for the rights of all citizens, and especially without making it impossible for rebels in arms to trample upon the rights of those then fighting the battles of the Union; that a government founded on military power, or having its origin in military orders, could not be "a republican form of government," and that its recognition would be contrary not only to the Constitution, but to that essential principle of government which, in the language of Jefferson, establishes "the supremacy of the civil over the military authority;" that in the states whose governments have already been vacated, a government founded upon an oligarchical class could not sustain itself without national support; that such a government was not competent, at that moment, to discharge the duties and execute the powers of a state, and that its recognition as a legitimate government would tend to enfeeble the Union, to postpone the day of reconciliation, and to endanger national tranquillity; that considerations of expediency are in harmony with the requirements of the Constitution and the dictates of justice and reason, especially since colored soldiers had shown their military value; that as their muskets had been needed for the national defence against rebels in the field, so would their ballots be yet more needed against the subtle enemies of the Union at home, and that without their support at the ballot-box the cause of human rights and of the Union itself would be in constant peril.[1]

Sumner asked to have this substitute printed, which was agreed to, and thus placed upon the record, a counter-manifesto or protest against the Amnesty Proclamation. The features of this manifesto are too prominent to be overlooked. The first one is that the old governments in the seceded states had been "vacated" by the existing rebellion, and that it was the duty of the United States to reëstablish "republican governments," but that no government should be recognized as republican which had its origin in military orders, and where the civil was subordinated to the military authority, or the rule of the majority repudiated; nor where such government was instituted by any executive officer, or by any one except the United States, and that the term "the United States" meant President *and* Congress. Inasmuch as Sumner, the day before, had replied to Henderson that "it was the bounden duty of the United States *by act of Congress* to guarantee complete freedom," the share which he meant Congress to take in the

[1] Cong. Globe, 2d Sess. 38th Cong., 1091.

division of this constitutional duty between the legislature and the Executive is clear. The manifesto provided for the exclusion of rebels, but there was one thing more exclusive than presidential proclamations, congressional enactments, state constitutions, or state laws, and that was a majority of votes. As this majority of votes could not be found among the whites, he sought it among the blacks. It is noticeable that for once there is no talk on Sumner's part about the "oligarchy of skin," or the rights of the negro. He does not cloud his object with mock philanthropy, but goes right to the root of the matter and lays it bare. It is this: If you mean to keep your power, you must outvote the Southerner in his home, and the only way to do that will be to swamp the ex-rebels with the votes of their ex-slaves. It was only four days before [1] that Henry Winter Davis had made his doleful prediction in the House, and had pictured the representatives and senators from the South *claiming* admission to Congress,[2] and Sumner, on his part, dropping even the pretence of philanthropy, at once raised the cry of warning in the Senate; "their ballots," said he, "are yet more needed against the subtle enemies of the Union at home, and without their support at the ballot-box the cause of human rights and of the Union itself will be in constant peril."

As the Republicans had all along appropriated to themselves the cause of human rights and of the Union, and had denounced without ceasing the Democrats as the subtle enemies of the Union, it is not

[1] February 21, 1865.

[2] Cong. Globe, 2d Sess. 38th Cong., 969.

straining the senator's language too far, in view of Davis' prediction, to read his warning after this fashion: "The ballots of the negroes are needed to prevent the reinforcement of the Democratic minority by their old allies, the Southerners, and without negro ballots at the ballot-box the supremacy of the Republican party will be in constant peril."

Howard then took the floor and asked the question where in the Constitution could authority be found enabling the President to assure one tenth part of the people of an insurrectionary state, that they, to the exclusion of all other portions of the population of that state, should be recognized as the state, and be entitled to all the benefits of the guarantee contained in the Constitution? Here was an attempt to stretch the executive authority beyond anything which the country had thus far witnessed, and he thought that it was time for Congress to lay hold of this subject, assert their power, and provide by a statute of uniform application for the reconstruction, as it was called, and readmission of these states. That was the right, the duty, of Congress; that was not the right, the duty, of the President of the United States. He went somewhat learnedly into the question, What is a state?[1] He rejected the idea that the rebellious states could be converted into territories, yet he said that he could not escape from the conclusion that the United States, as the party which had conquered the rebel country, and who held it necessarily in the iron grip of war, had the right, as the conqueror, to rule and govern the state as conquered country, subject for a time at least to their sole will.

[1] Howard took Penhallow's Case, 3 Dallas, 94, as a text.

This was to outdo himself, for all that Henderson had proved against Howard was, that he would keep the seceded states in a "tutelage" of one, five, ten, or twenty years; but now he went still farther, until he planted himself upon the merciless *vae victis* policy of Thaddeus Stevens. Better far had he adopted the position taken by Sumner in his resolution of February 11, 1862, and accorded the states the grace of being territories of the United States: for a territory of the United States is under the reign of law, but a conquered territory is under no law, and is subject to the mere will of a commander and to the sway of that commander's sword.

Reverdy Johnson followed,[1] and, after giving an epitome of the principal facts which led to the reorganization of Louisiana, astonished the Senate and particularly his Democratic comrades by accepting the presidential reconstruction of that state, and recognizing its government. He shed much light on the reason that led the committee to recommend the recognition. He said that the committee were of the opinion that it was not in the power of the President, under the circumstances, to bring the state back under the constitution of 1864, but that it was competent for Congress to do so. In taking this position, this astute lawyer anticipated events. He reviewed the objections to recognition, and answered them: First, that this government had been instituted at the instance and under the power of the military authorities of the United States. He admitted that the precedent was a bad one, but his conclusion was that no matter how the proceedings were instituted, if in point

[1] Cong. Globe, 2d Sess. 38th Congress, 1095.

of fact the people of the state acted voluntarily, and were competent to act under the original constitution, and were authorized to act by being loyal at the time they did act, it was the duty of the United States to receive them back. Whether they were brought together under the authority of the President's Amnesty Proclamation, or by the authority of General Banks, made no difference. If, coming together, they did an act which they would have been authorized to do if they had come together voluntarily, they should be received.

Another objection was that, however true it might be that it would be in the power of all the voters of the state to adopt a constitution for themselves, or to claim the right of coming back under the constitution existing at the inception of the rebellion, it was not true that it was in the power of 11,414 voters to take that course, when the entire voting population of the state was 51,000. It seemed to him that there was no evidence to show that a single citizen of Louisiana was excluded from the right of voting. It by no means followed that there was an exclusion, either in fact or in law, because the vote of 11,000 was much less than the vote that could have been cast before the rebellion occurred. The war began in 1861, and these proceedings were had in 1864. Now, the greater proportion of the fighting, and therefore of the voting population entered into the military service of the confederate government, and of these most had forfeited their lives on the battlefield, and of those over and under the age of military service some had gone elsewhere, or had stayed where they were, but as disloyal, not as loyal citizens. It by no means followed, therefore, that the number of votes cast was not a large majority of the actual number of voters to be found at that time in Louisiana. So then it was not only not certain, but it was quite improbable, that there was a single person excluded from the privilege of voting who should have been entitled to vote.

That being the case, another thing was to be considered: What was the condition of the loyal citizens of Louisiana, in the relation in which they stood to the federal government, by reason of the ordinance of secession? Nobody pretended that they had ceased to be citizens of the United States: and if loyal, nobody would say that they had forfeited any of the rights which belonged to them when the rebellion broke out.[1] When, then, the protection of the United States was afforded them, and they saw that they could speak their sentiments without hazard, they met at their election polls, organized their government under the existing constitution, and then, wishing to change it, met in convention and adopted the constitution now before Congress: why should this government not be reorganized?

Powell interrupted to ask the question: What right had the Senate to presume that there may not have been 12,000 loyal voters in Louisiana who were deprived of the right of voting because of the order of General Banks? As he understood it, no one could vote, no matter how loyal, although he had borne arms for the Union and had always been for the old flag and the old Union, unless he would take the oath pre-

[1] Thaddeus Stevens had discussed this point, and had expressly declared that it was the misfortune, though not the fault, of these loyal people to suffer the fate of the disloyal majority.

scribed by the President, and swear to support all proclamations in regard to African slavery which had been already issued, and all that might afterward be issued.

Johnson admitted that this was a difficulty which he had always felt. He asked, were these states to be governed as provinces? If so, there was no limitation to the power of Congress. If they were to be dealt with by the conqueror as he thought proper, what was to become of the loyal citizens? Where were the limitations thrown around the power of Congress? All gone. Were they to be governed as territories of the United States? If so, the right to meet in convention and establish a constitution for themselves without a law of Congress authorizing it could not be taken from them. It was the American doctrine that the people have a right, as against the government, to meet and establish a government for themselves.

Johnson then turned his attention to the amendment or substitute which Sumner had that morning laid on the table. He characterized some of its doctrine as most remarkable, and asked whither would it lead if true? Suppose the senator got Louisiana back under an act of Congress such as he would draw, saying to the people; "You are authorized to frame a constitution for yourselves, provided you will insert in it a clause that the right of suffrage shall be exercised by the black as well as by the white," and they were admitted; did he think that it would not be in their power to change that afterward? When Congress admits a state into the Union, it puts such a state on an equality with all the other states. Would the

Senator from Massachusetts deny that it would be in the power of Massachusetts that day to exclude the black? Yet, if an act of Congress placed it out of the power of the seceded states when they came back, under the authority of that act, to change the qualifications of electors, they would not come back as the equals of Massachusetts.

Sumner interposed with an inquiry concerning the power of a state organized under the ordinance prohibiting slavery throughout the Northwest Territory, and which was declared to be a perpetual compact, to set aside this ordinance. Johnson thought the state could do so, except so far as rights were vested. A sharp colloquy ensued, in which Sumner was manifestly unable to cope with Johnson, who forced his opponent to concede that Massachusetts had done wrong when she united with South Carolina in withdrawing from Congress authority to prohibit the slave trade for twenty years. He likewise exposed a gross mistake of Sumner, who attributed to General Washington advocacy of consolidation of the states. All that Washington meant, said Johnson, was that the Union existing under the Articles of Confederation was made a stronger and more consolidated Union than it had been under those Articles; not that Washington by this expression intended to announce as the true theory of the Constitution that the government of the United States was one government, possessed with all the powers that belonged to one single government. This brought forward Henderson, who read a part of the letter of Washington, which showed beyond cavil that Washington did not convey the idea Sumner had attributed to him, but had used the very words, "the consolidation of our *Union*." This incident did not enhance the credit of Sumner for ingenuousness. The next day, he made matters worse by reading a letter of Washington to John Jay, in which the writer recognized as essential to our national existence a power which would "pervade the whole Union in as energetic a manner as the authority of the state governments extends over the several states."

The debate drifted on in a colloquial way, with Clark, Pomeroy, Saulsbury, Sumner, Davis, Johnson, Wade, Powell, Henderson, Trumbull, Hendricks, Doolittle, half of the Senate, taking part, and grew more and more disputatious. Attempts were made to terminate it by motions to adjourn, to postpone, and to lay on the table, but were voted down. "The discordant elements of the Republican party are exhibiting themselves here," said Hendricks. "But four years ago, a solemn pledge was made to the people of this country that that party, when it came into power, would not undertake to interfere with the institutions of the states. As soon as the disturbed condition of the country gave the pretext for it, the undertaking was commenced; and now, when, in the judgment of some, it has been accomplished, there comes up the grave question, what is to be done, and what is to be the political condition of the 4,000,000 negroes when they are set free? And upon that question the real strife of to-night has been witnessed. That is the subject, and it need not be disguised: it is growing out of the discordant elements of the party that now governs the country. . . . There are senators upon the Republican side who feel that it is a very troublesome question. The Senator from Massachusetts (Sumner) is determined that none of these states shall ever be heard in the halls of Congress, until the men who speak from those states speak the voice of the negroes as well as that of the white men. Other senators say that shall not be. We Democrats are a unit upon that question. We believe that this government was made by white men for white men, and we expect to stand by that idea. Let the controversy go on." [1]

An adjournment being at last effected, the debate was renewed two days afterward, when Wade made one of his trenchant, denunciatory speeches against the recognition of Louisiana, and of its two senators, "representing nobody and nothing except the will of the commander-in-chief of the army of the United States," and against the plan and everything that was presidential. Sumner ended the debate with a burst of fury, in which he made the coarse but very effective assertion, much commented upon throughout the country, that the pretended state government of Louisiana was "a mere seven-months' abortion, begotten by the bayonet in criminal conjunction with the spirit of caste, and born before its time, rickety, unformed, unfinished — whose continued existence would be a burden, a reproach, and a wrong. That," said he, "is the whole case." [2]

With these scathing words, the debate upon the recognition of Louisiana closed. Sherman had made a motion that the pending rule be dispensed with, so as to take up the bill which had been made the

1 Cong. Globe, 2d Sess. 38th Cong., 1098.

1 Cong. Globe, 1129.

special subject of the day. He now insisted on the order of the Senate being enforced, or on abandoning his motion. "Senators must see now that to take up this controverted (Louisiana) question, in the face of the statements made here, is to exhaust the expiring hours of this session on a controversy in which the members of our own political party are divided." Thus did he accept and confirm the assertion of Hendricks that the Republican party was divided on the negro question, or rather the freedman question. The vote on Sherman's motion was regarded as a test vote on the pending question of the recognition of Louisiana; for if Sherman prevailed, there could be little hope that in the few days that were left of the session, Louisiana would obtain recognition. Accordingly, the Senate was marked by a very full attendance, four senators only being absent, and when the vote was taken on Sherman's motion, thirty-four voted aye, and twelve nay. Louisiana had failed to obtain recognition.

CHAPTER XIX.

WHAT CONSTITUTES A STATE OF THE AMERICAN UNION?

Debate in the Senate upon a resolution to reject from the Electoral College the states that had seceded — The case of Louisiana discussed.

It was a week only before the day fixed for the counting of the votes cast by the Electoral College for President and Vice-President in the presence of both branches of Congress, that is to say on February 1, 1865, that a joint resolution which had emanated from the House and had been passed there was reported with amendments to the Senate by Senator Trumbull, chairman of the Committee on the Judiciary. This resolution declared that the states named in the preamble, which were the eleven states that had seceded, having been in a condition of armed rebellion on the eighth of November, 1864, the day of election, were not entitled to representation in the College, and that no electoral votes should be received or counted from these states.[1]

It was evident at the very outset that the case of Louisiana was going to be the main theme of discussion, for Ten Eyck at once moved to strike out of the preamble the word "Louisiana." If this had been agreed to by both Houses, the effect would have been

[1] Cong. Globe, 533 *et seq.*

that the new government of this state, lately organized by General Banks at the instance of the President, and under the mode laid down in the Amnesty Proclamation, would have been recognized, and that the electoral vote of this state would have been counted, and would have had the same force as the vote of any other state. Ten Eyck frankly avowed that this was the object of his motion, which was the question pending before the Senate. But the Committee on the Judiciary, when they reported back the joint resolution, had accompanied it with an amendment, by which a statement that these states had continued in armed rebellion for more than three years was to be stricken out, and another substituted to the effect that "no valid election for President and Vice-President of the United States, according to the Constitution and laws thereof, was held therein on said day." The object of this amendment, according to Trumbull, was to avoid as far as possible any committal upon the subject which Ten Eyck's motion brought up, and to put the preamble in such form that, if it were adopted and the resolution passed, Congress would not have decided thereby whether Louisiana was in or out of the Union; whether she was or was not a state. For himself, he did not believe that there could have been an election in Louisiana according to the Constitution and laws of the United States, when a very considerable portion of the state was overrun by the enemy, and the legal voters had no opportunity to vote one way or the other. Moreover, the proclamation declaring the inhabitants of that state to be in rebellion had never been recalled, and, accordingly, these inhabitants were presumably still in a condition of insurrection. Ten

Eyck, in response, took the ground that these states were still in the Union, but that their governments were in abeyance, and that whenever these states, by the aid of the general government, or by the efforts of their own people, set their governments in action anew, it was proper to extend to them all the rights which the loyal people of a loyal state were entitled to. A committal of Congress should not be had against the interest of a state any more than in its favor; and the adoption of his amendment, he admitted, would be a declaration by Congress that Louisiana was in a condition to perform all the functions of a state government, and to appoint state officers and senators and members of the national House of Representatives: but the same question was involved in the resolution, and it would be determined against the state if the joint resolution passed as it stood, for Congress would then decide that this state was at that day in a condition of rebellion such as to deprive it of all the powers, rights, and privileges of a state.

Howe followed in support of Ten Eyck's proposition to except Louisiana from the rejected states, but for the reason contrary to the one given by Ten Eyck; because, on account of rebellion, "the American state was not there," and that it became the duty of Congress, in consequence, to supply the bereaved people with a government. In taking this view he evidently coincided with Judge Peabody.

On the next day, Doolittle appeared on the scene, especially charged with the care of the Presidential Plan of Reconstruction and its defence upon the floor of the Senate against any and all comers. His comrade, Trumbull, with wise prevision, it has been seen, had done his best to forestall adverse action upon the Louisiana case, for such a mishap would jeopardize the future of the Presidential Plan by subjecting it to what virtually would be a vote of lack of confidence. Whether the vote of Louisiana were counted or no, the result would not be affected one way or the other; Lincoln was sure to be President, and the main thing was to insure the future of the Presidential Plan; the present was secure. To imperil the future by a fruitless decision in the present, that, on the eighth of November, 1864, Louisiana was in a proper and lawful condition to vote for President, was to reënact the part of the dog in the fable; it was bad politics. Accordingly, he avoided all question and any decision upon what he must have felt could stand little scrutiny, by including the name of Louisiana among the rejected votes and thus keeping her in the place she had occupied during the rebellion. Why, in taking this course, he and Doolittle failed to act in concert, as was usual, does not appear, but on February second, Doolittle gained the floor, and proceeded to argue away the existence of any power in Congress over the counting of these electoral votes. Of course, if Congress had no power over the count, the votes would have to be received and counted as they had been returned, and no right of rejection would exist in Congress: the federal legislature could neither annul votes nor declare void votes that had been given. Hale denied the correctness of this position emphatically, and thought that it would be one of the strangest things that had ever occurred on earth, if Congress had not such power; whereupon Doolittle averred that Hale had stated his case for him too strongly, and that Congress did have power over the subject, but that it was restricted, and was limited to power over the question of choosing electors. Congress was not the tribunal to which the question of counting was referred, but the President of the United States Senate presiding over the joint convention of both Houses had been constituted such tribunal. A slight manifestation of feeling between Doolittle and Trumbull occurred, and the latter expressed his regret at seeing Doolittle exhibit it; a manifestation which Doolittle disclaimed. The debate proceeded, and Collamer proposed to settle the matter by an amendment to the effect that the people of no state declared in insurrection should be regarded as empowered to choose electors until a law of the United States had declared this insurrection to have ceased. Reverdy Johnson agreed with Trumbull and Collamer that the authority of Congress over the subject existed, and so did Howard, who looked upon it as the bounden duty of Congress to keep out of the Union every one of these eleven seceded states until it had become evident that there was a clear, absolute majority of the voters in each state "friendly to the government of the United States;" a phrase susceptible to divers interpretations, when it is considered that Howard was one of those who, like Wilson, had no faith in the loyalty of any one who did not vote the Republican ticket.

In the warmth of the debate, a good many questions foreign to the issue, as Davis complained, had been dragged into discussion. How the vote was to be counted, and by whom, were subjects much discussed. Powell, nevertheless, stuck to the subject of Louisiana, and strenuously opposed Ten Eyck's motion, and also Collamer's substitute, and scored General Banks unmercifully. The most pungent speech of the debate was, without question, Benjamin Wade's. This senator was a blunt man, and whenever he spoke, he spoke to the point and did not mince matters. He was a man of strong passion, was pugnacious, and one who did not easily forget an injury or forego an opportunity to strike back. He was the senator who had united with Henry Winter Davis in giving to the world the manifesto against the President when he had pocketed the Reconstruction Bill at the end of the preceding session. He never forgave Lincoln for that act; he did not fear him, he would not court favor of him, and he did not hesitate to give his opinion about the President whenever he had the chance to do so. This debate offered him an opportunity to unbosom himself, and accordingly he took the floor.

He began by saying that, a year before, Congress, wisely anticipating these questions, had framed a bill with which to meet them, but that it had been pocketed by the President. This the President had done in defence of his Amnesty Proclamation, declaring that when one tenth part of the people of a state would come back, they should be recognized as a state, — a proposition the most absurd and impracticable that ever had haunted the imagination of a statesman. In this the President had cut loose from the principle of the rule of the majority, and there was nothing left; all was open sea, all anarchy, all confusion, and this proclamation was the most contentious, the most anarchical, the most dangerous proposition that was ever put forth for the government of a free people.

Could any portion of the territory of a state attempt to govern the whole? Could the Senate be so blind as to suppose that, when these state officers were clothed by military power with authority to govern, it was a republican government? It was just as much a military government after as it had been before the farce of selecting those officers was gone through with. There was the military governor; had he ever been withdrawn from Louisiana? Or, if another had been substituted, by whom had he been substituted? By the commander-in-chief of all the armies of the United States. When the mandate went forth from the President to Hahn, "Be governor of that state," he did not consult the Senate, he did not consult anybody in particular, but the mandate issued from the President of the United States unaided, unknown, uncounseled by anybody.

"You need not talk to me about your one tenth," he exclaimed; "if a majority of a state was rebellious, a free government in that state is impossible. Was there any principle of free government that had decided that anything less than a majority of the people, or voters, of a state could govern its destinies? I speak not of the farce of a civil government overshadowed by a military governor, a wheel within a wheel, a military government dominating your whole political community, and inside of that and under it and subordinate to it, a civil government pretending to be a free government! I say it is a farce; it is unworthy of the American Senate to give it a moment's consideration. . . . It is a government of false pretences. Withdraw your army from Louisiana to-day, and what would be its condition? Have you any evidence as to what that people would do to-morrow, if you withdrew all your military force from there? Have they voted, have they given any evidence to show that they are loyal to the government of the United States? Not a lisp of it, not a word of it. More than four fifths of the territory of that state now is trampled down beneath the feet of military power, just where it ought to be for its rebellion, and you dare not withdraw your armies from there: and do you talk of free republican state government there! Sir, you cannot have it."

Doolittle weakly interposed, but was silenced in a moment by the provoked orator, who, like Henry Winter Davis, was astonished to find any difference of opinion in the body that had so unanimously passed the Reconstruction Bill less than a year before. Had anything occurred to change their opinions? Could they really claim that that portion of Louisiana was free even where their army was? and he sarcastically insinuated that the Border states themselves were under military domination, for the Senator from Kentucky, Powell, had told them that they did not govern there according to the laws of Kentucky, and that they did not even found the basis of government upon the laws of that state, but that the military authorities regulated the elective franchise there. Was there any freedom in that?

Wade evidently feared the extension of presidential usurpation over the Border states, and, perhaps, over the whole country, for he did not hesitate to say: "I make these observations, because I am exceedingly jealous of military power, and I never will consent that a people predominated over by a hostile military power shall found an American republican state. They cannot do it. To do it, they must be as free as air, and until they are in that condition, it is impossible to have a free government there. . . . Let us settle now and forever the principle, that the President of the United States cannot in times of civil war, whenever he happens to have an army in a state, improvise by military force a legislature, and call it the power of a state, in such a sort as to count that semblance in his favor as a fact. If it were attempted, I know for one that I would not put up with it."

There were two things which seemed to weigh upon Wade's mind. One was, that a result of leaving the reorganization of a state to a mere fraction like one tenth might be, indeed would be, to invite eventually the political destruction of a feeble minority by the nine tenths, when the return of peace had reinstated the majority. "When the general government abandons them," said he, "when it leaves the one tenth in the hands and under the domination of the nine tenths, what will be their condition?" This apprehension, he declared, was shared by Andrew Johnson, the Vice-President elect, and by other Unionists in the southern states. This calamity, he insisted, had been provided against by the Reconstruction Bill, which had required a majority of the loyal people to effect the reorganization.

The other thing which predominated in Wade's speech was dread of presidential usurpation. He did not delude himself with the notion that the aggrandizement of power was distasteful to the President, or that he had assumed it unwillingly and would as willingly lay it down the moment the necessity for it had passed away. The pretext of necessity and the pushing away the crown could not deceive him in view of Lincoln's secret letter to Banks, and his curt investiture of Governor Hahn with military power *after* this governor's election and inauguration. Nor did he overlook Powell's allusion to the military rule of Kentucky, a Border state, and one separated from his own state by the river Ohio only. This was getting too near home.

As soon as Wade halted for breath, Wright moved to adjourn, but the Senate refused to do so, and a running colloquy ensued until another motion to adjourn was made, which in its turn was voted down. A motion was then made to postpone this joint resolution indefinitely, but the Senate had no mind at this stage to get rid of the question; they preferred to meet it, and so they refused to postpone. Having done this, the Senate adjourned.

When the pending question came up as the special business of the next day, Doolittle took the floor, and it was evident from his statement that the pending question would have no practical effect whatever in disposing of the presidential canvass, and that there was no necessity for fixing the law that day more than at any time within the next four years, that perhaps he had become convinced overnight of Trumbull's sagacity in letting the sleeping dog lie. He set bravely to work, but it was not long before he lost his temper, and coupling together Wade, the radical, with Powell, the conservative and strict-constructionist, he remarked upon the strange spectacle presented when the two extremes of the Senate came together in this way. "One would suppose," he cried, "that

Pilate and Herod had joined hands both to attack the administration in its policy on this subject, and to see if they could crucify the free state of Louisiana."

Doolittle was one of the most accomplished orators and debaters then in the Senate: he was withal a fair man, self-controlled, and one who respected himself and others. But even such men cannot always maintain their balance, and he lost his when he lost his temper. His taunt brought him no good, for Powell retorted that he did not know whether the honorable senator had likened him to Herod or to Pilate, but the senator had said that the Senator from Kentucky and the Senator from Ohio, like Herod and Pilate, desired to crucify the state of Louisiana. He was not aware before that Herod had much to do with the crucifixion. He knew that Pontius Pilate judged on that occasion, and that his judgments had been deemed infamous. He had told the Senator from Ohio that he might take either; if he thought he had been likened to Pilate, he might defend Pilate, and if he thought that he, Powell, had been likened to Herod, he would stand on that: but the Senator from Ohio had answered that he did not care a toss of the copper which. Here the Senate forgot its gravity and roared; while Powell added that, if the comparison should be applied to anybody, it ought to be applied to the President and General Banks.

Powell, who had already made some clear-headed remarks, now proceeded to discuss the pending question at length. He brought out the military character of the Louisiana reorganization with great effect, dwelling particularly upon the conduct of Banks, and he exemplified the dangers of military interference by showing that Banks had even deliberately exceeded his orders: an excess of zeal which, it was significant, had not been rebuked by his superior. He had, too, something to say of the usurpation of the President, and, at a time when this and kindred words were used with looseness and indefiniteness, to characterize the President's action, he did the political world a service by defining the word "usurper," and by indicating its proper application. He divested it of its quality as a malignant epithet, and gave it its proper signification. "I use the word 'usurper,' to indicate those who administer the functions of their offices in violation of law. It was a maxim of the Athenians that all who administered the functions of their offices in violation of law were usurpers. It is in that sense that I use the term. However good their intentions may have been, I say that in their [the President and General Banks] exercise of power in Louisiana they overthrew the Constitution and laws of their country which they had sworn to support; and hence, in my judgment, they are technically usurpers."

It is noticeable throughout these debates in the Senate that, with the exception of general denials, and these even rarely expressed, there was no attempt to contradict the reiterated accusations of presidential usurpation. It is true that these accusations were frequently made in the excitement of the moment, when it would have invested them with gravity too great had the orderly course of debate been interrupted in order to answer them. On the other hand, they were made usually with all the seriousness and earnestness the subject demanded; not in a captious spirit, but with the most sober sense of responsibility and with pressing warning, and yet, except such denials as Doolittle afforded an instance of in this very debate, mere counter-assertions in fact, they were allowed to pass without answer. The inference is, that as the House was silenced on this subject by the bitter sarcasm of Thaddeus Stevens when a member was bold enough to claim constitutionality for the President's interference in southern reconstruction, so the Senate was silenced by the self-evident truth which these accusations carried with them.[1] They could not be controverted, for the repudiation of the principle that the will of the majority, lawfully exercised and expressed, shall rule, and of the principle that the military power must be subordinate to civil government, — this was unwarranted by the Constitution or by any principle of representative democracy, and, under Powell's definition, which will hardly be gainsaid, the course of the President must be considered one in which powers were usurped.

In this debate Doolittle took positive ground in favor of the doctrine that the states in rebellion were not out of the Union. Indeed, he went out of his way to controvert "the fine-spun theories advocated in certain other quarters," that such states, by virtue of their insurrection, had ceased to exist as states of the Union.[2] He was very denunciatory of this doctrine,

[1] In his speech on the recognition of Louisiana (Cong. Globe, 2d Sess. 38th Cong., 1061) Powell declared, without contradiction, that he had heard the Amnesty Proclamation commented upon in the Senate by numerous senators, and had heard no senator maintain that the President could legitimately exercise the power he had assumed in that proclamation.

[2] Cong. Globe, p. 578.

maintaining that it was "one huge, infernal, constitutional lie, that would stamp all our conduct from the beginning as murder, and cover us all over with blood. And I tell you that, whatever fine-spun theories politicians may adopt here at Washington or elsewhere, when the Convention came to meet at Baltimore, freshly representing the people of the United States, they trampled the miserable humbug under their feet by nominating Andrew Johnson, of Tennessee, as Vice-President of the United States — Tennessee, still a state of the United States."

Such was Doolittle's opinion of the principle underlying the relations of the seceded states to the general government, and such, in his view, was the motive which the people had for nominating Andrew Johnson, whose great ally and henchman he was soon to be. It is singular that Sumner, who was to become Johnson's unrelenting adversary, took this occasion to give his opinion of his former co-member of the Senate, who was then Vice-President elect. It was to this effect: "I presume nobody ever questioned that Andrew Johnson was a great and loyal citizen of the United States."

Ten Eyck's motion was lost,[1] and finally the joint resolution was passed on February fourth,[2] and was returned to the House, where the Speaker signed it.[3] The eleven states, therefore, were debarred from representation in the Electoral College. Nevertheless, the end was not yet, for, though the President returned the joint resolution with his signature, he accompanied it with a message which gave his adversaries on the

[1] By a vote of 22 to 15; not voting, 14.

[2] By a vote of 29 to 10; absent, 12.

[3] February 6, 1865.

floors of Congress fresh occasion to accuse him of disrespect towards the legislative branch of the government. He said that he had signed the resolution in deference to the views of Congress implied in its passage and presentation to him. In his own view, however, the convened Houses of Congress had complete power to exclude from a count all electoral votes deemed by them to be illegal; and that it was not competent for the Executive to defeat or obstruct that power by a veto, as would be the case if his action were at all essential in the matter. He disclaimed all right of the Executive to interfere in any way in the matter of canvassing or counting electoral votes, and he also denied that, by signing the resolution, he had expressed any opinion on the recitals of the preamble, or any judgment of his own upon the subject of the resolution.

It was evident that the President had taken the matter sorely, and the supposition was that he regarded the joint resolution as a legislative censure of his plan of reconstruction; but that, as Congress had undertaken to convey to him their opinion of him and his methods, he had embraced the same occasion to show them that his indifference towards what they said and did was as great then as it was on the day he pocketed the Reconstruction Bill. For the Republicans to express their feelings would be to make public their family quarrel. Accordingly, they remained dumb, while Reverdy Johnson, whose position as a Democrat imposed no restrictions upon him in this respect, gave utterance to the general feeling on what he characterized the extraordinary course of the President, and a reflection upon the Senate and Congress.

If the President was sincere in thinking that it was not a subject for the legislation of Congress, he ought to have disapproved the resolution, but in the speaker's judgment the President was entirely wrong in point of law. Johnson recalled the manifesto of the President after pocketing the Reconstruction Bill, in which he had said that there were some good things in the bill passed by Congress, and some bad ones; and that as far as they were good he would act upon them, but as far as they were not as good as the things he himself proposed, he would be governed by his own judgment. It seemed to Johnson that the President had read Congress a lecture — and so it seemed to the world, and thus for the second time in seven months, or in a period really of sixty days only of congressional session, Lincoln had snubbed the legislature. The Executive had become too strong for the legislative branch of the government; he felt his power, and his contempt of the representatives of the states and the people grew apace; in fact, he made no attempt at concealment. As for the people, everything that the President did pleased them: they looked not to conclusions, and what could be more amusing than to see "Old Abe get ahead of the politicians"?

CHAPTER XX.

CONCLUSION.

THIS account of the President's course with reference to slavery and the seceded states, the opinions held by the dominant party in Congress respecting the relations of the federal government towards the seceded states, and the short life and untimely fate of the Reconstruction Bill, are sufficient to indicate the departure of the Republicans from the position they occupied at the outbreak of hostilities, and their repudiation of the sentiments expressed in the President's Inaugural Address and First Message, and by the vote of Congress on the Crittenden resolution in July, 1861. This rupture with old doctrine had been speedy, and this repudiation had been emphatic: indeed, the time came when every Republican member that had been in Congress during 1861 seemed to make it a point, in season and out of season, to repudiate his vote on this resolution; while every new member made haste to show to the world how truly he was "abreast of the times," or in advance of them.

The secret of this change in the temper and sentiment of the Republican party is to be found in the change of temper and sentiment which the people themselves had undergone as the war continued. During the first part of the war, the North had to sustain a succession of reverses in the field. Never in the history of any modern people can there be found so many and so great failures as appeared, one after another, among the federal commanders of armies. They followed thick and fast, and were of all species of incompetency. The Army Register seemed to have been ransacked for weak material, and the people, as they saw army after army paralyzed or crippled, at last lost patience and became soured and vengeful. They became soured towards the authorities at Washington, executive and legislative, and vengeful towards the South. The spectacle of vast numbers of northern soldiers rotting in southern prisons, with their own government apparently indifferent to their fate, exasperated them beyond measure. It was natural, for it was easier and safer, to lay all the blame at the door of the rebels, and to regard them as enemies to be punished after success had placed it in the power of the North to do so. This object attained, it mattered little to the unthinking masses whether the President considered the rebellious states in the Union, or whether Stevens looked upon them as out of the Union.

The Republican party was not at heart a constitutional party. There stood the Constitution, and it would not down : but it could be used, and when not used for their purposes, it could be, for the moment, argued away or ignored. Nothing more clearly reveals the unadaptability of this party to the Constitution than its manner of treating that instrument when it came to ascertain and settle the relations of the seceded states to the federal government. The harmony which conformity with a common standard characterizes was wanting ; three distinct and conflicting views of the situation appeared, and three separate and distinct plans of reconstruction struggled for supremacy within the limits of this party. There was the Presidential view, which, on the face of it, could not have had its origin in any provision of the Constitution, for a new government was to be imposed upon the state, and not created by the people of the state; it was not, therefore, a popular government: it was to be created, ostensibly, by a small fraction of the people, one tenth; it could not, therefore, be a government of the majority, nor a republican form of government: and it was to be inaugurated and indefinitely controlled by the army, and therefore was in violation of the constitutional principle which subordinates the military to the civil power.

Of the two factions which struggled for supremacy on the Republican side of Congress, one faction maintained that the states were in the Union in spite of secession, but that the people of the state had, by their act of secession, forfeited their federal rights; *i. e.*, that the states were still "in," but that the people were "out;" and the other that they were out of the Union by virtue of secession that was maintaining armed resistance successfully enough to entitle them to be considered as belligerents, with the penalty of subjection if worsted in the fight: neither of these factions found support in the Constitution, though one of them made use of the "republican form of government" clause.[1]

If those who asserted that these states were still in the Union had carried this doctrine to its logical conclusion, they would have had to concede that, under any circumstances, those of reconstruction included,

[1] Art. IV. sec. 4.

their right of self-government had survived inviolate, and therefore that their restoration depended upon themselves. But these legislators would not grant this consequence, and were forced to the untenable position that, though these states were still members of the Federal Union, and their citizens had not ceased to be citizens of the United States, these citizens had become incapable of exercising political privileges. The defects of this position are manifest: in the first place, it involved the contradiction that while certain states were in, their citizens were out, and, secondly, in order to establish a constitutional ground, they adopted for this purpose the clause of the Constitution ordaining that "the United States shall *guarantee* to every state in *this* Union a republican form of government." As a guarantee implies a preëxisting government, and can refer only to such a one, they were met with the difficulty that the state governments in question were not only republican, but that this republican form had been recognized in every instance already by the United States, and that, as there was no evidence of their having been changed in form, this article could not apply to the seceded states: moreover, the term "this Union" could have no reference to any other Union than that formed under the Constitution, and from which these states had seceded. It could not mean "*a* Union," or "*another* Union," or, as Doolittle asserted, "a *better* Union."

Coupled with this error was the claim of Congress to paramount and absolute authority in matters of reconstruction. This claim was founded upon the sovereignty of the people of the United States, to which was relegated all power affecting the Union. But the reconstruction of a state is the creation of a state, and the power to create does not belong to the people of the United States, but to the people of the state to be created. No state can be the creature or the creator of its fellows: New York cannot impose a constitution, directly or indirectly, upon Vermont, and if New York cannot do so, neither can any other state, nor, consequently, can all the states combined. The fact remained as it always had existed that, great as the powers of Congress may be respecting the affairs of the Union, they could not be extended so as to enlarge, diminish, create, or extinguish a state. So far as the internal affairs of the Union are concerned, Congress is merely the legislature of the Union, and as each House of this legislature has by direct provision and limitation of the Constitution the right to be the judge of the elections, returns, and qualifications of its own members, its power even to recognize is limited when these conditions are satisfactory to it. The recognition cannot be a qualified one, for when the members and senators take their seats, the state that sent them has been recognized unconditionally as a member of the Federal Union. Congress may delay admission, but when the Constitution has been complied with, it cannot refuse recognition and complete recognition. Hence the necessity of Congress to find constitutional ground for its claim to absolute power. It had already set aside the article forbidding any new state to be formed or created within the jurisdiction of any other state, when it sanctioned the creation and admission of West Virginia. In casting about for ground upon which it could proceed to the absolute control of the South, it fixed upon the section next succeeding the one it had violated: this section[1] could be adapted to the present circumstances with reason, only in case a republican form of government were adjudged to be so incompatible with slavery that this form of government could not exist where slavery existed. But the history of the United States since the Declaration of Independence was in direct contradiction of such a notion; for when independence was declared, slavery was a feature of all of the new-born states save one, and where it had been abolished since that time, it had been abolished by the states and not by the federal government, and then there could be no question of each state having control over its own institutions (the distinguishing feature of a free and independent state, and of one, too, which must be republican), otherwise it could not have been, during its whole existence as a state, a member of the Federal Union. Nor was the present less striking than the past in its contradiction of such an interpretation of this constitutional clause, for how could slavery be incompatible with a republican form of government when it still remained an institution in several of the states which had not seceded, which were supporting the Union, and of whose republican form of government there was no question? But, to sweep away any claim resting upon such ground, it is enough merely to point out the undeniable fact that slavery is not a form of government, republican or otherwise; it is an institution merely. So far adrift was the only faction in the Republican party which pretended a regard for the Constitution.

[1] Article IV. sec. 4.

Much more manly and less dangerous were those who asserted that the seceded states, by the act of secession and by maintaining this secession by force of arms, had placed themselves outside of the Union, and had become mere territories over which the federal government might exercise the rights of conquest. They knew well that any policy which had for its foundation the inequality of the states, the interference of the federal government in the affairs of a state within the Union, the subordination of the civil to the military power, and the abrogation of the rule of the majority, had no countenance from anything within the four corners of the Constitution, and was in violation of the spirit as well as of the tenor of the bond of Union. Accordingly, they did not hesitate to say so, and to make the abrogation of the Constitution coördinate with the dissolution of the Union, which they accepted so far as the states in armed resistance were concerned. This view placed the states without the pale of the Union and the Constitution; it made their soil conquered territory, to be disposed of as the United States should think fit, and making the rebels belligerents, handed them over when conquered to the mercy of the federal government. This party exercised its severity under the cry of "humanity,"—war was to be waged for the enfranchisement of the slave; this accomplished, it would be for the subjected whites to meet the day of reckoning. It is due to the people of the North to say that, while this *vae victis* policy swayed many in its direction, it never got possession of their minds and hearts until a late day. "There's too much negro in it," and "blood, after all, is thicker than water," were common sayings even among those upon whom the war had fallen with a heavy hand.

It is idle to speak of constitutional standards and positions when discussing those who openly avowed their independence of the Constitution, and who, like Stevens, took malign pleasure in pointing out to their less radical colleagues how these fine-spun theories were as much outside of the Constitution as were their own bold and radical views. Nothing delighted Stevens, the Mephistopheles of the Republican party, more than to add to the confusion of his colleagues by taunting them with their broken-down constitutionism, or to complete the discomfiture of the President's party by winding up a bitter attack on the Executive with the question, where the President found in the Constitution, to which he was constantly alluding, his authority for creating military governments at the South, or for creating any government at all, and where the Constitution authorized him, or any one else, to set the minority above the majority.[1] The radical faction boldly maintained that the states were out of the Union; that, when conquered, their terri-

1 "Where does he [the President] find anything in the Constitution to warrant that? If he must look there alone for authority, then all these acts are flagrant usurpations, deserving the condemnation of the community. . . . I understand that these proceedings all take place, not under any pretence of legal or constitutional right, but in virtue of the laws of war; and by the laws of nations these laws are just what we choose to make them, so that they are not inconsistent with humanity. I say, then, that we may admit West Virginia as a new state, not by virtue of any provision of the Constitution, but under our absolute power which the laws of war give us in the circumstances in which we are placed. I shall vote for this bill upon that theory, and upon that alone; for I will not stultify myself by supposing that we have any warrant in the Constitution for this proceeding." December 9, 1862: Cong. Globe, 50.

tories and the property of their citizens were subject to confiscation, and that the citizens themselves were subject to punishment at the will of the conqueror; and they snapped their fingers at a Constitution which all but themselves professed to reverence but never obeyed, and which was upheld by none except the "copperheads."

The defectiveness of the radical view of the situation, judged from the standpoint of the Constitution, is apparent. That the Constitution is a compact irrefragable by anything except successful revolution is the view taken by northern constitutionists. President Lincoln, in his first Inaugural Address, expressed this matter very tersely and clearly when he said that: "The Union is perpetual. . . . It follows from these views that no state, upon its own mere motion, can lawfully get out of the Union; that resolves and ordinances to that effect are legally void; and that acts of violence within any state or states against the authority of the United States are insurrectionary or revolutionary according to circumstances." This notion was not confined to the North; it had been widely entertained throughout the South, but there it was universally held also that no power existed, by which, under the Constitution, the coercion of one state by another, or by the federal government, was permissible. If this view of the irrefragability of the Union be conceded, it follows that the effect given by the radical Republicans in Congress to the maintenance of armed resistance in the seceded states was to grant that secession had accomplished dissolution of the Union. This was going as far as the most radical secessionist himself could go. It was conceding the very point at issue, and allowing the secessionist to depart in peace. But at this point the radical claimed that the secessionist was a belligerent, and that it was the duty of the federal government to subject the South to its authority. It is difficult to see, if the secessionist could abandon our Constitution and make a new one for himself, and if his act of secession were rendered valid by his successful resistance to our arms, why he should not be allowed to do so in his acknowledged right to "the pursuit of happiness;" or what was left to us but to lay down our arms, to gather the fragments of the old Union together, and provide for the future as best we could. Granting this effect of secession, asserted by the radicals, what right had we, in this event, to pursue the secessionist with force of arms? "He was guilty of an act of treason and rebellion," replied Stevens; "all these crimes were committed before the rebels became belligerents." If all these crimes had been committed before the perpetrators became belligerents, then the recognition by the federal government of the perpetrators as belligerents did away with their character as criminals, and rendered punishment after subjection out of the question. If to recognize them as belligerents was to lose authority over the insurgent states, what pretext had the federal government to continue the war, for authority was the very basis of its action; it was waging war against those who, it asserted, owed obedience to its authority, but who were openly denying this authority. "Who ever heard," retorted Thomas, of Massachusetts, "as a matter of public law, that the authority of a government over its rebellious subject was lost until that revolution was successful, — was a fact accomplished?"

Thus, like his brethren whom he had taunted, Stevens found himself in the midst of contradictions, and, like them, he floundered in the attempt to gain a solid footing. The radicals, who had made merry over the confusion of their colleagues who still professed a regard for the Constitution, had in turn to face the fact that throwing the compass and chart overboard was not the most judicious way of making port.

APPENDIX A.

The following extracts from the credentials of the delegates from the different colonies to the Congress of 1774,[1] show how single was the object sought, and how strictly advisory was the character of this body. It will be observed that of governmental powers there were none: the Congress was a mere Council.

New Hampshire. "To devise, consult, and adopt such measures as may have the most likely tendency to extricate the colonies from their present difficulties; to secure and perpetuate their rights, liberties, and privileges, and to restore that peace, harmony, and mutual confidence, which once happily subsisted between the parent country and her colonies."

Massachusetts. "To consult on the present state of the colonies, and the miseries to which they are, and must be reduced, by the operation of certain acts of Parliament respecting America; and to deliberate and determine upon wise and proper measures to be by them recommended to all colonies, for the recovery and establishment of their just rights and liberties, civil and religious, and the restoration of union and harmony between Great Britain and the colonies, most ardently desired by all good men."

Rhode Island. "To consult on proper measures to obtain a repeal of the several acts of the British Parliament for levying tax on his Majesty's subjects in America without their consent, and upon proper measures to establish the rights and liberties of the colonies upon a just and solid foundation, agreeably to instructions given by the General Assembly."

[1] Journals, I, 2-9.

Connecticut. "To consult and advise on proper measures for advancing the best good of the colonies, and such conference to report from time to time to the Colonial House of Representatives."

New Jersey. "To represent the colony in the General Congress."

Pennsylvania. "To form and adopt a plan for the purposes of obtaining redress of American grievances, ascertaining American rights upon the most solid and constitutional principles, and for establishing that union and harmony between Great Britain and the colonies which is indispensably necessary to the welfare and happiness of both."

Delaware. "To consult and advise with the deputies from the other colonies, to determine upon all such prudent and lawful measures as may be judged most expedient for the colonies immediately and unitedly to adopt, in order to obtain relief for an oppressed people, and the redress of our general grievances."

Maryland. "To attend a general congress, to effect one general plan of conduct operating on the commercial connection of the colonies with the mother country, for the relief of Boston, and the preservation of American liberty."

Virginia. "To consider of the most proper and effectual manner of so operating on the commercial connection of the colonies with the mother country, as to procure redress for the much injured province of Massachusetts Bay, to secure British America from the ravage and ruin of arbitrary taxes, and speedily to procure the return of that harmony and union, so beneficial to the whole empire, and so ardently desired by all British America."

North Carolina. "To take such measures as they may deem prudent to effect the purpose of describing with certainty the rights of Americans, repairing the breach made in those rights, and for guarding them for the future against any such violations done under the sanction of public authority."

South Carolina. "To consider the acts lately passed,

and bills depending in Parliament with regard to the port of Boston, and the colony of Massachusetts Bay; which acts and bills, in the precedent and consequences, affect the whole Continent of America. Also the grievances under which America labors, by reason of the several acts of Parliament that impose taxes or duties for raising a revenue, and lay unnecessary restraints and burdens on trade; and of the statutes, parliamentary acts, and royal instructions, which make an invidious distinction between his Majesty's subjects in Great Britain and America, with full power and authority to concert, agree to, and prosecute such legal measures, as in the opinion of said deputies, so to be assembled, shall be most likely to obtain a repeal of the said acts, and a redress of those grievances."

Neither New York nor Georgia was represented in this Congress. Delegates from certain counties of New York appeared, but none representing the colony, nor elected by it as a colony.

It is also worthy of remark that the Congress of 1774 had no agents of its own in foreign countries, but employed those of the several colonies; and see the resolutions for delivering the Address to the King, October 25, 1774, and Letter to the agents, approved the following day.

That the powers granted to the delegates to the second Congress were substantially the same with those granted to the delegates to the first will appear from the following extracts from their credentials: —

New Hampshire. "To consent and agree to all measures which said Congress shall deem necessary to obtain redress of American grievances." Delegates were appointed by a convention.

Massachusetts. "To concert, agree upon, direct, and order" (in concert with the delegates of the other colonies) "such further measures as to them shall appear to be the best calculated for the recovery and establishment of American rights and liberties, and for restoring harmony between Great Britain and the colonies." Delegates were appointed by Provincial Congress.

Connecticut. "To join, consult, and advise with the other colonies in British America, on proper measures for advancing the best good of the colonies." Delegates were appointed by the Colonial House of Representatives.

Pennsylvania. "To attend the general Congress." Delegates appointed by Provincial Assembly.

New Jersey. "To attend the Continental Congress, and to report their proceedings at the next session of the General Assembly." Delegates were appointed by the Colonial Assembly.

Delaware. "To concert and agree upon such further measures, as shall appear to them best calculated for the accommodation of the unhappy differences between Great Britain and the colonies on a constitutional foundation, which the House most ardently wish for, and that they report their proceedings to the next session of General Assembly." Delegates were appointed by the Assembly.

Maryland. "To consent and agree to all measures, which said Congress shall deem necessary and effectual to obtain a redress of American grievances; and this province bind themselves to execute to the utmost of their power, all resolutions which the said Congress may adopt." Delegates were appointed by convention, and subsequently approved by the General Assembly.

Virginia. "To represent the colony in general Congress, to be held," etc. Delegates were appointed by convention.

North Carolina. "Such powers as may make any acts done by them, or any of them, or consent given in behalf of this province, obligatory in honor upon every inhabitant thereof." Delegates were appointed by convention and approved in General Assembly.

South Carolina. "To concert, agree to, and effectually prosecute such measures as in the opinion of the said deputies, and the deputies to be assembled, shall be most likely to obtain a redress of American grievances." Delegates were appointed by Provincial Congress.

The credentials of the delegates from Rhode Island are not to be found in the copy of the Journals of Congress from which the foregoing are taken.

New York was not represented as a colony in the Congress of 1775; Georgia was not represented until September, 1775. Georgia's delegates were authorized "to do, transact, join, and concur with the several delegates from the other colonies and provinces upon the continent, on all such matters and things as shall appear eligible and fit, at this alarming time, for the preservation and defence of our rights and liberties, and for the restoration of harmony, upon constitutional principles, between Great Britain and America."

Some of the colonies appointed their delegates only for limited times, at the expiration of which they were replaced by others, but without any material change in their powers. The delegates were, in all things, subject to the orders of their respective colonies.[1]

It is perfectly clear from these extracts, 1, That each colony acted in its own individual capacity, without reference to any other, and that the colonies made common cause, only because the principles at stake affected all alike, and the objects to be attained were the same. 2. That each colony appointed its own delegates, giving them precisely such power and authority as suited its own views. 3. That no colony gave any power or authority except for advisement only. 4. That the purposes set forth were, not to establish a new government, but to preserve the old, by effecting harmony with Great Britain on constitutional principles. 5. That the Continental Congress was organized by the colonies as such, and generally through their ordinary legislatures, and always with a careful regard to their separate and independent rights and powers.[2]

[1] Extracted from notes to Upshur's The Federal Government, ed. 1868, pp. 47, 48, 49, 53, 54, 55.

[2] Adapted from Upshur, p. 49 n.

APPENDIX B.

EXTRACTS FROM THE KENTUCKY AND VIRGINIA RESOLUTIONS OF 1798 AND 1799.

KENTUCKY RESOLUTIONS.

1. *Resolved*, That the several states composing the United States of America are united on the principle of unlimited submission to their General Government; but that, by a compact under the style and title of a Constitution for the United States, and of Amendments thereto, they constituted a General Government for special purposes, — delegated to that Government certain definite powers, reserving, each state to itself, the residuary mass of right to their own self-government; and that whensoever the General Government assumes undelegated powers, its acts are unauthoritative, void, and of no force: that to this compact each state acceded as a state, and is an integral party, its co-states forming, as to itself, the other party: that the Government created by this compact was not made the exclusive or final judge of the extent of the powers delegated to itself; since that would have made its discretion, and not the Constitution, the measure of its powers; but that, as in all other cases of compact among powers having no common judge, each party has an equal right to judge for itself, as well of infractions as of the mode and measure of redress.

7. *Resolved*, That the construction applied by the General Government (as is evidenced by sundry of their proceedings) to those parts of the Constitution of the United States which delegate to Congress a power "to lay and collect taxes, duties, imports, and excises, to pay the debts and provide for the common defence and general welfare of the United States," and "to make all laws which shall be necessary and proper for carrying into execution the powers vested by the Constitution in the Government of the United

States, or in any department or officer thereof," goes to the destruction of all limits prescribed to their power by the Constitution: that words meant by the instrument to be subsidiary only to the execution of limited powers ought not to be so construed as themselves to give unlimited powers, nor a part to be so taken as to destroy the whole residue of that instrument: that the proceedings of the General Government under color of these articles will be a fit and necessary subject of revisal and correction, at a time of greater tranquillity, while those specified in the preceding resolutions call for immediate redress.

8. *Resolved*, That a Committee of conference and correspondence be appointed, who shall have in charge to communicate the preceding resolutions to the Legislatures of the several states; to assure them that this commonwealth continues in the same esteem of their friendship and union which it has manifested from that moment at which a common danger first suggested a common union: that it considers union for specified national purposes, and particularly to those specified in their late federal compact, to be friendly to the peace, happiness, and prosperity of all the states: that faithful to that compact, according to the plain intent and meaning in which it was understood and acceded to by the several parties, it is sincerely anxious for its preservation: that it does also believe, that to take from the states all the powers of self-government and transfer them to a general and consolidated government, without regard to the special delegations and reservations solemnly agreed to in that compact, is not for the peace, happiness, or prosperity of these states; and that therefore this commonwealth is determined, as it doubts not its co-states are, to submit to undelegated, and consequently unlimited powers in no man, or body of men on earth: that in cases of an abuse of the delegated powers, the members of the General Government, being chosen by the people, a change by the people would be the constitutional remedy; but where powers are assumed which have not been delegated, a nullifica-

tion of the act is the rightful remedy: that every State has a natural right in cases not within the compact (casus non foederis), to nullify of their own authority all assumptions of power by others within their limits: that without this right, they would be under the dominion, absolute and unlimited, of whosoever might exercise this right of judgment for them: that nevertheless, this commonwealth, from motives of regard and respect for its co-states, has wished to communicate with them on the subject: that with them alone it is proper to communicate, they alone being parties to the compact, and solely authorized to judge in the last resort of the powers exercised under it, Congress being not a party, but merely the creature of the compact, and subject as to its assumptions of power to the final judgment of those by whom, and for whose use, itself and its powers were all created and modified: . . . That this Commonwealth does therefore call on its co-states for an expression of their sentiments on the acts concerning aliens, and for the punishment of certain crimes hereinbefore specified, plainly declaring whether these acts are or are not authorized by the federal compact. And it doubts not that their sense will be so announced as to prove their attachment unaltered to limited government, whether general or particular. And that the rights and liberties of their co-states will be exposed to no dangers by remaining embarked in a common bottom with their own. That they will concur with this commonwealth in considering the said acts as so palpably against the Constitution as to amount to an undisguised declaration that that compact is not meant to be the measure of the powers of the General Government, but that it will proceed in the exercise over these states of all powers whatsoever: that they will view this as seizing the rights of the states, and consolidating them in the hands of the General Government, with a power assumed to bind the states (not merely as the cases made federal (casus foederis), but in all cases whatsoever, by laws made, not with their consent, but by others against their consent): that this would be to surrender the form of government we have chosen, and live under one deriving its powers from its own will, and not from our authority: and that the co-states, recurring to their natural right in cases not made federal, will concur in declaring these acts void, and of no force, and will each take measures of its own for providing that neither these acts, nor any others of the General Government not plainly and intentionally authorized by the Constitution, shall be exercised within their respective territories.

9. *Resolved*, That the said committee be authorized to communicate by writing or personal conferences, at any time or places whatever, with any person or persons who may be appointed by any one or more co-states to correspond or confer with them, and that they lay their proceedings before the next session of Assembly.

VIRGINIA RESOLUTIONS.

In the Virginia House of Delegates, Friday, December 21, 1798.

Resolved, That the General Assembly of Virginia doth unequivocally express a firm resolution to maintain and defend the Constitution of the United States, and the constitution of this state, against every aggression either foreign or domestic; and that they will support the government of the United States in all measures warranted by the former.

That this Assembly most solemnly declares a warm attachment to the Union of the states, to maintain which it pledges its powers; and, that for this end, it is their duty to watch over and oppose every infraction of those principles which constitute the only basis of that Union, because a faithful observance of them can alone secure its existence and the public happiness.

That this Assembly doth explicitly and peremptorily declare, that it views the powers of the Federal Government, as resulting from the compact to which the states are parties, as limited by the plain sense and intention of the instrument constituting that compact, as no further valid than they are authorized by the grants enumerated in that compact; and that, in case of a deliberate, palpable, and dangerous exercise of other powers, not granted by the said compact, the states, who are parties thereto, have the right, and are in duty bound, to interpose, for arresting the progress of the evil, and for maintaining, within their respective limits, the authorities, rights, and liberties appertaining to them.

That the General Assembly doth also express its deep regret that a spirit has, in sundry instances, been manifested by the Federal Government, to enlarge its powers by forced constructions of the constitutional charter which defines them; and that indications have appeared of a design to expound certain general phrases (which, having been copied from the very limited grant of powers in the former Articles of Confederation, were the less liable to be misconstrued) so as to destroy the meaning and effect of the particular enumeration which necessarily explains and limits the general phrases, and so as to consolidate the states, by degrees, into one Sovereignty, the obvious tendency and inevitable result of which would be, to transform the present republican system of the United States into an absolute, or, at best, a mixed monarchy. . . .

That the good people of this commonwealth, having ever felt, and continuing to feel, the most sincere affection for their brethren of the other states; the truest anxiety for establishing and perpetuating the union of all; and the most scrupulous fidelity to that Constitution, which is the pledge of mutual friendship, and the instrument of mutual happiness; the General Assembly doth solemnly appeal to the like dispositions in the other states, in confidence that they will concur with this commonwealth in declaring, as it does hereby declare, that the acts aforesaid are unconstitutional; and that the necessary and proper measures will be taken by each for coöperating with this state, in maintaining unimpaired the authorities, rights, and liberties reserved to the states respectively, or to the people.

That the governor be desired to transmit a copy of the foregoing resolutions to the executive authority of each of the other states, with a request, that the same may be communicated to the legislature thereof; and that a copy be furnished to each of the senators and representatives representing this state in the Congress of the United States.

APPENDIX C.

PROCLAMATION.

Whereas, At the late session, Congress passed a bill to guarantee to certain states whose governments have been usurped or overthrown a republican form of government, a copy of which is hereunto annexed;

And whereas, The said bill was presented to the President of the United States for his approval less than one hour before the *sine die* adjournment of said session, and was not signed by him;

And whereas, The said bill contains, among other things, a plan for restoring the states in rebellion to their proper practical relation in the Union, which plan expressed the sense of Congress upon that subject, and which plan it is now thought fit to lay before the people for their consideration;

Now, therefore, I, Abraham Lincoln, President of the United States, do proclaim, declare, and make known that while I am — as I was in December last, when by proclamation I propounded a plan for restoration — unprepared by a formal approval of this bill to be inflexibly committed to any single plan of restoration; and while I am also unprepared to declare that the free-state constitutions and governments already adopted and installed in Arkansas and Louisiana shall be set aside and held for naught, thereby repelling and discouraging the loyal citizens who have set up the same as to further effort, or to declare a constitutional competency in Congress to abolish slavery in the states, but am at the same time sincerely hoping and expecting that a constitutional amendment abolishing slavery throughout the nation may be adopted;

Nevertheless, I am fully satisfied with the system for restoration contained in the bill, as one very proper for the loyal people of any state choosing to adopt it; and that I am, and at all times shall be, prepared to give the Executive aid and assistance to any such people, so soon as military resistance to the United States shall have been suppressed in any such state, and the people thereof shall have sufficiently returned to their obedience to the Constitution and the laws of the United States — in which cases military governors will be appointed, with directions to proceed according to the bill.

In testimony whereof, I have hereunto set my hand, and caused the seal of the United States to be affixed.

Done at the City of Washington, this 8th day of July, in the year of our Lord one thousand eight hundred and sixty-four, and of the independence of the United States the eighty-ninth.

(L. S.) ABRAHAM LINCOLN.

PROTEST OF SENATOR WADE AND H. WINTER DAVIS, M. C.

To the supporters of the Government:

We have read without surprise, but not without indignation, the proclamation of the President of the 8th of July, 1864.

The supporters of the Administration are reponsible to the country for its conduct; and it is their right and duty to check the encroachments of the Executive on the authority of Congress, and to require it to confine itself to its proper sphere.

It is impossible to pass in silence this proclamation without neglecting that duty; and, having taken as much responsibility as any others in supporting the Administration, we are not disposed to fail in the other duty of asserting the rights of Congress.

The President did not sign the bill "to guarantee to certain states whose governments have been usurped, a republican form of government" —passed by the supporters of his Administration in both Houses of Congress after mature deliberation.

The bill did not therefore become a law; and it is, therefore, nothing.

The proclamation is neither an approval nor a veto of the bill; it is, therefore, a document unknown to the Laws and Constitution of the United States.

So far as it contains an apology for not signing the bill, it is a political manifesto against the friends of the Government.

So far as it proposes to execute the bill which is not a law, it is a grave Executive usurpation.

It is fitting that the facts necessary to enable the friends of the Administration to appreciate the apology and the usurpation be spread before them.

The proclamation says: —

"And whereas the said bill was presented to the President of the United States for his approval less than one hour before the *sine die* adjournment of said session, and was not signed by him" —

If that be accurate, still this bill was presented with other bills which were signed.

Within that hour the time for the *sine die* adjournment was three times postponed by the votes of both Houses; and the least intimation of a desire for more time by the President to consider this bill would have secured a further postponement.

Yet the committee sent to ascertain if the President had any further communication for the House of Representatives reported that he had none; and the friends of the bill, who had anxiously waited on him to ascertain its fate, had already been informed that the President had resolved not to sign it.

The time of presentation, therefore, had nothing to do with his failure to approve it.

The bill had been discussed and considered for more than a month in the House of Representatives, which it passed on the 4th of May. It was reported to the Senate on the 27th of May, without material amendment, and passed the Senate absolutely as it came from the House on the 2d of July.

Ignorance of its contents is out of the question.

Indeed, at his request, a draft of a bill substantially the same in material points, and identical in the points objected to by the proclamation, had been laid before him for his consideration in the winter of 1862–1863.

There is, therefore, no reason to suppose the provisions of the bill took the President by surprise.

On the contrary, we have reason to believe them to have been so well known that this method of preventing the bill from becoming a law without the constitutional responsibility of a veto had been resolved on long before the bill passed the Senate.

We are informed by a gentleman entitled to entire confidence, that before the 22d of June, in New Orleans, it was stated by a member of General Banks' staff, in the presence of other gentlemen in official position, that Senator Doolittle had written a letter to the department that the House Reconstruction Bill would be staved off in the Senate to a period too late in the session to require the President to veto it in order to defeat it, and that Mr. Lincoln would retain the bill, if necessary, and thereby defeat it.

The experience of Senator Wade, in his various efforts to get the bill considered in the Senate, was quite in accordance with that plan; and the fate of the bill was accurately predicted by letters received from New Orleans before it had passed the Senate.

Had the proclamation stopped there, it would have been only one other defeat of the will of the people by the Executive perversion of the Constitution.

But it goes further. The President says: —

"And whereas the said bill contains, among other things,

a plan for restoring the States in rebellion to their proper practical relation in the Union, which plan expresses the sense of Congress upon that subject, and which plan it is now thought fit to lay before the people for their consideration" —

By what authority of the Constitution? In what forms? The result to be declared by whom? With what effect when ascertained?

Is it to be a law by the approval of the people, without the approval of Congress, at the will of the President?

Will the President, on his opinion of the popular approval, execute it as a law?

Or is this merely a device to avoid the serious responsibility of defeating a law on which so many loyal hearts reposed for security?

But the reasons now assigned for not approving the bill are full of ominous significance.

The President proceeds: —

"Now, therefore, I, Abraham Lincoln, President of the United States, do proclaim, declare, and make known that, while I am (as I was in December last, when by proclamation I propounded a plan for restoration) unprepared by a formal approval of this bill to be inflexibly committed to any single plan of restoration."

That is to say, the President is resolved that people shall not *by law* take *any* securities from the rebel states against a renewal of the rebellion, before restoring their power to govern us.

His wisdom and prudence are to be our sufficient guarantees! He further says: —

"And while I am also unprepared to declare that the free-state constitutions and governments already adopted and installed in Arkansas and Louisiana shall be set aside and held for naught, thereby repelling and discouraging the loyal citizens who have set up the same as to further effort" —

That is to say, the President persists in recognizing those

shadows of governments in Arkansas and Louisiana which Congress formally declared should not be recognized — whose representatives and senators were repelled by formal votes of both Houses of Congress — which it was declared formally should have no electoral vote for President and Vice-President.

They are mere creatures of his will. They are mere oligarchies, imposed on the people by military orders under the form of election, at which generals, provost marshals, soldiers, and camp-followers were the chief actors, assisted by a handful of resident citizens, and urged on to premature action by private letters from the President.

In neither Louisiana nor Arkansas, before Banks' defeat, did the United States control half the territory or half the population. In Louisiana, General Banks' proclamation candidly declared: "The fundamental law of the state is martial law."

On that foundation of freedom he erected what the President calls "the free constitution and government of Louisiana."

But of this state, whose fundamental law was martial law, only sixteen parishes out of forty-eight parishes were held by the United States; and in five of the sixteen we held only our camps.

The eleven parishes we substantially held had 233,185 inhabitants; the residue of the State not held by us, 575,617.

At the farce called an election, the officers of General Banks returned that 11,346 ballots were cast; but whether any or by whom, the people of the United States have no legal assurance; but it is probable that 4000 were cast by soldiers or employés of the United States, military or municipal, but none according to any law, state or national, and 7000 ballots represent the state of Louisiana.

Such is the free constitution and government of Louisiana; and like it is that of Arkansas. Nothing but the failure of a military expedition deprived us of a like one in the swamps of Florida; and before the Presidential election, like ones may be organized in every rebel state where the United States have a camp.

The President, by preventing this bill from becoming a law, holds the electoral votes of the rebel states at the dictation of his personal ambition.

If those votes turn the balance in his favor, is it to be supposed that his competitor, defeated by such means, will acquiesce?

If the rebel majority assert their supremacy in those states, and send votes which elect an enemy of the Government, will we not repel his claims?

And is not that civil war for the Presidency inaugurated by the votes of rebel states?

Seriously impressed with these dangers, Congress, "the proper constitutional authority," formally declared that there are no state governments in the rebel states, and provided for their erection at a proper time; and both the Senate and the House of Representatives rejected the senators and representatives chosen under the authority of what the President calls the free constitution and government of Arkansas.

The President's proclamation "holds for naught" this judgment, and discards the authority of the Supreme Court, and strides headlong toward the anarchy his proclamation of the 8th of December inaugurated.

If electors for President be allowed to be chosen in either of those states, a sinister light will be cast on the motives which induced the President to "hold for naught" the will of Congress rather than his government in Louisiana and Arkansas.

That judgment of Congress which the President defies was the exercise of an authority exclusively vested in Congress by the Constitution, to determine what is the established government in a state, and in its own nature and by the highest judicial authority binding on all other departments of the government.

The Supreme Court has formally declared that, under the 4th section of the IVth article of the Constitution, requiring the United States to guarantee to every state a republican form of government, "it rests with Congress to decide what government is the established one in a state;" and "when senators and representatives of a state are admitted into the councils of the Union, the authority of the Government under which they are appointed, as well as its republican character, is recognized by the proper constitutional authority, and its decision is binding on every other department of the Government, and could not be questioned in a judicial tribunal. It is true that the contest in this case did not last long enough to bring the matter to this issue; and as no senators or representatives were elected under the authority of the Government of which Mr. Dorr was the head, Congress was not called upon to decide the controversy. Yet the right to decide is placed there."

Even the President's proclamation of the 8th of December formally declares that "whether members sent to Congress from any state shall be admitted to seats constitutionally rests exclusively with the respective Houses, and not to any extent with the Executive."

And that is not the less true because wholly inconsistent with the President's assumption in that proclamation of a right to institute and recognize state governments in the rebel states, nor because the President is unable to perceive that his recognition is a nullity if it be not conclusive on Congress.

Under the Constitution, the right to senators and representatives is inseparable from a state government.

If there be a state government, the right is absolute.

If there be no state government, there can be no senators or representatives chosen.

The two Houses of Congress are expressly declared to be the sole judges of their own members.

When, therefore, senators and representatives are admitted, the state government under whose authority they were chosen is conclusively established; when they are rejected, its existence is as conclusively rejected and denied; and to this judgment the President is bound to submit.

The President proceeds to express his unwillingness "to declare a constitutional competency in Congress to abolish slavery in States" as another reason for not signing the bill.

But the bill nowhere proposes to abolish slavery in the States.

The bill did provide that all *slaves* in the rebel states should be *manumitted.*

But as the President had already signed three bills manumitting several classes of slaves in the states, it is not conceived possible that he entertained any scruples touching *that* provision of the bill respecting which he is silent.

He had already himself assumed a right by proclamation to free much the larger number of slaves in the rebel states, under the authority given him by Congress to use military power to suppress the rebellion; and it is quite inconceivable that the President should think Congress could vest in him a discretion it could not exercise itself.

It is the more unintelligible from the fact that, except in respect to a small part of Virginia and Louisiana, the bill covered only what the proclamation covered — added a congressional title and judicial remedies by law to the disputed title under the proclamation, and perfected the work the President professed to be so anxious to accomplish.

Slavery as an institution can be abolished only by a change of the Constitution of the United States, or of the law of the States; and this is the principle of the bill.

It required the new constitution of the State to provide for that prohibition; and the President, in the face of his own proclamation, does not venture to object to insisting on that condition. Nor will the country tolerate its abandonment — yet he defeated the only provision imposing it.

But when he describes himself, in spite of this great blow at emancipation, as "sincerely hoping and expecting that a constitutional amendment abolishing slavery throughout the nation may be adopted," we curiously inquire on what his expectation rests, after the vote of the House of Representatives at the recent session, and in the face of the political complexion of more than enough of the states to prevent the possibility of its adoption within any reasonable time; and why he did not indulge his sincere hopes with so large an instalment of the blessing as his approval of the bill would have secured?

After this assignment of his reasons for preventing the bill from becoming a law, the President proceeds to declare his purpose to execute it as a law by his plenary dictatorial power.

He says: "Nevertheless, I am fully satisfied with the system for restoration contained in the bill, as one very proper for the loyal people of any state choosing to adopt it; and that I am, and at all times shall be, prepared to give the Executive aid and assistance to any such people, as soon as military resistance to the United States shall have been suppressed in any such state, and the people thereof shall have sufficiently returned to their obedience to the Constitution and laws of the United States — in which cases military governors will be appointed, with directions to proceed according to the bill."

A more studied outrage on the legislative authority of the people has never been perpetrated.

Congress passed a bill; the President refused to approve it, and then by proclamation puts as much of it in force as he sees fit, and proposes to execute those parts by officers unknown to the laws of the United States, and not subject to the confirmation of the Senate.

The bill directed the appointment of provisional governors by and with the advice and consent of the Senate.

The President, after defeating the law, proposes to appoint, without law and without the advice and consent of the Senate, military governors for the rebel states!

He has already exercised this dictatorial usurpation in Louisiana, and defeated the bill to prevent its limitation.

Henceforth we must regard the following precedent as the Presidential law of the rebel states: —

EXECUTIVE MANSION,
WASHINGTON, March 15, 1864.

His Excellency Michael Hahn, Governor of Louisiana:

Until further orders you are hereby invested with the powers exercised hitherto by the military governor of Louisiana. Yours,

ABRAHAM LINCOLN.

This Michael Hahn is no officer of the United States; the President, without law, without the advice and consent of the Senate, by a private note not even countersigned by the Secretary of State, makes him dictator of Louisiana!

The bill provided for the civil administration of the laws of the state, — but it should be in a fit temper to govern itself, — repealing all laws recognizing slavery, and making all men equal before the law.

These beneficent provisions the President has annulled. People will die, and marry, and transfer property, and buy and sell; and to these acts of civil life courts and officers of the law are necessary. Congress legislated for these necessary things, and the President deprives them of the protection of the law!

The President's purpose to instruct his military governors "to proceed according to the bill" — a makeshift to calm the disappointment its defeat has occasioned — is not merely a grave usurpation, but a transparent delusion.

He cannot "proceed according to the bill" after preventing it from becoming a law.

Whatever is done will be at his will and pleasure, by persons responsible to no law, and more interested to secure the interests and execute the will of the President than of the people; and the will of Congress is to be "held for naught," "unless the loyal people of the rebel states choose to adopt it."

If they should graciously prefer the stringent bill to the easy proclamation, still the registration will be made under no legal sanction; it will give no assurance that a majority of the people of the states have taken the oath; if administered, it will be without legal authority and void; no indictment will lie for false swearing at the election, or for admitting bad or rejecting good votes; it will be the farce of Louisiana and Arkansas acted over again, under the forms of this bill, but not by authority of law.

But when we come to the guarantees of future peace which Congress meant to enact, the forms as well as the substance of the bill must yield to the President's will that none should be imposed.

It was the solemn resolve of Congress to protect the loyal men of the nation against three great dangers: (1) the return to power of the guilty leaders of the rebellion; (2) the continuance of slavery; and (3) the burden of the rebel debt.

Congress required assent to those provisions by the convention of the state; and, if refused, it was to be dissolved.

The President "holds for naught" that resolve of Congress, because he is unwilling "to be inflexibly committed to any one plan of restoration," and the people of the United States are not to be allowed to protect themselves unless their enemies agree to it.

The order to proceed according to the bill is therefore merely at the will of the rebel states; and they have the option to reject it, accept the proclamation of the 8th of December, and demand the President's recognition!

Mark the contrast! The bill requires a majority, the proclamation is satisfied with one tenth; the bill requires one oath, the proclamation another; the bill ascertains voters by registering, the proclamation by guess; the bill exacts adherence to existing territorial limits, the proclamation admits of others; the bill governs the rebel states *by law*, equalizing all before it, the proclamation commits them to the lawless discretion of military governors and provost marshals; the bill forbids electors for President, the proclamation and defeat of the bill threaten us with civil war for the admission or exclusion of such votes; the bill exacted exclusion of dangerous enemies from power and the relief of the nation from the rebel debt, and the prohibition of slavery forever, so that the suppression of the rebellion will double our resources to bear or pay the national debt, free the masses from the old domination of the rebel leaders, and eradicate the cause of the war; the proclamation secures neither of these guarantees.

It is silent respecting the rebel debt and the political exclusion of rebel leaders; leaving slavery exactly where it was by law at the outbreak of the rebellion, and adds no guarantee even of the freedom of the slaves he undertook to manumit.

It is summed up in an illegal oath, without sanction, and therefore void.

The oath is to support all proclamations of the President, during the rebellion, having reference to slaves.

Any government is to be accepted at the hands of one tenth of the people not contravening that oath.

Now that oath neither secures the abolition of slavery, nor adds any security to the freedom of the slaves the President declared free.

It does not secure the abolition of slavery; for the proclamation of freedom merely professed to free certain slaves while it recognized the institution.

Every constitution of the rebel states at the outbreak of the rebellion may be adopted without the change of a letter: for none of them contravene that proclamation; none of them establish slavery.

It adds no security to the freedom of the slaves; for their title is the proclamation of freedom.

If it be unconstitutional, an oath to support it is void. Whether constitutional or not, the oath is without authority of law, and therefore void.

If it be valid and observed, it exacts no enactment by

the state, either in law or constitution, to add a state guarantee to the proclamation title; and the right of a slave to freedom is an open question before the state courts on the relative authority of the state law and the proclamation.

If the oath binds the one tenth who take it, it is not exacted of the other nine tenths who succeed to the control of the state government, so that it is annulled instantly by the act of recognition.

What the state courts would say of the proclamation, who can doubt?

But the master would not go into court — he would seize his slaves.

What the Supreme Court would say, who can tell?

When and how is the question to get there?

No *habeas corpus* lies for him in a United States Court; and the President defeated with this bill the extension of that writ to his case.

Such are the fruits of this rash and fatal act of the President, — a blow at the friends of his Administration, at the rights of humanity, and at the principles of republican government.

The President has greatly presumed on the forbearance which the supporters of his Administration have so long practised, in view of the arduous conflict in which we are engaged, and the reckless ferocity of our political opponents.

But he must understand that our support is of a cause, and not of a man; that the authority of Congress is paramount and must be respected; that the whole body of the Union men of Congress will not submit to be impeached by him of rash and unconstitutional legislation; and if he wishes our support, he must confine himself to his Executive duties, — to obey and execute, not make the laws, — to suppress by arms armed rebellion, and leave political reorganization to Congress.

If the supporters of the Government fail to insist on this, they become responsible for the usurpations which they fail to rebuke, and are justly liable to the indignation of the people whose rights and security, committed to their keeping, they sacrifice.

Let them consider the remedy of these usurpations, and, having found it, fearlessly execute it.

B. F. Wade,
Chairman Senate Committee.
H. Winter Davis,
Chairman Committee House of Representatives on the rebellious states.

INDEX.

www.ingramcontent.com/pod-product-compliance
Lightning Source LLC
Chambersburg PA
CBHW032259280326
41932CB00009B/622

* 9 7 8 3 3 3 7 0 0 9 1 2 0 *